The Complete COSORI Air Fryer Cookbook

600 Easy & Delicious Frying Recipes for 1000 Days - with Tips & Tricks to Fry the Most Flavorful Foods More Healthy

By Ride Terrison

Legal & Disclaimer

The content and information in this book is consistent and truthful, and it has been provided for informational, educational and business purposes only.

The content and information contained in this book has been compiled from reliable sources, which are accurate based on the knowledge, belief, expertise and information of the Author. The author cannot be held liable for any omissions and/or errors.

Table of Content

Introduction 1

Chapter 1 Understanding Cosori Air Fryer 2

Why Buy Cosori Air Fryer 2   Cleaning and Care................................ 5

User Guide 3   Conclusion 6

Chapter 2 Breakfast 8

Bread Boat Eggs with Mushroom 8   Quiche Cups with Pork Sausage........................ 17

Berry Pancake Muffins 8   Spicy Hash Browns 17

Sweet Pumpkin Donut Holes............................ 8   Fried Potatoes with Onion and Bell Peppers....... 17

Cheesy Egg English Muffins............................. 9   Cheddar and Ham Muffins............................... 18

Crispy Tofu with Tamari 9   Chickpeas Donuts 18

Coconut Donut Holes 9   Maple French Toast Sticks 18

Egg and Turkey Sausage Roll-Ups 10   Cinnamon French Toast Sticks......................... 18

Chocolate Crescent Rolls with Almond............... 10   Coated Eggs with Sausage 19

Red Rolls with Meat..................................... 10   Blueberry Muffins... 19

Asparagus, Bell Pepper and Carrot Strata 11   Salmon and Spinach Frittata 19

Breakfast Cherry Tarts.................................. 11   Authentic Quesadillas.................................... 19

Glazed Apple Cider Doughnut Holes.................. 11   Simple Blueberry Muffins................................. 20

Cranberry Bran Muffins 12   Cheesy Vegetables Egg Cups........................... 20

Carrot and Raisin Muffins with Brown Sugar....... 12   Ham and Tomato Sandwiches........................... 20

Sweet Cinnamon-Glazed Butter-Pecan Roll 12   Cinnamon Apples Stuffed with Granola.............. 20

Fluffy Oat Bran Muffins 13   Eggs in a Bread 21

Butternut Squash Frittata with Ricotta 13   Spicy Barbecue Chicken Flatbreads 21

Cheesy Eggs with Bacon and Tomato Sauce...... 13   Chicken Sausage and Cream Cheese Biscuits... 21

Scotch Eggs with Sausage............................. 14   Asparagus and Goat Cheese Frittata 21

Fried PB&J with Banana................................. 14   Salmon and Pork Sausage Omelet 22

Quick Shakshuka with Tomato Sauce 14   Cinnamon Sweet Potato Toast 22

Crispy Bacon 15   Quick Hard-Boiled Eggs 22

Apple and Walnut Muffins............................... 15   Hard-Cooked Eggs 22

Cheddar Muffins with Bacon........................... 15   Spinach and Turkey Bacon Rollups................... 22

Fluffy Fruity Beignets.................................... 15   Quick Breakfast Bacon Sandwiches................... 22

Simple Veggie Omelet................................... 17   Easy Cinnamon Rolls 23

Cinnamon Egg Porridge 23
Eggs Florentine with Spinach 23

Easy French Toast...23

Chapter 3 Vegetable... 25

Chile Cornbread with Cheddar 25
Cinnamon Butternut Squash 25
Mashed Potato Tots with Bacon 25
Tart and Spicy Potatoes.....................................26
Crispy Latkes with Sour Cream and Applesauce 26
Green Tomatoes with Sriracha Mayo 26
Yuca Roots Fries 27
Bell Peppers Salad with Feta 27
Hasselback with Sour Cream and Pesto.............27
Breaded Okra 28
Breaded Yellow Squash.....................................28
Fried Smashed Red Potatoes 28
Blackened Zucchini with Kimchi Sauce...............29
Mole-Braised Cauliflower with Sesame Seeds....29
Simple Caesar Whole Cauliflower 29
Easy Asparagus with Tarragon 30
Air-Fried Cauliflower with Tahini Sauce 30
Fingerling Potatoes with Parsley 30
Spicy Turkish Leek Fritters 30
Cheesy Corn in a Cup 31
Cheddar Red Potato Pot 31
Chiles Rellenos with Tomato Sauce 31
Button Mushrooms 33
Sweet Glazed Carrot 33
Onion Rings..33
Potato Wedges 33

Garlicky Baby Carrot with Sesame Seeds...........34
Spicy Indian Okra 34
Bottom Rice with Pistachios 34
Parmesan Broccoli Crust with Alfredo Sauce 34
Green Peas with Lettuce 35
Pearl Onions with Rosemary 35
Air-Fried Green Beans and Bacon 35
Air-Fried Brussels Sprouts.................................35
Broccoli Salad with Bacon 35
Stuffed Eggplant Shell with Spinach...................35
Air-Fried Corn on the Cob 36
Super Colorful Vegetable Rolls...........................36
Maple Cheery Tomatoes with Thyme 36
Bella Mushrooms with Bacon 36
Fragrant Jerk Rubbed Corn on the Cob 36
Quick Lemony Cauliflower..................................37
Sesame Broccoli Florets....................................37
Easy Parmesan Coated Artichokes....................37
Parmesan Zucchini Gratin with Parsley..............37
Fluffy Cheddar Mushroom Loaf..........................37
Heirloom Carrots with Orange Zest 38
Classic Gobi Manchurian....................................38
Mushroom and Carrot with Grated Eggs 38
Fried Shallots..38
Sweet Butternut Squash....................................39
Spicy Green Beans..39

Chapter 4 Poultry 41

Garlic Chicken Tender 41
Buttermilk-Fried Chicken Drumsticks 41
Spicy Chicken Chimichangas 41
Simple Chicken Hand Pies 42

Fiesta Chicken Plate with Refried Beans 42
Breaded Chicken with Spaghetti and Marinara Sauce
....42
Chicken Cordon Bleu with Ham.........................43

Golden Panko-Crusted Chicken Nuggets...........43

Coconut Chicken Tender with Apricot-Ginger Sauce 43

Black Bean and Turkey Burgers with Cumin-Avocado Spread 44

General Tso's Chicken....................................44

Fried Chicken Breast with Buttermilk Waffles......45

Buffalo Egg Rolls with Blue Cheese Dip............45

Herbed Turkey Breast....................................46

Lemony Chicken Souvlaki 46

Herbed Turkey Breast with Cherry Glaze...........46

Butter Coated Chicken Breast.........................47

Peanut Butter-BBQ Chicken............................47

Authentic Taquitos 47

Quick Marinaded Chicken Strips 48

Poblano Pepper with Turkey............................48

Lime Curried Chicken with Coconut Rice............48

Chicken Breast with Dark Cherries...................49

Simple Spicy Chicken Thighs...........................49

Chicken and Dill Pickle with Nashville Hot Sauce 49

Airy Breaded Chicken.....................................50

Chili Peanut Chicken 50

Buttermilk-Fried Chicken 50

Marinara Chicken Breast Parmesan...................52

Turkey and Zucchini Meatballs with Chili Sauce .52

Lemony Chicken with Sage 52

Sweet Chicken Drumsticks..............................53

Cheesy Chicken Breast...................................53

Paprika Fried Chicken 53

Italian Lemony Chicken Thighs 54

Sweet Gochujang Chicken Wings 54

Garlic Cream Chicken Thighs...........................54

Chicken and Onion with Pineapple.....................55

Spicy Chicken Fries..55

Peruvian-Style Chicken with Herb-Mayonnaise ..55

Super Cheesy Chicken....................................56

Mozzarella Chicken Fritters with Garlic Dip.........56

Quick Buffalo Chicken Wings 56

Chicken and Bell Peppers Fajita Roll-Ups..........56

Easy Turkey Wings...57

Simple Seasoned Cornish Hen 57

Greek Chicken Salad with Kalamata Olives........57

Garlic Breaded Chicken Breast 57

Honey Glazed Cornish Hens 57

Simple Mustard Chicken Tenders......................58

Teriyaki Paprika Chicken Legs 58

Spicy Chicken and Corn Stir-Fry 58

Easy Turkey Burgers 58

Spinach and Cheese Stuffed Chicken.................58

Simple Herbed Turkey Breasts.........................59

BBQ Chicken Thighs 59

Hoisin Duck Breast...59

Smoked Paprika Chicken Breasts......................59

BBQ Chicken Burgers 59

Mayo Chicken and Carrot Salad........................59

Chinese Chicken Patties 60

Garlic Honey Chicken Wings............................60

Five-Spice Chicken Drumsticks.........................60

Garlic Chicken Breasts 60

Breaded Fried Chicken Drumsticks....................61

Quick Panko-Crusted Chicken Chunks...............61

Chapter 5 Pork 63

Lemony Breaded Schnitzel...............................63

Spicy Vietnamese Pork Sausages 63

Thin Pork Cutlets with Aloha Salsa....................63

Air-Fried Pork and Creamer Potatoes 64

Vietnamese Pork Shoulder with Roasted Peanuts 64

Pork Tenderloin, Plum and Apricot Kebabs 64

Sweet-Sour Pork Chunks 64

Bacon Lettuce Salad with Croutons 65

Tasty Pork Bulgogi...65

Caribbean-Style Pork Patties with Brioche
Hamburger Buns 65

Chili Breaded Pork Chops 65

Pork Butt with Fresh Rosemary..........................66

Hot Center Cut Pork Roast..................................66

Picnic Ham with Tamari Sauce 66

Paprika Pork Loin Roast......................................66

Pork Loin with Dijon Mustard..............................66

Pork Dinner Rolls...66

Orange Glazed Pork Chops 67

Mexican-Style Pork and Chile Tacos..................67

Coconut Pork Chops with Salad..........................67

Garlic St. Louis-Style Ribs..................................67

Tasty Souvlaki..67

Spicy Pork Gyros...67

Garlic Rosemary Pork Loin Roast 68

Sweet Pork Spareribs..68

Breaded Pork Sirloin Chops 68

BBQ Pork Butt 68

Hot Pork Rib Roast..68

Cuban Cheesy Pork Sandwich............................68

Easy Beer Pork Loin..70

Chinese Pork Back Ribs......................................70

Dijon Pork Burgers 70

Pork Sausage and Fennel....................................70

Pork Center Cut with Red Pepper 70

Chinese Slab Baby Back Ribs.............................70

Spareribs with Sriracha Sauce 71

Herbed Pork Butt...71

Honey-Lemon Pork Tenderloin 71

Herbed Pork Belly..71

Country-Style Ribs with Red Wine 71

Mustard Breaded Pork Tenderloin......................71

Paprika Pork Loin Chops.....................................72

Pulled Pork Sliders with Fish Sauce...................72

Pork Loin Ribs with Zucchini 72

Country-Style Ribs with Sriracha........................72

Pork Chops and Bell Peppers 72

Cheesy Pork Taquitos..72

Pepper Pork Loin Chops with Onions..................73

Chinese-Style Pork Loin Porterhouse 73

Worcestershire Center-Cut Pork Chops 73

Pork Shoulder Chops with Rosemary..................73

Tasty Tortilla Chips Coated Pork Cutlets 73

Pork Loin Fillets and Mushroom with Blue Cheese
....73

Honey Bratwurst and Brussels Sprouts...............74

Pork, Eggplant and Bell Pepper Skewers............74

Pork Tenderloin with Apple 74

Balsamic Pork Loin with Red Pepper 74

Sliced Pork Tenderloin and Mixed Greens Salad 74

Smoked Pork Sausage with Onions Rings..........75

Country-Style Pork Belly with Tomato Sauce 75

Paprika Baby Back Ribs 75

Chapter 6 Beef 77

Beef Satay with Cilantro 77

Authentic Carne Asada..77

Ritzy Beef Steak with Mushroom Gravy 77

Beef, Mushroom and Broccoli 78

Beef, Orange and Pineapple Stir-Fry 78

Cheesy Lasagna..78

Glazed Beef Cheese Cups 79

Cheddar Roasted Stuffed Bell Peppers...............79

Light Herbed Beef Meatballs 79

Spicy Beef with Fajita Veggie 79

Saucy Mongolian Beef...80

Salsa Sirloin Tip Steak..80

Beef Taco Wraps 80

Spicy Beef and Brown Rice Stuffed Bell Peppers 80

Peruvian Stir-Fried Beef and Tomato with Fries ..81

Beef and Bell Pepper Risotto 81

Sherry Beef Steak and Broccoli...........................81

Classic Onion Beef Brisket...................................82

Quick Ribeye Steak..82

Herbed Roast Beef...82

Garlic Skirt Steak...82

Garlic Ribeye Steak..82

Simple Beef Empanadas 82

French Filet Mignon..83

Skirt Steak Sliders with Mustard..........................83

Old-Fashioned Shallot Meatloaf 83

Herbed New York Strip Steak 83

Parsley Roast Beef...83

Authentic Mexican Carnitas.................................83

Traditional Montreal Ribeye Steak 85

Italian Rump Roast with Onion 85

Ketchup Pulled Beef...85

Mustard Filet Mignon..85

Classic BBQ Cheeseburgers...............................85

Parsley Top Round Roast.....................................85

Quick Paprika Flank Steak 86

Classic Corned Beef Brisket.................................86

Thai Curry Lime Beef Meatballs 86

Tasty Barbecue Beef Brisket 86

Beef Sausage and Bell Peppers...........................86

Parsley London Broil 86

Parsley Coulotte Roast..87

Traditional Mexican-Style Meatloaf 87

Tasty Beef Burgers 87

Simple Beef Sliders 87

Brandy Paprika Rump Roast.................................87

Lemon Marinated London Broil 87

Beef Patties with Mushroom.................................88

Sicilian Beef and Tomato Stuffed Peppers 88

Beef Shoulder and Onion 88

Garlicky Chuck Roast 88

T-Bone Steak and Tomato Salad 89

Sirloin Roast with Carrots and Herbs 89

Tenderloin Steaks with Mushrooms......................89

Spicy Beef Burgers..89

Chuck Eye Roast with Jalapeno Pepper 89

Herbed Filet Mignon 90

Juicy Tomahawk Steaks with Bell Pepper 90

Chinese-Style Spiced Beef Tenderloin 90

Garlic Pulled Beef..90

Ribeye Steak with Blue Cheese 90

Chapter 7 Fish and Seafood 92

Fish Fillet with Crumb Coating.............................92

Pesto White Fish and Spinach Pie 92

Coconut Shrimp and Tomato Po' Boys 92

Spicy Bang Bang Shrimp......................................93

Fried Shrimp with Peanut Mix..............................93

Authentic Cajun Fried Shrimp with Remoulade...93

Honey Mustard Breaded Salmon Fillet................94

Marinaded Shrimp and Grits................................94

Lush Stuffed Tail-on Shrimp 94

Louisiana Shrimp Po Boy with Remoulade 95

Crispy Marinaded Shrimp.....................................95

One-Pot Shrimp and Egg Fried Rice 95

Lime Mackerel Fillets..96

Chili Pollock 96

Lemon Cilantro Swordfish Steak 96

Buttery Garlic Sea Scallops..................................96

Mediterranean Cheesy Squid 96

Basil Mahi-Mahi Fillets..96

Buttery Halibut Steaks 97

Chili Squid with Capers 97

Garlic Calamari with Sherry Wine.......................97

Lemon Shrimp and Broccoli Floret 97

Exotic Hot Paprika Fried Prawns........................97

Mustard Coated Calamari...................................97

Parsley Calamari 98

Quick Fried Calamari Rings................................98

Classic Mediterranean Calamari 98

Pepper Air-Fried Shrimp....................................98

Herb Salmon Fillets 98

Cheesy Tilapia Fish Fillets Burgers 98

Garlic Orange Roughy Fillets 100

Chili Calamari with Red Chili 100

Mayonnaise King Prawn Salad.........................100

Sea Scallops with Rosemary............................100

Buttermilk Coconut Shrimp...............................100

Sea Scallop and Tomato Salad 100

Simple Tilapia Fillet and Chips 101

Jumbo Shrimp with Chives 101

Pink Salmon Patties 101

Breaded Sea Scallops.......................................101

Tandoori Shrimp with Cilantro...........................101

Panko Breaded Shrimp 102

Herbed Tilapia Fillet Nuggets 102

Breaded Cod Fish Fingers.................................102

Codfish Fillet Tacos with Avocado-Mayonnaise...102

Cheesy English Muffin Tuna..............................102

Italian-Style Sea Bass with White Wine..............103

Garlic Halibut Burgers 103

Swordfish Steaks with Red Wine.......................103

Old-Fashioned Fish and Olive Salad..................103

Light Asian Tuna Steak......................................103

Old Bay Tiger Prawns with Sherry Wine.............104

Easy Old Bay Calamari 104

Buttery Lobster Tail 104

Tuna and Spinach Salad with a Twist.................104

Coated Tilapia Fillet 104

Greek Monkfish Fillet Pita with Avocado 105

Shrimp and Cucumber Salad Sandwich.............105

Italian Cheesy Monkfish Fingers 105

Panko-Crusted Shrimp with Bang Bang Sauce...105

Chapter 8 Bread, Sandwiches and Pizza 107

Cheddar and Mango Chutney Puff Pie................107

Spicy Chimichurri Beef Empanadas....................107

Fluffy Mini Pita Breads.......................................107

Healthy Banana Bread 108

Cheesy Pull-Apart Bread with Anchovies 108

Honey Rosemary Knots.......................................108

Garlic Bacon Cheese Pizza.................................109

Healthy Corn Bread 109

Garlicky Parmesan Bread Ring 109

Cheesy Salami and Kale Pizza 110

Coconut Banana Chia Bread................................110

Samosa Potato Pot Pie 110

Strawberry Bread..112

Healthy Crushed Tomato Pizza 112

Paprika Lamb, Green Olive and Cheese Pizza...112

Zucchini Chocolate Bread 112

Smoked Mozzarella and Oyster Mushroom Pizza
....113

Cinnamon Pumpkin Loaf 113

Peanut Butter Banana Bread.............................113

Cheesy Olives and Roasted Red Pepper Bread .113

Chicken English Muffin Sandwiches...................114

Traditional Tuscan Toast....................................114

Mayonnaise Egg Salad Sandwich 114

Sweet Cornbread...114

Cheesy Broccoli Cornbread...............................114

Sweet Italian Sausage Sandwich 115

Chili BLT Sandwich..115

Cheesy Beef Sandwich 115

Cheesy Mushroom and Tomato Pita Pizza..........115

Chapter 9 Snacks and Appetizers 117

Cheesy Bacon Wrapped Jalapeño Peppers........117

Buffalo Cheesy Meatballs...................................117

Cheesy Spinach Dip with Bread Knots................117

Shrimp Cucumber Pirogues 118

Beef Steak Sliders with Horseradish Mayonnaise
....118

Asian Rice Logs with Orange Marmalade 118

Quick Mozzarella Cheese Sticks 119

Pepper-Brined Fried Calamari............................119

Crispy Potato with Spicy Tomato Ketchup...........119

Honey Glazed Chicken Wings............................120

Cinnamon Apple Wedges 120

Masala Onion Rings with Lemon-Mayo Dip 120

Stuffed Onion with Garlic-Lemon Breadcrumb 121

Cheesy Dill Pickles 121

Sesame Seasoned Sausage Rolls 121

Crispy Carrot Chips 122

Loaded Potato Skins with Bacon.......................122

Crispy Avocado Fries...122

Crispy String Bean Fries....................................122

Simple Curried Chickpeas 124

Crispy Fried Peaches 124

Crispy Yellow Potato Chips.................................124

Panko Breaded Eggplant Fries...........................124

Lemony Pita Chips 125

Hot Fried Dill Pickles 125

Sweet-Spicy Chicken Wings...............................125

Cheddar Cheese Bites 125

Ranch Chickpeas 126

Potatoes Wedges 126

Greek Street Feta and Hummus Tacos 126

Turkey, Pineapple and Bell Pepper Burger Sliders
....126

Authentic Tomatillo Salsa Verde 127

Garlic Coated Chicken Wings.............................127

Asian-Style Chicken Wings 127

Chicken Tender with Blue Cheese......................127

Spicy Red Beets Chips 128

Parmesan Zucchini Fries 128

Bread Crumbs Stuffed Button Mushrooms..........128

Sweet Cinnamon Bagel Chips............................128

Crispy Potato Chips...128

Mozzarella Eggplant Chips.................................129

Chapter 10 Desserts 131

Tasty Caramelized Peach Shortcakes.................131

Strawberry Scone Shortcake with Powdered Sugar
....131

Coconut Almond Chocolate Cake.......................132

Spoon Chocolate Brownies 132

Persian Doughnuts with Saffron Syrup...............132

Lemony Apple Cake 133

Frosted Chocolate Cookie with Peanut Butter.....133

Raisin Apple Turnovers.......................................133

Lavender Lemon Doughnuts 134

Simple Brownies with a Twist 134

Lemony Apple Pie..134

Cinnamon Coconut Pancake Cups 135

Pumpkin Bread Pudding....................................135

Coconut Chia Chocolate Cake 135

Honey Basil Strawberry Tart...............................135

Vanilla Apple Wedges 137

Vanilla Pumpkin Cake.................................137

German Giant Apple Pancake............................137

Buttery Vanilla French Toast..............................137

Cinnamon Peaches 137

Chocolate Cupcakes 137

Brown Sugar Fried Plums..................................138

Authentic Thai Goreng Pisang...........................138

Classic Spanish Churros 138

Homemade Banana Fritters 138

Simple Colorful Fruit Skewers 138

Classic American-Style Crullers 138

Indian Unnakai Malabar....................................139

Pumpkin Cake with Honey 139

Autumn Walnut Pumpkin Pie.............................139

Sweet Vanilla Pears in Red Wine.......................139

Homemade Cinnamon Rolls................................139

Chocolate Cupcakes with Raisin 139

Buttery Pears Sticks 140

Banana Fritters 140

Healthy Blueberry Fritters..................................140

Cinnamon Banana Slices 140

Simple Beignets..140

Old-Fashioned Stuffed Apples with Pecans 140

Quick French Dessert...141

Honey Yogurt and Walnut Stuffed Pears 141

Cinnamon Cherry 141

Favorite Chocolate Fudge Cake.........................141

Appendix 1: Measurement Conversion Chart 142

Appendix 2: Recipes Index... 143

Introduction

Air fryers have made oil-free cooking a reality, and today there are millions of people around the world who rely on this technology to cook all sorts of oil-free healthy meals at home. Cosori has emerged as a trusted air fryer manufacturer over the years; the cooking technology and the user interface used in the appliances created by Cosori have garnered much appreciation and positive reviews from its customers. And when it comes to recommending an air fryer for every household, the multipurpose 11-in-1 Cosori 5.8 quarts Air Fryer always comes to mind. The reason is the ease and comfort of cooking and the effective results it offers. Not once was I disappointed with its cooking functions? So I had a thought, why not share the amazing recipes that I tried using this air fryer and help you all  create a great menu out of it-as I did? So here comes a Cosori Air Fryer recipes cookbook which has a complete range of Cosori-cooked meals, including 500 recipes for breakfast, crispy snacks, entrees, desserts and much more.

Chapter 1 Understanding Cosori Air Fryer

With the Cosori Air Fryer resting on your countertop, you don't need to turn to your deep-fryers to enjoy crispy food. Now you can cook almost any meal in this air fryer, and it will taste equally delicious and far healthier than the oil-soaked deep-fried food. The efficient cooking techniques used in the Cosori Air fryers are known for good and consistent results. And the most striking feature of the Cosori Air Fryer is that it offers you cooking functions that are hard to find in other models of air fryers in this range. There are several new features that have been introduced to make it more user-friendly. When you buy the Cosori 5.8 quarts Air Fryer, you will get the following:

- A 5.8 quarts cooking capacity
- Large enough to cook a serving of 3-5 people at a time
- The size of the inner air fryer basket is large enough to fit 5-6 pounds of whole chicken
- The inner basket size is 9 x 9 x 3.75 inches
- With the overall dimensions of 11.8 x 11.8 x 12.6 inches, the appliance makes a portable appliance that can perfectly sit on your countertop without taking up much space.

Why Buy Cosori Air Fryer

It might be difficult to consistently serve foods that are both enjoyable and healthful for the family. Even though we know there are healthier options, we sometimes turn to deep-fried foods. That may soon be a thing of the past, as air fryers have arrived to save the day, allowing you to enjoy guilt-free fried meals without sacrificing flavor. The Cosori Air Fryer Pro, with its amazing features, has a lot to offer to those who want to enjoy oil-free meals:

Great Design

The design of the Cosori Air Fryer is possibly one of its most distinguishing features. It includes an angled display with simple presets and a compact design that allows it to fit directly on your counter. It comes in three colors: sleek black, stylish burgundy red, and white color. And they are perfect for adding elegance to the whole kitchen ambience. The design is simple and suggestive, with a modern touchscreen panel that lights up while in use. The Cosori Air Fryer's surface is also fingerprint-resistant, so it will stay smudge-free even after a lot of use, keeping its lovely appearance intact.

Better Controls

When looking at the controls on the Digital Cosori Air Fryer, it may appear that there are too many buttons. But, upon closer inspection, it actually looks quite simple to use. Its control panel is a one-touch LED screen that is very easy to operate. The temperature & time manual buttons, the on/off button, a keep warm button, and the start & pause button are all located in the centre of the panel under the display screen. The READY sign on the LED lights up when you need to add the food to the air fryer.

Amazing Presets

The presets on this Cosori Air Fryer are the next intriguing feature. Steak, fish, chicken, shrimp, frozen meals, bacon, French fries, root vegetables, veggies, desserts, and bread are among the 11 one-touch presets. You may quickly select your desired setting with the one-tap display, and you're ready to cook! Your recipes can also have their own temperature and time settings. That means you may air fry your meals manually at 170 to 400 degrees F for 1 to 60 minutes.

Shake and Keep Warm Options

While we're on the subject of presets, the Cosori Air Fryer features a handy shake and keep warm option that reminds you to shake or flip the food once it is cooked halfway through. This is one approach to ensure that your food is correctly cooked and will not stick. While you're waiting for your dinner to be served, use the keep-warm option to keep the food fresh. It is important to mention here that only a few of the preset settings of this Air Fryer display the shaking sign during cooking; for others, you will have to check in on the food to flip or toss it once it is cooked halfway through.

Dishwasher Safe Air Fryer Baskets

A non-stick-coated and dishwasher-safe detachable basket is also included with the Cosori Air Fryer. The basket is easy to separate, wash (dishwasher safe), and clean, and you may use it to place food on the table or wherever you are preparing dinner. This basket provides for simple food preparation and maintenance, ensuring that you get the most out of it.

Automatic Shutoff

It's fine if you tend to forget to switch off your cooking appliance after each use because the automatic shutoff system of the Cosori Air Fryer has that in control. The air fryer shuts itself off within 3 minutes of inactivity.

Overheating Protection

Another great safety feature of this appliance is that it shuts itself off whenever it is overheated. If this air fryer shuts downs automatically during cooking, without beeping, it means that it is overheated. Let your air fryer cool down for a few minutes, then restart again for cooking.

Health Benefits

When compared to a regular deep-fried dinner, this air fryer keeps the fat content of the food less than 85 percent. And it will not compromise the taste and texture of the food. That is why air fryers are always a good investment when it comes to your family's health. Deep fryers consume 50 times more oil than air fryers, which will undoubtedly have a negative influence on your health. Instead, the appliance cooks your favorite meals using sophisticated air circulation technology.

User Guide

These days there are several air fryers that come with preset settings for various foods. The Cosori Air Fryer comes with 11 preset settings, including seafood, bread, bacon, root vegetables, and French fries, which give you the right options to cook your meals. The controls of the Cosori Air Fryer are simple to understand and operate. It is a digital appliance, and you can select any cooking preset by pressing the buttons given on the touch panel. The central power button is pressed to switch on the appliance. Then the temperature and time are adjusted to begin cooking. The Cosori Air Fryer beeps at the end of each cooking cycle. When you pull out the drawer in the middle of a cooking session, the air fryer automatically pauses and resumes when the drawer is placed back again.

Setting Up the Air Fryer

The air fryer must be kept in a place where there is another heating appliance or element near it. It has to be 5 inches away from any nearby surface. The top of the air fryer heats up during use, so make sure that nothing is covering the top.

After unboxing the air fryer, place it over a sturdy surface, which has to be heat resistant which means that plastic tables are not a good place to keep your air fryer. Once the air fryer is set in place, remove the baskets and their plastic from the inside. Separate the inner basket from the outer basket by pressing the button. You need to wash both baskets separately and then wipe them with a clean cloth to dry them up. Now put both the baskets back in place. Your Cosori Air Fryer is now ready for use.

Preheating

Almost all the air fryer companies recommend preheating, and it is best for the taste and texture of the food cooked inside. The great thing about this Cosori Air Fryer is that it comes with a PREHEAT button which you can press to select the preheat settings and then press the START/PAUSE key to start preheating.

You can either preheat on the default setting, which is 400 degrees F temperature for 5 minutes, or you can manually preheat the appliance on a different temperature setting, then here are the recommended timings:

- 400 degrees F : 5 minutes.
- 390 degrees F : 5 minutes.
- 380 degrees F : 5 minutes.
- 370 degrees F : 4 minutes.
- 360 degrees F : 4 minutes.
- 350 degrees F : 4 minutes.
- 340 degrees F : 4 minutes.
- 330 degrees F : 3 minutes.

When your Cosori Air Fryer is done with the preheating, it will beep three times, and the display will show the READY sign, which indicates that you can now add food to the inner air fryer basket.

Air Frying

The Cosori Air Fryer 5.8 quarts come with two options for cooking; you can either use the different preset settings or manually adjust the time and temperature to air fry your food.

Preset

There are a total of 11 presets you can use when you have Cosori Air Fryer Pro. Each preset has its own default time and temperature settings. Besides that, the shake reminder of the appliance also works for a few of those presets. They all have their respective symbols. Here is the list of all the presets and their respective default settings.

Meals	Shake Reminder	Cooking Time	Cooking Temperature
Bacon	-	8 minutes	320 degrees F
Bread	-	8 minutes	320 degrees F
Chicken	-	25 minutes	380 degrees F
Desserts	-	30 minutes	300 degrees F
French Fries	-	25 minutes	380 degrees F
Frozen Food	Yes	10 minutes	350 degrees F
Root Vegetables	Yes	12 minutes	400 degrees F
Seafood	-	8 minutes	350 degrees F
Shrimp	Yes	8 minutes	370 degrees F
Steak	-	6 minutes	400 degrees F
Vegetables	Yes	10 minutes	300 degrees F

The presets that do not have the SHAKE food feature do not display the SHAKE sign on display, so you will have to check on the food on your own and flip it once it is cooked quarter or halfway through.

Manual Air Frying

If you are not comfortable using the presets, then you can manually adjust the settings and cook your food at the desired temperature. For that, you will have to first preheat the appliance as per the guidelines I shared earlier. Once preheated, your device will flash the READY sign on display. Now instead of pressing any of the PRESET, simply press the TEMP/TIME button for once, then use the + or – buttons to increase or decrease the value between 170-400 degrees or 77- 205 degrees C.

Press the TEMP/TIME button again for the second time, and now use the + or – buttons to adjust the value from 1-60 minutes. After that, press the button with the START/PAUSE symbol on it. At the end of this cooking cycle, the air fryer will beep 3 times, and you can either remove the baskets to serve the food or press the KEEP WARM button to keep the food in the air fryer.

Cleaning and Care

Regular cleaning keeps your air fry forever young, and that calls for cleaning the interior of the air fryer after every season of cooking. If you want to make after-cook cleaning easy, then make sure to line the outer basket of your air fryer with a foil sheet, In this way, you can simply remove the foil to discard the drippings, and the basket won't need any cleaning at all. Similarly, you can place parchment paper under stick food before cooking; this will keep any food from sticking over the base of the air fryer basket. To clean your Cosori Air Fryer, here is what you need to do:

1. Cleaning a hot air fryer can be a great mistake, so unplug it after cooking and allow the interior and exterior of your air fryer to cool down your air fryer. For quick cooling, remove the air fryer basket from the main unit and keep it aside.

2. If there are any dust or food particles sticking over the exterior of the air fryer, then don't try to wash it off or scrub it. Take a lightly damp clean kitchen towel and wipe the exterior with it. The exterior can

be cleaned once or twice a week. It does not require daily cleaning. Never dip or immerse this unit in water or any liquid for cleaning.

3. The interior of the air fryer, however, must be properly cleaned after each use. The baskets inside the air fryer drawer are dishwasher safe which means you can simply remove them after cooling them down and then place them in your dishwasher to wash and dry.

4. If you don't have a dishwasher, then no worries! You can wash the basket with soapy water. Avoid scrubbing the baskets with hard scrubbers as they may damage their non-stick coating. If there is any stubborn food particle stuck on the basket, then soak it in lukewarm water for almost 10-15 minutes to soften the food particles, then lightly remove them using a non-abrasive sponge.

5. Stubborn grease is a tough one to wash, and it does not just go away with soapy water. Here is the company recommended method to remove that stubborn grease from the baskets: Mix 2 tablespoons of masking with 1 tablespoon of water to make a paste. Apply this paste over the stubborn grease and lightly scrub it over the grease with a soft sponge. Leave this paste on for 15 minutes, then rinse it off. Now when you wash the baskets with soap and water, that grease will be gone.

6. Before putting the air fryer basket back into its drawer, make sure to dry it well. The heating coil must be completely dry before you plug in the device and restart it for more cooking.

Conclusion

It's time to plug in that Cosori Air Fryer of yours and start making some finger-licking delicious meals every day. The 5.8 quarts 11-in-1 versatile Cosori Air Fryer makes air frying super quick and easy with its smart cooking technology, the shake and keep warm features and user-friendly control and presets. You can cook from the smallest of the serving size to a total of 5 people serving in this countertop kitchen appliance. From breakfast to snacks, poultry, meat, seafood, and desserts, you can cook it all in your Cosori Air Fryer. You just need the right recipes and the perfect combination of ingredients to get the most out of it. This Cosori Air Fryer cookbook comes with a wide range of air fryer recipes that you can try at home. Pick and choose your favorite recipes and give them a try. Make sure to follow through with the general guidelines and the tips shared before the recipes to start off on the right note. The cooking time and temperature for the basic ingredients are also shared there, so you can get a perfectly cooked meal every time. Once the meal is cooked, you can then use the keep warm feature of your air fryer to keep it fresh to serve at any time. So, stop waiting around, set up your Cosori Air Fryer and start enjoying the perks of oil-free cooking every day.

Chapter 2 Breakfast

Bread Boat Eggs with Mushroom

Prep time: 10 minutes | Cook time: 13 minutes | Serves 4

4 pistolette rolls	1 tsp. butter
4 eggs	½ tsp. dried onion flakes
¼ cup diced fresh mushrooms	½ tsp. salt
	¼ tsp. dried dill weed
1 tbsp. milk	¼ tsp. dried parsley

1. Cut a rectangle in the top of each roll and scoop out the center, leaving a ½-inch shell on the sides and bottom.
2. Place mushrooms, butter and dried onion in air fryer basket and air fry for 1 minute. Stir and cook for 3 more minutes.
3. In a medium bowl, beat together the eggs, dill, parsley, salt and milk. Pour the mixture into the air fryer basket with mushrooms.
4. Air fry for about 2 minutes at 390ºF (200ºC). Stir. Continue cooking for 3 or 4 minutes, stirring every minute, until eggs are scrambled to your liking.
5. Remove the air fryer basket from the air fryer and fill rolls with scrambled egg mixture.
6. Place filled rolls in air fryer basket and air fry at 390ºF (200ºC) for 3 minutes or until rolls are lightly browned.

Berry Pancake Muffins

Prep time: 15 minutes | Cook time: 28 minutes | Serves 4

Cooking spray	¼ tsp. salt
1 egg, beaten	24 foil muffin cups
1 cup buttermilk	**FOR THE SUGGESTED**
1 cup flour	**FILLINGS:**
2 tbsps. sugar (optional)	1 tbsp. fresh blueberries
2 tbsps. melted butter	or strawberries
½ tsp. baking soda	1 tsp. of jelly or fruit
1 tsp. baking powder	preserves
1 tsp. pure vanilla extract	

1. In a large bowl, stir together flour, baking soda, baking powder, optional sugar and salt.
2. In a small bowl, combine egg, butter, buttermilk and vanilla. Mix well.
3. Pour the egg mixture into dry ingredients and stir to mix well but don't overbeat.
4. Double up the muffin cups and remove the paper liners from the top cups. Spray the foil cups lightly with cooking spray.
5. Put 4 sets of muffin cups in the air fryer basket. Pour just enough batter into each cup to cover the bottom. Sprinkle with your desired filling. Pour in more batter to cover the filling and fill the cups about ¾ full.
6. Air fry for about 7 to 8 minutes at 330ºF (165ºC).
7. Repeat steps 5 and 6 for the remaining pancake muffins.

Sweet Pumpkin Donut Holes

Prep time: 10 minutes | Cook time: 5 minutes | Makes 12 donut holes

1 cup whole-wheat pastry flour, plus more as needed	more as needed
	2 tbsps. unsalted butter, melted
⅓ cup canned no-salt-added pumpkin purée	1 tsp. low-sodium baking powder
1 egg white	½ tsp. ground cinnamon
3 tbsps. packed brown sugar	Powdered sugar (optional)
3 tbsps. 2% milk, plus	

1. In a medium bowl, mix the pastry flour, cinnamon, brown sugar and baking powder.
2. In a small bowl, beat the pumpkin, butter, milk and egg white until combined well. Place the pumpkin mixture to the dry ingredients and mix until combined. You may need to place more flour or milk to form a soft dough.
3. Evenly divide the dough into 12 pieces. With floured hands, shape each piece into a ball.
4. Cut a piece of parchment paper or aluminum foil to fit inside the air fryer basket but about 1 inch smaller in diameter. Poke holes in the paper or foil and put it in the basket.
5. Place 6 donut holes into the basket, leaving some space around each. Air fry for about 5 to 7 minutes, or until the donut holes reach an internal temperature of 200ºF (95ºC) and are firm and light golden brown.
6. Allow to cool for 5 minutes. Remove from the basket and roll in powdered sugar, if desired. Repeat this process with the remaining donut holes and serve.

Cheesy Egg English Muffins

Prep time: 5 minutes | Cook time: 8 minutes | Serves 4

Olive oil
4 eggs
4 English muffins, split
1 cup shredded Colby

Jack cheese
4 slices ham or Canadian bacon
Salt and pepper, to taste

1. Preheat air fryer to 390ºF (200ºC).
2. Beat together eggs and add salt and pepper to taste. Spray air fryer basket lightly with oil and add eggs. Air fry for about 2 minutes, stir and continue cooking for 3 or 4 minutes, stirring every minute, until eggs are scrambled to your preference. Remove the air fryer basket from the air fryer.
3. Put the bottom halves of English muffins in air fryer basket. Take half of the shredded cheese and distribute it among the muffins. Top each with a slice of ham and one-quarter of the eggs. Sprinkle the remaining cheese on top of the eggs. Press the cheese into the egg a little with a fork so it doesn't slip off before it melts.
4. Air fry at 360ºF (180ºC) for 1 minute. Place English muffin tops and cook for 2 to 4 minutes to heat through and toast the muffins.

Crispy Tofu with Tamari

Prep time: 15 minutes | Cook time: 14 minutes | Serves 4

Cooking oil spray (sunflower, safflower, or refined coconut)
2 tsps. neutral-flavored oil (such as sunflower, safflower, or melted refined coconut)
1 (8-ounce / 227-g) package firm or extra-firm tofu
2 tbsps. nutritional yeast

4 tsps. tamari or shoyu
2 tsps. arrowroot (or cornstarch)
1 tsp. dried rosemary
1 tsp. dried dill
1 tsp. onion granules
½ tsp. garlic granules
½ tsp. turmeric powder
¼ tsp. freshly ground black pepper

1. Slice the tofu into slices and press out the excess water.
2. Cut the slices into ½-inch cubes and put in a bowl. Sprinkle with the tamari and gently toss to coat. Keep aside for a few minutes.
3. Toss the tofu again, then place the garlic, onion, turmeric and pepper. Gently toss to thoroughly coat.
4. Add the nutritional yeast, dill, rosemary and arrowroot. Toss gently to coat.
5. Finally, drizzle with the oil and toss one last time.

Lightly spray the air fryer basket with the oil. Arrange the tofu in the air fryer basket and air fry for about 7 minutes. Remove, shake gently (so that the tofu cooks evenly), and cook for 7 minutes more, or until the tofu is crisp and browned.

Coconut Donut Holes

Prep time: 15 minutes | Cook time: 8 minutes | Makes 12 donut holes

Cooking oil spray (refined coconut, sunflower, or safflower)
1½ cups whole-wheat pastry flour or all-purpose gluten-free flour
¾ cup coconut sugar, divided
¼ cup nondairy milk, unsweetened
2 tbsps. neutral-flavored

oil (sunflower, safflower, or refined coconut)
1 tbsp. ground flaxseed
1½ tbsps. water
2½ tsps. cinnamon, divided
1½ tsps. vanilla
¾ tsp. baking powder
½ tsp. nutmeg
¼ tsp. sea salt

1. In a medium bowl, stir the flaxseed with the water and keep aside for about 5 minutes, or until gooey and thick.
2. Add the oil, milk and vanilla. Stir well and set this wet mixture aside.
3. In a small bowl, combine the ½ cup coconut sugar, flour, ½ tsp. cinnamon, nutmeg, salt and baking powder. Stir very well. Place this mixture to the wet mixture and stir together—it will be stiff, so you'll need to knead it lightly, just until all of the ingredients are thoroughly combined.
4. Lightly spray the air fryer basket with oil. Pull off bits of the dough and roll into balls (about 1 inch in size each). Place in the basket, leaving room in between as they'll increase in size a smidge. (You'll need to work in batches, as you probably won't be able to cook all 12 at once.) Spray the tops with oil and air fry for about 6 minutes.
5. Remove the pan, spray the donut holes with oil again, flip them over, and spray them with oil again. Cook them for another 2 minutes, or until golden-brown.
6. During the last 2 minutes of cooking, put the remaining 4 tbsps. coconut sugar and 2 tsps. cinnamon in a bowl, and stir to combine well.
7. When the donut holes are done cooking, take them one at a time and coat them as follows: Spray with oil again and toss with the cinnamon-sugar mixture. Spray one last time, and coat with the cinnamon-sugar one last time. Serve warm.

Egg and Turkey Sausage Roll-Ups

Prep time: 10 minutes | Cook time: 22 minutes | Serves 3

Cooking spray oil
2 eggs
6 links turkey sausage
6 slices of white bread, crusts removed
½ cup milk

1 tbsp. butter, melted
½ tsp. ground cinnamon
½ tsp. vanilla extract
Powdered sugar (optional)
Maple syrup, for serving

1. Preheat the air fryer to 380ºF (195ºC) and add a little water to the bottom of the air fryer drawer. (This will help prevent the grease that drips into the bottom drawer from burning and smoking.)
2. Air Fry the sausage links at 380ºF (195ºC) for 8 to 10 minutes, turning them a couple of times during the cooking process. (If you have pre-cooked sausage links, omit this step.)
3. Roll each sausage link in a piece of bread, pressing the finished seam tightly to seal shut.
4. Preheat the air fryer to 370ºF (188ºC).
5. Combine the eggs, cinnamon, milk and vanilla in a shallow dish. Dip the sausage rolls in the egg mixture and let them soak in the egg for 30 seconds. Lightly spray or brush the bottom of the air fryer basket with oil and take the sausage rolls to the air fryer basket, seam side down.
6. Air Fry the rolls at 370ºF (188ºC), and set time to 9 minutes. Brush melted butter over the bread, flip the rolls over and air fry for another 5 minutes. Remove the French toast roll-ups from the basket and dust with powdered sugar, if using. Serve with maple syrup.

Chocolate Crescent Rolls with Almond

Prep time: 5 minutes | Cook time: 8 minutes | Serves 4 to 6

Butter or oil
⅔ cup semi-sweet or bittersweet chocolate chunks
1 (8-ounce / 227-g) tube of crescent roll dough

1 egg white, lightly beaten
¼ cup sliced almonds
Powdered sugar, for dusting

1. Preheat the air fryer to 350ºF (180ºC).
2. Unwrap the crescent roll dough and separate it into triangles with the points facing away from you. Put a row of chocolate chunks along the bottom edge of

the dough. (If you are using chips, make it a double row.) Roll the dough up around the chocolate and then arrange another row of chunks on the dough. Roll again and finish with one or two chocolate chunks. Be sure to leave the end free of chocolate so that it can adhere to the rest of the roll.
3. Brush the tops of the crescent rolls with the lightly beaten egg white and sprinkle the almonds on top, carefully pressing them into the crescent dough so they adhere.
4. Brush the bottom of the air fryer basket with butter or oil and take the crescent rolls to the air fryer basket. Air fry for about 8 minutes at 350ºF (180ºC), in multiple batches if necessary. Remove and let the crescent rolls cool before dusting with powdered sugar and serving.

Red Rolls with Meat

Prep time: 10 minutes | Cook time: 15 minutes | Serves 6

1 tbsp. sesame oil
7 cups minced meat
1 packet spring roll sheets
1 cup mixed vegetables
2 ounces (57 g) Asian

noodles
1 small onion, diced
3 cloves garlic, crushed
2 tbsps. water
1 tsp. soy sauce

1. Cook the noodles in hot water until they turn tender. Drain and cut to your desired length.
2. Lightly grease the wok with sesame oil. Place it over a medium-high heat and fry the minced meat, mixed vegetables, onion and garlic, stirring regularly to ensure the minced meat cooks through. The cooking time will vary depending on the pan you are using – allow 3 to 5 minutes if using a wok, and 7 to 10 minutes if using a standard frying pan.
3. Drizzle in the soy sauce and add to the noodles, tossing well to let the juices spread and absorb evenly.
4. Scoop the stir-fry diagonally across a spring roll sheet and fold back the top point over the filling. Fold over the sides. Before folding back the bottom point, brush it with cold water, which will act as an adhesive.
5. Repeat the step 4 until all the filling and sheets are used.
6. Preheat your Air Fryer at 360ºF (180ºC).
7. If desired, drizzle a small amount of oil over the top of the spring rolls to enhance the taste and ensure crispiness.
8. Air fry for about 8 minutes, in multiple batches if necessary. Serve warm and enjoy.

Asparagus, Bell Pepper and Carrot Strata

Prep time: 10 minutes | Cook time: 15 minutes | Serves 4

3 egg whites
1 egg
8 large asparagus spears, trimmed and cut into 2-inch pieces
½ cup chopped red bell pepper
⅓ cup shredded carrot
2 slices low-sodium whole-wheat bread, cut into ½-inch cubes
3 tbsps. 1 percent milk
½ tsp. dried thyme

1. In a 6-by-2-inch pan, combine the asparagus, red bell pepper, carrot and 1 tbsp. of water. Air fry for about 3 to 5 minutes in the air fryer, or until crisp-tender. Drain well.
2. Put the bread cubes to the vegetables and gently toss.
3. In a medium bowl, whisk the milk, egg whites, egg and thyme until frothy.
4. Pour the egg mixture into the pan. Air fry for 11 to 15 minutes, or until the strata is slightly puffy and set and the top starts to brown. Serve warm.

Breakfast Cherry Tarts

Prep time: 10 minutes | Cook time: 20 minutes | Serves 6

FOR THE TARTS:
Cooking oil
⅓ cup cherry preserves
2 refrigerated piecrusts
1 tsp. cornstarch
FOR THE FROSTING:
1 ounce (28 g) cream cheese
½ cup vanilla yogurt
1 tsp. stevia
Rainbow sprinkles, for garnish

MAKE THE TARTS:
1. Put the piecrusts on a flat surface. Cut each piecrust into 3 rectangles with a knife or pizza cutter, for 6 total. (I discard the unused dough left from slicing the edges.)
2. Combine the preserves and cornstarch in a small bowl. Mix well.
3. Spoon 1 tbsp. of the preserves mixture onto the top half of each piece of piecrust.
4. Gently fold the bottom of each piece up to close the tart. Press along the edges of each tart to seal with the back of a fork.
5. Spray the breakfast tarts with cooking oil and arrange them in the air fryer. I do not recommend stacking the breakfast tarts. They will stick together if stacked.

You may need to prepare them in two batches. Air fry for 10 minutes.
6. Let the breakfast tarts cool fully before removing from the air fryer.
7. If necessary, repeat steps 5 and 6 for the remaining breakfast tarts.
MAKE THE FROSTING:
8. In a small bowl, combine the cream cheese, yogurt and stevia. Mix well.
9. Spread the breakfast tarts with frosting. Top with sprinkles and serve.

Glazed Apple Cider Doughnut Holes

Prep time: 15 minutes | Cook time: 6 minutes | Makes 10 mini doughnuts

FOR THE DOUGHNUT HOLES:
Vegetable oil, for brushing
1 large egg, lightly beaten
1½ cups all-purpose flour
¼ cup plus 2 tbsps. buttermilk, chilled
2 tbsps. apple cider (hard or nonalcoholic), chilled
2 tbsps. granulated sugar
2 tsps. baking powder
1 tsp. baking soda
½ tsp. kosher salt
Pinch of freshly grated nutmeg
FOR THE GLAZE:
2 tbsps. unsweetened applesauce
½ cup powdered sugar
¼ tsp. vanilla extract
Pinch of kosher salt

MAKE THE DOUGHNUT HOLES:
1. In a bowl, whisk together the granulated sugar, flour, baking powder, baking soda, salt and nutmeg until smooth. Place the buttermilk, cider and egg and stir with a small rubber spatula or spoon until the dough just comes together.
2. Using a 1-ounce ice cream scoop or 2 tablespoons scoop and drop 10 balls of dough into the air fryer basket, spaced evenly apart, and brush the tops lightly with oil. Air fry for 6 minutes at 350ºF (180ºC), until the doughnut holes are golden brown and fluffy. Take the doughnut holes to a wire rack to cool completely.
MAKE THE GLAZE:
3. In a small bowl, stir together the applesauce, powdered sugar, vanilla and salt until smooth.
4. Dip the tops of the doughnuts holes in the glaze, then allow to stand until the glaze sets before serving. If you're impatient and want warm doughnuts, have the glaze ready to go while the doughnuts cook, then use the glaze as a dipping sauce for the warm doughnuts, fresh out of the air fryer.

Cranberry Bran Muffins

Prep time: 10 minutes | Cook time: 30 minutes | Makes 8 muffins

1 egg
1½ cups bran cereal flakes
1 cup plus 2 tbsps. whole-wheat pastry flour
1 cup 2 percent milk
½ cup dried cranberries
3 tbsps. safflower oil or peanut oil
3 tbsps. packed brown sugar
1 tsp. low-sodium baking powder

1. In a medium bowl, mix the pastry flour, cereal, brown sugar and baking powder.
2. In a small bowl, whisk the oil, milk and egg until combined well.
3. Stir the egg mixture into the dry ingredients until just combined.
4. Gently stir in the cranberries.
5. Double up 16 foil muffin cups to make 8 cups. Place 4 cups into the air fryer and fill each three-fourths full with batter. Air fry for 15 minutes, or until the muffin tops spring back when lightly touched with your finger.
6. Repeat the step 5 with the remaining muffin cups and batter.
7. Allow to cool on a wire rack for 10 minutes before serving.

Carrot and Raisin Muffins with Brown Sugar

Prep time: 10 minutes | Cook time: 12 minutes | Makes 8 muffins

3 tbsps. safflower oil
1 egg
2 egg whites
1½ cups whole-wheat pastry flour
⅔ cup almond milk
½ cup finely shredded carrots
⅓ cup golden raisins, chopped
⅓ cup brown sugar
1 tsp. low-sodium baking powder
½ tsp. ground cinnamon

1. In a medium bowl, combine the flour, brown sugar, baking powder and cinnamon and mix well.
2. In a small bowl, combine the almond milk, egg, egg whites and oil and beat until combined well. Stir the egg mixture into the dry ingredients just until combined. Don't overbeat; some lumps should be in the batter—that's just fine.
3. Stir the shredded carrot and chopped raisins slowly into the batter.

4. Double up 16 foil muffin cups to make 8 cups. Place 4 of the cups into the air fryer and fill ¾ full with the batter.
5. Air fry for about 12 to 17 minutes or until the tops of the muffins spring back when lightly touched with your finger.
6. Repeat with remaining muffin cups and the remaining batter. Allow to cool the muffins on a wire rack for 10 minutes before serving.

Sweet Cinnamon-Glazed Butter-Pecan Roll

Prep time: 15 minutes | Cook time: 25 minutes | Serves 2

All-purpose flour, for dusting
8 ounces (227 g) pizza dough
½ cup powdered sugar
¼ cup chopped pecans
¼ cup packed dark brown sugar
1 ounce (28 g) cream
cheese, at room temperature
2 tbsps. unsalted butter, melted
1 tbsp. maple syrup, or dark agave syrup
1 tbsp. milk
¼ tsp. kosher salt
⅛ tsp. ground cinnamon

1. Roll the pizza dough out on a lightly floured work surface into a rough 12 x 8-inch rectangle with a rolling pin. Brush the dough all over with the melted butter, then sprinkle evenly with the pecans, brown sugar and salt, then drizzle with the syrup. Cut the rectangle lengthwise into 8 equal strips with a pizza cutter or knife. Roll up one strip like a snail shell, then continue rolling each spiral up in the next strip until you have one giant spiral.
2. Cut a piece of parchment paper or foil to the size of the bottom of your air fryer basket and line the bottom with it. Slowly lay the spiral in the air fryer and cover with a round of foil cut to fit the size of the spiral. Air fry for 15 minutes at 325ºF (160ºC). Take the foil from the top and cook the roll until golden brown and cooked through in the middle, about 10 minutes more.
3. At the same time, in a bowl, whisk together the powdered sugar, milk, cream cheese and cinnamon until smooth.
4. Once the roll is cooked, allow it to cool in the basket for 10 minutes, then carefully lift it out of the air fryer using the parchment paper bottom as an aid. Take the roll to a plate and pour the icing over the roll to cover it completely. Allow the roll and icing to cool together for at least 10 more minutes to set before cutting into wedges to serve.

Fluffy Oat Bran Muffins

Prep time: 10 minutes | Cook time: 20 minutes | Makes 8 muffins

Cooking spray
2 tbsps. canola oil
1 egg
⅔ cup oat bran
½ cup flour
½ cup buttermilk
¼ cup brown sugar

½ cup chopped dates, raisins or dried cranberries
1 tsp. baking powder
½ tsp. baking soda
⅛ tsp. salt
24 paper muffin cups

1. Preheat air fryer to 330ºF (165ºC).
2. In a large bowl, combine the oat bran, brown sugar, flour, baking powder, baking soda and salt.
3. In a small bowl, beat together the egg, buttermilk and oil.
4. Pour the buttermilk mixture into the bowl with dry ingredients and stir just until moistened. Do not beat.
5. Slowly stir in dried fruit.
6. Use triple baking cups to help muffins hold shape during baking. Spray them with cooking spray, put 4 sets of cups in air fryer basket at a time, and fill each one ¾ full of batter.
7. Air fry for about 10 to 12 minutes, until the top springs back when lightly touched and toothpick inserted in the center comes out clean.
8. Repeat this work for the remaining muffins.

Butternut Squash Frittata with Ricotta

Prep time: 10 minutes | Cook time: 13 minutes | Serves 2

2 tbsps. olive oil
1 cup cubed (½-inch) butternut squash
6 large eggs, lightly beaten
½ cup ricotta cheese
4 fresh sage leaves,

thinly sliced
Cayenne pepper, for garnish
Kosher salt and freshly ground black pepper, to taste

1. In a bowl, toss the squash with the olive oil and season with salt and ground black pepper until coated evenly. Sprinkle the sage on the bottom of a 7-inch round cake pan insert, metal cake pan or foil pan and put the squash on top. Arrange the pan in the air fryer and air fry for about 10 minutes at 400ºF (205ºC). Stir to incorporate the sage, then cook until the squash is soft and lightly caramelized at the edges, about 3 minutes more.
2. Pour the eggs over the squash, dollop the ricotta

all over and scatter with cayenne. Air fry at 300ºF (150ºC) until the eggs are set and the frittata is golden brown on top, about 20 minutes. Take the pan from the air fryer and cut the frittata into wedges to serve.

Cheesy Eggs with Bacon and Tomato Sauce

Prep time: 10 minutes | Cook time: 27 minutes | Serves 1

1 tsp. olive oil
2 slices of bacon, chopped
2 large eggs
1 (14-ounce / 397-g) can crushed or diced tomatoes
¼ cup grated Cheddar cheese

2 tbsps. finely chopped onion
1 tsp. chopped fresh oregano
Fresh parsley, chopped
pinch crushed red pepper flakes
Salt and freshly ground black pepper, to taste

1. Start by making the tomato sauce. Preheat a medium saucepan over medium heat on the stovetop. Pour in the olive oil and sauté the onion, oregano and pepper flakes for about 5 minutes. Place the tomatoes and bring to a simmer. Season with salt and pepper and simmer for about 10 minutes.
2. At the same time, preheat the air fryer to 400ºF (205ºC) and pour a little water into the bottom of the air fryer drawer. (This will help prevent the grease that drips into the bottom drawer from burning and smoking.) Arrange the bacon in the air fryer basket and air fry at 400ºF (205ºC) for 5 minutes, shaking the basket every once in a while.
3. When the bacon is almost crispy, remove it to a paper-towel lined plate and rinse out the air fryer drawer, draining away the bacon grease.
4. Take the tomato sauce to a shallow 7-inch pie dish. Crack the eggs on top of the sauce and scatter the cooked bacon back on top. Season with salt and pepper and transfer the pie dish into the air fryer basket. You can use an aluminum foil sling to complete this by taking a long piece of aluminum foil, folding it in half lengthwise twice until it is roughly 26-inches by 3-inches. Put this under the pie dish and hold the ends of the foil to move the pie dish in and out of the air fryer basket. Tuck the ends of the foil beside the pie dish while it cooks in the air fryer.
5. Air fry for about 5 minutes at 400ºF (205ºC), or until the eggs are almost cooked to your liking. Sprinkle the cheese on top and air-fry for 2 minutes more. When the cheese has melted, remove the pie dish from the air fryer, garnish with a little chopped parsley and let the eggs cool for a few minutes.

Scotch Eggs with Sausage

Prep time: 10 minutes | Cook time: 15 minutes | Serves 4

Vegetable oil spray
1 pound (454 g) bulk pork sausage
4 hard-cooked large eggs, peeled
1 cup shredded Parmesan cheese
2 tbsps. finely chopped fresh parsley
1 tbsp. finely chopped fresh chives
⅛ tsp. freshly grated nutmeg
⅛ tsp. kosher salt
⅛ tsp. black pepper
Coarse mustard, for serving

1. In a large bowl, gently mix the sausage, chives, nutmeg, parsley, salt and pepper until well combined. Form the mixture into four equal-size patties.
2. Put one egg on each sausage patty and shape the sausage around the egg, covering it completely. Dredge each sausage-covered egg in the shredded cheese to cover completely, pressing lightly to adhere. (Make sure the cheese is well adhered to the meat so shreds of cheese don't end up flying around in the air fryer.)
3. Place the Scotch eggs in the air fryer basket. Spray lightly with vegetable oil spray. Air fry for about 15 minutes at 400ºF (205ºC). Halfway through the cooking time, turn eggs and spray again.
4. Serve with the mustard.

Fried PB&J with Banana

Prep time: 10 minutes | Cook time: 7 minutes | Serves 4

Oil for misting or cooking spray
8 slices oat nut bread or any whole-grain, oversize bread
2 medium bananas, cut into ½-inch-thick slices
1 egg, beaten
½ cup cornflakes, crushed
¼ cup shredded coconut
6 tbsps. peanut butter
6 tbsps. pineapple preserves

1. Preheat air fryer to 360ºF (180ºC).
2. In a shallow dish, mix together the coconut and cornflake crumbs.
3. For each sandwich, spread one bread slice with 1½ tbsps. of peanut butter. Top with banana slices. Evenly spread another bread slice with 1½ tbsps. of preserves. Combine to make a sandwich.
4. Using a pastry brush, brush the top of the sandwich lightly with beaten egg. Sprinkle with about 1½ tbsps. of crumb coating, tightly pressing it in to make it stick. Spray with oil.

5. Turn sandwich over and repeat to coat and spray the other side.
6. Cooking 2 at a time, arrange sandwiches in air fryer basket and air fry for about 6 to 7 minutes or until the coating is golden brown and crispy. If the sandwich doesn't brown enough, spray with a little more oil and air fry at 390ºF (200ºC), and set time to another minute.
7. Slice cooked sandwiches in half and serve warm.

Quick Shakshuka with Tomato Sauce

Prep time: 15 minutes | Cook time: 30 minutes | Serves 2

FOR THE TOMATO SAUCE:
3 tbsps. extra-virgin olive oil
1 can (28-ounce / 794-g) whole plum tomatoes with juice
1 jalapeño pepper, seeded and minced
1 red bell pepper, diced
1 small yellow onion, diced
2 cloves garlic, minced
1 tbsp. tomato paste
2 tsps. granulated sugar
1 tsp. cumin
1 tsp. sweet paprika
Salt to taste
Pinch cayenne pepper
FOR THE SHAKSHUKA:
4 eggs
1 tbsp. chopped cilantro
1 tbsp. heavy cream
crusty bread for serving
Kosher salt and pepper, to taste

1. In a large, deep skillet, heat the olive oil over medium heat. Add the onion and peppers, season with salt, and sauté until softened, for about 10 minutes. Add the garlic and spices and sauté for a few additional minutes until fragrant. Place the tomato paste and stir to combine well. Pour the plum tomatoes along with their juice—breaking up the tomatoes with a spoon—and the sugar. Turn the heat to high and bring the mixture to a boil. Turn the heat down and simmer until the tomatoes are thickened, about 10 minutes. Turn off the heat. (May be done in advance. Refrigerate the sauce if not use right away.)
2. Crack the eggs into a 7-inch round cake pan and insert for the air fryer. Take 1 cup of the tomato sauce from the skillet and scoop it over the egg whites only, leaving the yolks exposed. Drizzle the cream over the yolks.
3. Arrange the cake pan in the air fryer and air fry for about 10 to 12 minutes at 300ºF (150ºC), until the egg whites are set and the yolks still runny. Remove the pan from the air fryer and garnish with chopped cilantro. Season with salt and pepper to taste.
4. Serve warm with crusty bread to mop up the sauce.

Crispy Bacon

Prep time: 5 minutes | Cook time: 5 minutes | Serves 5

10 slices bacon

1. Slice the bacon slices in half, so they will fit in the air fryer.
2. Put the half-slices in the air fryer basket in a single layer. (You may need to cook the bacon in more than one batch.)
3. Select the Bacon function, adjust time to 5 minutes, then press Start/Pause.
4. Open the air fryer and check the bacon. (The power of the fan may have caused the bacon to fly around during the cooking process. If so, rearrange the slices with a fork or tongs.)
5. Reset the timer and cook for 5 minutes more.
6. When the cooking time is complete, check the bacon again. If you like your bacon crispier, cook for another 1 to 2 minutes.

Cheddar Muffins with Bacon

Prep time: 5 minutes | Cook time: 20 minutes | Serves 1

1 slice cooked bacon (cured, pan-fried, cooked)	1 ounce (28 g) Cheddar cheese
1 medium egg	Salt and black pepper, to taste
¼ cup heavy cream	

1. Preheat your fryer to 350ºF (180ºC).
2. Mix the eggs with the cream, salt and pepper in a bowl.
3. Spread into muffin tins and fill the cups half full.
4. Put 1 slice of bacon into each muffin hole and half ounce of cheese on top of each muffin.
5. Air fry for about 15 to 20 minutes or until slightly browned.
6. Place another ½ ounce of cheese onto each muffin and cook until the cheese is slightly browned. Serve warm!

Apple and Walnut Muffins

Prep time: 15 minutes | Cook time: 20 minutes | Makes 8 muffins

1 egg	1 tsp. cinnamon
1 cup flour	1 tsp. baking powder
¾ cup unsweetened applesauce	½ tsp. vanilla extract
⅓ cup sugar	¼ tsp. baking soda
¼ cup chopped walnuts	¼ tsp. salt
¼ cup diced apple	¼ tsp. ginger
2 tbsps. pancake syrup, plus 2 tsps.	¼ tsp. nutmeg
2 tbsps. melted butter, plus 2 tsps.	8 foil muffin cups, liners removed and sprayed with cooking spray

1. Preheat air fryer to 330ºF (165ºC).
2. In a large bowl, stir together flour, baking powder, baking soda, sugar, salt, cinnamon, ginger and nutmeg.
3. In a small bowl, beat the egg until frothy. Add butter, syrup, applesauce and vanilla and mix well.
4. Pour egg mixture into dry ingredients and stir just until moistened.
5. Slowly stir in nuts and diced apple.
6. Distribute batter among the 8 muffin cups.
7. Put 4 muffin cups in air fryer basket and air fry for about 9 to 11 minutes at 330ºF (165ºC), or until toothpick inserted in center comes out clean.
8. Repeat with remaining 4 muffins.

Fluffy Fruity Beignets

Prep time: 10 minutes | Cook time: 8 minutes | Makes 16 beignets

1 egg	3 tbsps. packed brown sugar
1½ cups whole-wheat pastry flour	2 tbsps. unsalted butter, melted
⅓ cup buttermilk	1 tsp. active quick-rising dry yeast
3 tbsps. chopped dried cherries	Powdered sugar, for dusting (optional)
3 tbsps. chopped golden raisins	

1. In a medium bowl, mix the yeast with 3 tbsps. of water. Allow it to stand for 5 minutes, or until it bubbles.
2. Stir in the b brown sugar, buttermilk and egg until well mixed.
3. Stir in the pastry flour until well combined.
4. With your hands, work the raisins and cherries into the dough. Let the mixture stand for about 15 minutes.
5. Pat the dough into an 8-by-8-inch square and cut into 16 pieces. Carefully shape each piece into a ball.
6. Drizzle the balls with the melted butter. Arrange them in a single layer in the air fryer basket so they don't touch. You may have to cook these in batches. Air fry for about 5 to 8 minutes, or until puffy and golden brown.
7. Dust with powdered sugar before serving, if desired.

Cheesy Vegetables Egg Cups, page 20

Eggs Florentine with Spinach, page 23

Spicy Hash Browns, page 17

Eggs in a Bread, page 21

Simple Veggie Omelet

Prep time: 5 minutes | Cook time: 10 minutes | Serves 2

3 eggs
½ cup finely chopped vegetables of your

choosing
Pinch of cayenne or black pepper

1. In a pan on high heat, stir-fry the vegetables in extra-virgin olive oil until lightly crispy.
2. Air fry for about 10 minutes at 350ºF (180ºC). Cook the eggs with one tbsp. of water and a pinch of pepper.
3. When almost cooked, put the vegetables on top and flip to cook briefly.
4. Serve warm.

Quiche Cups with Pork Sausage

Prep time: 5 minutes | Cook time: 22 minutes | Makes 10 quiche cups

Cooking spray
3 eggs
¼ pound all-natural ground pork sausage

¾ cup milk
4 ounces (113 g) sharp Cheddar cheese, grated
20 foil muffin cups

1. Divide sausage into 3 portions evenly and shape each into a thin patty.
2. Put patties in air fryer basket and air fry for about 6 minutes at 390ºF (200ºC).
3. While the sausage is cooking, prepare the egg mixture. A large measuring cup or bowl with a pouring lip works best. Combine the eggs and milk and whisk until well blended. Set aside.
4. When sausage has cooked fully, take patties from the basket, drain well, and crumble the meat into small pieces with a fork.
5. Double the foil cups into 10 sets. Remove paper liners from the top muffin cups and lightly spray the foil cups with cooking spray.
6. Divide crumbled sausage among the 10 muffin cup sets.
7. Top each with grated cheese, distribute evenly among the cups.
8. Arrange 5 cups in air fryer basket.
9. Pour egg mixture into each cup, filling until each cup is at least ⅔ full.
10. Air fry for 8 minutes and test for doneness. A knife inserted into the center shouldn't have any raw egg on it when removed.
11. If needed, cook for another 1 to 2 minutes, until the egg completely sets.
12. Repeat steps 8 through 11 for the remaining quiches.

Spicy Hash Browns

Prep time: 5 minutes | Cook time: 20 minutes | Serves 4

Cooking oil
4 russet potatoes
1 tsp. paprika

Salt, to taste
Pepper, to taste

1. Peel the potatoes with a vegetable peeler. Shred the potatoes with a cheese grater. If your grater has different size holes, use the area of the tool with the largest holes.
2. Arrange the shredded potatoes in a large bowl of cold water. Allow to sit for 5 minutes. Cold water helps remove excess starch from the potatoes. Stir to help dissolve the starch.
3. Drain the potatoes and dry with paper towels or napkins. Make sure the potatoes are completely dry.
4. Season the potatoes with paprika, salt and pepper to taste.
5. Lightly spray the potatoes with cooking oil and take them to the air fryer. Air fry for 20 minutes, shaking the basket every 5 minutes (a total of 4 times).
6. Let cool before serving.

Fried Potatoes with Onion and Bell Peppers

Prep time: 10 minutes | Cook time: 23 minutes | Serves 4

1 tbsp. canola oil
1 tbsp. extra-virgin olive oil
3 large russet potatoes
1 cup chopped onion
1 cup chopped red bell

pepper
1 cup chopped green bell pepper
1 tsp. paprika
Salt, to taste
Pepper, to taste

1. Cut the potatoes into ½-inch cubes. Put the potatoes in a large bowl of cold water and let them soak for at least 30 minutes, preferably an hour.
2. Drain the potatoes and dry thoroughly with paper towels. Take them back to the empty bowl.
3. Add the canola and olive oils, paprika, and salt and pepper to taste. Toss to evenly coat the potatoes.
4. Transfer the potatoes to the air fryer. Air fry for 20 minutes, shaking the air fryer basket every 5 minutes (a total of 4 times).
5. Place the onion and red and green bell peppers to the air fryer basket. Air fry for 3 to 4 minutes more, or until the potatoes are cooked through and the peppers are tender.
6. Let cool before serving.

Cheddar and Ham Muffins

Prep time: 10 minutes | Cook time: 12 minutes | Makes 8 muffins

1 egg, beaten
¾ cup yellow cornmeal
½ cup milk
½ cup shredded sharp Cheddar cheese
½ cup diced ham
¼ cup flour

2 tbsps. canola oil
1½ tsps. baking powder
¼ tsp. salt
8 foil muffin cups, liners removed and sprayed with cooking spray

1. Preheat air fryer to 390ºF (200ºC).
2. In a medium bowl, stir together the flour, cornmeal, baking powder and salt.
3. Add oil, egg and milk to dry ingredients and mix well.
4. Stir in shredded cheese and diced ham.
5. Divide batter evenly among the muffin cups.
6. Place 4 filled muffin cups in air fryer basket and air fry for 5 minutes.
7. Reduce temperature to 330ºF (165ºC) and cook for about 1 to 2 minutes or until toothpick inserted in center of muffin comes out clean.
8. Repeat steps 6 and 7 to cook remaining muffins.

Chickpeas Donuts

Prep time: 10 minutes | Cook time: 10 minutes | Serves 6

1 tbsp. coconut oil, melted
1 cup flour
¼ cup milk
¼ cup sugar, plus extra for dusting
2 tbsps. aquafaba or

liquid from canned chickpeas
1 tsp. baking powder
¼ tsp. cinnamon, plus extra for dusting
½ tsp. salt

1. Put the flour, sugar and baking powder in a bowl and combine well. Mix in the salt and cinnamon.
2. In a separate bowl, combine the milk, aquafaba and coconut oil.
3. Gently pour the dry ingredients into the wet ingredients and combine well to create a sticky dough.
4. Refrigerate for at least an hour.
5. Preheat your Air Fryer at 370ºF (188ºC).
6. Shape the dough into several small balls with your hands and put each one inside the fryer. Air fry for about 10 minutes, refraining from shaking the basket as they cook.
7. Lightly dust the balls with sugar and cinnamon and serve with a hot cup of coffee.

Maple French Toast Sticks

Prep time: 10 minutes | Cook time: 15 minutes | Serves 4

Oil for misting or cooking spray
2 eggs
6 slices sandwich bread, each slice cut into 4 strips

¾ cup crushed cornflakes
½ cup milk
½ tsp. pure vanilla extract
⅛ tsp. salt
Maple syrup or honey, for serving

1. In a small bowl, beat together eggs, milk, vanilla and salt.
2. Put the crushed cornflakes on a plate or in a shallow dish.
3. Dip bread strips in egg mixture, shake off excess, and gently roll in cornflake crumbs.
4. Lightly spray both sides of bread strips with oil.
5. Arrange bread strips in air fryer basket in single layer.
6. Air fry for 5 to 7 minutes at 390ºF (200ºC), or until they're dark golden brown.
7. Repeat steps 5 and 6 to cook remaining French toast sticks.
8. Serve warm with maple syrup or honey for dipping.

Cinnamon French Toast Sticks

Prep time: 10 minutes | Cook time: 13 minutes | Makes 12 sticks

Cooking oil
4 slices Texas toast (or any thick bread, such as challah)
1 egg

¼ cup milk
1 tbsp. butter
1 tsp. ground cinnamon
1 tsp. stevia
1 tsp. vanilla extract

1. Slice each slice of bread into 3 pieces (for 12 sticks total).
2. Put the butter in a small, microwave-safe bowl. Microwave for 15 seconds, or until the butter has melted.
3. Take the bowl from the microwave. Add the egg, cinnamon, stevia, milk and vanilla extract. Whisk until fully combined.
4. Lightly spray the air fryer basket with cooking oil.
5. Dredge each of the bread sticks in the egg mixture.
6. Arrange the French toast sticks in the air fryer. It is okay to stack them. Spray the French toast sticks with cooking oil. Air fry for 8 minutes.
7. Open the air fryer and flip each of the French toast sticks. Cook for another 4 minutes, or until the French toast sticks are crisp.
8. Let cool before serving.

Coated Eggs with Sausage

Prep time: 10 minutes | Cook time: 20 minutes | Serves 4

Oil for misting or cooking spray
1 pound (454 g) ground breakfast sausage
4 hard boiled eggs, peeled
¾ cup flour, plus extra 2 tbsps.
1 raw egg
1 tbsp. water
Crumb Coating

1. Combine ¾ cup flour with ground sausage and mix thoroughly.
2. Divide into 4 equal portions evenly and mold each around a hard boiled egg so the sausage completely covers the egg.
3. Beat together the raw egg and water in a small bowl.
4. Dip sausage-covered eggs in the remaining flour, then the egg mixture, then roll in the crumb coating.
5. Air fry for about 10 minutes at 360ºF (180ºC). Spray eggs with oil, turn, and spray the other side.
6. Continue cooking for another 10 to 15 minutes or until the sausage is well done.

Blueberry Muffins

Prep time: 10 minutes | Cook time: 14 minutes | Serves 10

¾ cup fresh blueberries
⅔ cup all-purpose flour
1 egg
⅓ cup low-fat milk
3 tbsps. unsalted butter,
melted
2 tbsps. sugar
1 tsp. baking powder
2 tsps. vanilla extract

1. In a medium mixing bowl, combine the flour, sugar, egg, baking powder, vanilla, milk and melted butter and mix well.
2. Gently fold in the blueberries.
3. Coat the inside of an air fryer muffin tin with cooking spray.
4. Fill each muffin cup about two-thirds full.
5. Set the muffin tin into the air fryer basket. (You may need to cook the muffins in more than one batch.)
6. Air fry for about 14 minutes at 320ºF (160ºC).
7. Insert a toothpick into the center of a muffin; if it comes out clean, they are done. If batter clings to the toothpick, cook the muffins for another 2 minutes and check again.
8. When the muffins are cooked through, remove the muffin tin from the air fryer basket with silicone oven mitts. Turn out the muffins onto a wire rack to cool slightly before serving.

Salmon and Spinach Frittata

Prep time: 10 minutes | Cook time: 15 minutes | Serves 4

Olive oil, for greasing the pan
1 egg
4 egg whites
½ cup cooked, flaked salmon
½ cup fresh baby spinach
½ cup cooked brown rice
¼ cup chopped red bell pepper
1 tbsp. grated Parmesan cheese
½ tsp. dried thyme

1. Rub a 6-by-2-inch pan with a bit of olive oil and keep aside.
2. In a small bowl, beat the egg whites, egg and thyme until well mixed.
3. In the prepared pan, stir together the brown rice, spinach, salmon and red bell pepper.
4. Pour the egg mixture over the rice mixture and sprinkle with the Parmesan cheese.
5. Air fry for about 15 minutes at 350ºF (180ºC), or until the frittata is puffed and golden brown. Serve.

Authentic Quesadillas

Prep time: 10 minutes | Cook time: 18 minutes | Serves 4

Oil for misting or cooking spray
4 flour tortillas
4 eggs
2 ounces (57 g) Cheddar cheese, grated
½ small avocado, peeled and thinly sliced
4 tbsps. salsa
2 tbsps. skim milk
Salt and pepper, to taste

1. Preheat air fryer to 270ºF (132ºC).
2. Beat together eggs, milk, salt and pepper in a bowl.
3. Lightly spray a 6 x 6-inch air fryer basket with cooking spray and add egg mixture.
4. Air fry for about 8 to 9 minutes, stirring every 1 to 2 minutes, until eggs are scrambled to your liking. Remove and keep aside.
5. Spray one side of each tortilla with oil or cooking spray. Flip over.
6. Divide eggs, cheese, salsa and avocado among the tortillas, covering only half of each tortilla.
7. Fold each tortilla in half and press down lightly.
8. Arrange 2 tortillas in air fryer basket and air fry for 3 minutes at 390ºF (200ºC), or until the cheese melts and outside feels slightly crispy. Repeat with the remaining two tortillas.
9. Cut each cooked tortilla into halves or thirds and serve warm.

Simple Blueberry Muffins

Prep time: 10 minutes | Cook time: 28 minutes | Makes 8 muffins

1⅓ cups flour
1 egg
½ cup milk
⅔ cup blueberries, fresh or frozen and thawed
⅓ cup canola oil
½ cup sugar
2 tsps. baking powder
¼ tsp. salt
8 foil muffin cups including paper liners

1. Preheat air fryer to 330ºF (165ºC).
2. In a medium bowl, stir together flour, baking powder, sugar and salt.
3. In a separate bowl, combine oil, milk and egg and mix well.
4. Add egg mixture to dry ingredients and stir just until moistened.
5. Gently stir in blueberries.
6. Scoop batter evenly into muffin cups.
7. Arrange 4 muffin cups in air fryer basket and air fry for 12 to 14 minutes at 330ºF (165ºC), or until tops spring back when touched lightly.
8. Repeat previous step to cook the remaining muffins.

Cheesy Vegetables Egg Cups

Prep time: 10 minutes | Cook time: 19 minutes | Serves 2

Vegetable oil, for greasing
2 large eggs
½ cup shredded sharp Cheddar cheese
½ cup mixed diced vegetables, such as onions, bell peppers,
mushrooms and tomatoes
2 tbsps. half-and-half
1 tbsp. chopped fresh cilantro (or other fresh herb of your choice)
Kosher salt and black pepper, to taste

1. Lightly grease two 6-ounce ramekins with vegetable oil.
2. In a medium bowl, whisk together the vegetables, eggs, ¼ cup of the cheese, the half-and-half, cilantro, salt and pepper. Distribute the mixture between the prepared ramekins.
3. Place the ramekins in the air fryer basket. Air fry for 15 minutes at 300ºF (150ºC).
4. Top the cups with the remaining ¼ cup cheese. Air fry for another 4 minutes at 400ºF (205ºC), until the cheese on top is melted and lightly browned.
5. Serve right away, or store in an airtight container in the refrigerator up to a week.

Ham and Tomato Sandwiches

Prep time: 5 minutes | Cook time: 8 minutes | Serves 2

1 tsp. butter
4 thick slices tomato
4 slices smoked country
ham
4 slices bread
4 slices Cheddar cheese

1. Evenly spread ½ tsp. of butter onto one side of 2 slices of bread. Each sandwich will have 1 slice of bread with butter and 1 slice without.
2. Layer 2 slices of ham, 2 slices of cheese and 2 slices of tomato on the unbuttered pieces of bread to assemble each sandwich. Place the other bread slices buttered side up, on top.
3. Put the sandwiches in the air fryer buttered-side down. Air fry for 4 minutes.
4. Open the air fryer. Flip the grilled cheese sandwiches. Cook for 4 minutes more.
5. Cool before serving. Cut each sandwich in half and enjoy.

Cinnamon Apples Stuffed with Granola

Prep time: 5 minutes | Cook time: 20 minutes | Serves 4

4 Granny Smith or other firm apples
1 cup granola
1 cup water or apple juice
2 tbsps. unsalted butter, melted
2 tbsps. light brown sugar
¾ tsp. cinnamon

1. Working one apple at a time, cut a circle around the apple stem and spoon out the core, taking care not to cut all the way through to the bottom. (This should leave an empty cavity in the middle of the apple for the granola.) Repeat with the remaining apples.
2. Combine the granola, brown sugar and cinnamon in a small bowl. Pour the melted butter over the ingredients and stir with a fork. Divide the granola mixture among the apples, packing it tightly into the empty cavity.
3. Arrange the apples in the air fryer basket and insert for the air fryer. Pour the water or juice around the apples. Air fry for about 20 minutes at 350ºF (180ºC), until the apples are tender all the way through. (If the granola begins to scorch before the apples are fully cooked, cover the top of the apples with a small piece of aluminum foil.)
4. Serve hot with a dollop of crème fraîche or yogurt, if desired.

Eggs in a Bread

Prep time: 5 minutes | Cook time: 6 minutes | Serves 1

1 egg
1 thick slice country, sourdough, or Italian bread

2 tbsps. (28 g) unsalted butter, melted
Kosher salt and pepper, to taste

1. Brush the bottom of the air fryer basket insert and both sides of the bread with melted butter. Cut a hole out of the middle of the bread with a small round cookie or biscuit cutter and keep it aside.
2. Arrange the slice of bread in the air fryer basket insert. Crack the egg into the hole in the bread, taking care not to break the yolk. Season with salt and pepper to taste. Put the cut-out bread hole next to the slice of bread. Arrange the basket insert into the air fryer.
3. Air fry for 6 to 8 minutes at 300ºF (150ºC), until the egg white is set but the yolk is still runny. Remove the bread slice to a plate with a silicone spatula. Serve warm with the cut-out bread circle on the side or place it on top of the egg.

Spicy Barbecue Chicken Flatbreads

Prep time: 10 minutes | Cook time: 10 minutes | Serves 2 to 4

2 prepared naan flatbreads
2 cups chopped cooked chicken
¾ cup shredded Mozzarella cheese
¾ cup prepared barbecue

sauce
½ cup shredded smoked Gouda cheese
½ small red onion, halved and thinly sliced
2 tbsps. chopped fresh cilantro

1. Toss together the chicken and ¼ cup of the barbecue sauce in a medium bowl.
2. Spread half the remaining barbecue sauce on one of the flatbreads. Top with half the chicken and half each of the Mozzarella and Gouda cheeses. Sprinkle with half the red onion. Slowly press the cheese and onions onto the chicken with your fingers.
3. Gently place one flatbread in the air fryer basket. Air fry for about 10 minutes at 400ºF (205ºC), until the bread is browned around the edges and the cheese is bubbling and golden brown. If not, air fry for 2 minutes more. Take the flatbread to a plate and repeat this process to cook the second flatbread.
4. Garnish with the chopped cilantro before serving.

Chicken Sausage and Cream Cheese Biscuits

Prep time: 5 minutes | Cook time: 15 minutes | Serves 5

12 ounces (340 g) chicken breakfast sausage

1 (6-ounce/ 170-g) can biscuits
⅛ cup cream cheese

1. Shape the sausage into 5 small patties.
2. Arrange the sausage patties in the air fryer. Air fry for 5 minutes.
3. Open the air fryer. Flip the patties. Air fry for another 5 minutes.
4. Take the cooked sausages from the air fryer.
5. Separate the biscuit dough into 5 biscuits.
6. Put the biscuits in the air fryer. Air fry for 3 minutes.
7. Open the air fryer. Flip the biscuits. Air fry for 2 minutes more.
8. Remove the cooked biscuits from the air fryer.
9. Split each biscuit in half. Spread 1 tsp. of cream cheese onto the bottom of each biscuit. Place a sausage patty and the other half of the biscuit on top and serve warm.

Asparagus and Goat Cheese Frittata

Prep time: 10 minutes | Cook time: 25 minutes | Serves 2 to 4

1 tsp. vegetable oil
6 eggs
1 cup asparagus spears, cut into 1-inch pieces
2 ounces (57 g) goat cheese

1 tbsp. milk
1 tbsp. minced chives (optional)
Kosher salt and pepper, to taste

1. In a small bowl, toss the asparagus pieces with the vegetable oil. Arrange the asparagus in a 7-inch round air fryer cake pan insert and put the pan in the air fryer. Air fry for about 5 minutes at 400ºF (205ºC), until the asparagus is softened and slightly wrinkled. Remove the pan.
2. Whisk together the eggs and milk and pour the mixture over the asparagus in the pan. Crumble the goat cheese over the top of the eggs and put the chives, if using. Season with a pinch of salt and pepper to taste. Take the pan back to the air fryer and cook for 20 minutes at 320ºF (160ºC), until the eggs are set and cooked through. Serve warm.

Salmon and Pork Sausage Omelet

Prep time: 5 minutes | Cook time: 10 minutes | Serves 2

3 eggs
1 smoked salmon
3 links pork sausage
¼ cup provolone cheese
¼ cup onions, chopped

1. Whisk the eggs and pour them into the basket.
2. Air fry for 10 minutes at 350ºF (180ºC).
3. Add the salmon, onions and half of cheese before turning the omelet over.
4. Scatter the omelet with the remaining cheese and serve with the sausages on the side.

Cinnamon Sweet Potato Toast

Prep time: 5 minutes | Cook time: 8 minutes | Makes 6 to 8 slices

Oil, for misting
1 small sweet potato, cut into ⅜-inch slices
Ground cinnamon, to taste

1. Preheat air fryer to 390ºF (200ºC).
2. Spray both sides of sweet potato slices lightly with oil. Sprinkle both sides with cinnamon to taste.
3. Arrange potato slices in air fryer basket in a single layer.
4. Air fry for about 4 minutes, turn, and cook for 4 more minutes or until the potato slices are barely fork tender.

Quick Hard-Boiled Eggs

Prep time: 5 minutes | Cook time: 15 minutes | Serves 6

6 eggs

1. Place the eggs in the air fryer basket. (You can put the eggs in an oven-safe bowl if you are worried about them rolling around and breaking.)
2. Air fry for about 15 minutes at 250ºF (120ºC) (if you prefer a soft-boiled egg, reduce the cooking time to 10 minutes).
3. At the same time, fill a medium mixing bowl half full of ice water.
4. Remove the eggs from the air fryer basket with tongs, and transfer them to the ice water bath.
5. Allow the eggs to sit for about 5 minutes in the ice water.
6. Peel and eat on the spot or refrigerate for up to 1 week.

Hard-Cooked Eggs

Prep time: 5 minutes | Cook time: 15 minutes | Serves 6

6 large eggs

1. Fit a rack into the air-fryer basket. Place the eggs on the rack.
2. Air fry at 250ºF (120ºC) for about 15 minutes for large eggs (20 minutes for extra-large or jumbo eggs).
3. At the same time, fill a large bowl with ice and water.
4. At the end of the cooking time, very carefully take the hot eggs from the rack and put them in the ice bath for 5 minutes. When the eggs are cool to the touch, drain them, peel and eat them warm!

Spinach and Turkey Bacon Rollups

Prep time: 5 minutes | Cook time: 8 minutes | Serves 4

4 (6- or 7-inch) flour tortillas
1 cup baby spinach
leaves
4 slices turkey bacon
4 slices Swiss cheese

1. Preheat air fryer to 390ºF (200ºC).
2. On each tortilla, put one slice of cheese and ¼ cup of spinach.
3. Roll up tortillas and wrap each with a strip of bacon. Secure each end with a toothpick.
4. Arrange rollups in air fryer basket, leaving a little space in between them.
5. Air fry for 4 minutes. Turn and rearrange rollups (for more even cooking) and cook for 4 to 5 minutes more, or until the bacon is crisp.

Quick Breakfast Bacon Sandwiches

Prep time: 5 minutes | Cook time: 8 minutes | Serves 4

Cooking oil
8 slices Canadian bacon
4 English muffins
4 slices cheese

1. Separate each English muffin. Assemble the breakfast sandwiches by layering 2 slices of Canadian bacon and 1 slice of cheese onto each English muffin bottom. Place the other half of the English muffin on top.
2. Put the sandwiches in the air fryer. Lightly spray the top of each with cooking oil. Air fry for about 4 minutes.
3. Open the air fryer and flip the sandwiches. Cook for another 4 minutes.
4. Let cool before serving.

Easy Cinnamon Rolls

Prep time: 5 minutes | Cook time: 12 minutes | Makes 8 cinnamon rolls

1 can of cinnamon rolls

1. Spray the air fryer basket with olive oil.
2. Separate the canned cinnamon rolls and put them in the air fryer basket. (You may need to cook these in 2 batches.)
3. Air fry for about 6 minutes at 340ºF (170ºC).
4. Flip the cinnamon rolls with tongs. Reset the timer and cook for another 6 minutes.
5. When the rolls are done cooking, use tongs to remove them from the air fryer. Take them to a platter and spread them with the icing that comes in the package.

Cinnamon Egg Porridge

Prep time: 5 minutes | Cook time: 10 minutes | Serves 1

2 tbsps. grass-fed butter	⅓ cup organic heavy cream without food additives
2 organic free-range eggs	
2 packages of your preferred sweetener	Ground organic cinnamon, to taste

1. In a bowl, add the cream, eggs and sweetener and mix together.
2. In a saucepan over a medium heat, melt the butter. Lower the heat once the butter is melted.
3. Combine together with the egg and cream mixture.
4. Air fry for about 10 minutes at 350ºF (180ºC). While Cooking, mix until it thickens and curdles.
5. Pour the porridge into a bowl. Sprinkle cinnamon on top and serve warm.

Eggs Florentine with Spinach

Prep time: 5 minutes | Cook time: 15 minutes | Serves 2

2 eggs	Parmesan cheese
1 cup washed, fresh spinach leaves	1 tbsp. white vinegar
2 tbsps. freshly grated	Sea salt and pepper, to taste

1. Air fry the spinach in the air fryer until wilted.
2. Scatter with Parmesan cheese and seasoning.
3. Slice into bite-size pieces and arrange on a plate.
4. Simmer a pan of water and pour the vinegar. Stir quickly with a spoon.
5. Break an egg into the center. Remove from the heat and cover until set.
6. Repeat with the second egg.
7. Put the eggs on top of the spinach and serve warm.

Easy French Toast

Prep time: 10 minutes | Cook time: 6 minutes | Serves 2

Nonstick cooking spray	Pinch of cinnamon
4 slices bread of your choosing	Pinch of ground nutmeg
	Pinch of ground cloves
2 eggs, lightly beaten	Pinch of salt
2 tbsps. soft butter	Sugar, for serving

1. In a shallow bowl, mix together the salt, eggs and spices.
2. Butter each side of the slices of bread and cut into strips. You may also use cookie cutters for this step.
3. Set your air fryer to 350ºF (180ºC) and let warm up briefly.
4. Dredge each strip of bread in the egg and take to the fryer. Air fry for 2 minutes, ensuring the toast turns golden brown.
5. At this point, spritz the tops of the bread strips with cooking spray, flip, and cook for 4 minutes more on the other side. Top with a light dusting of sugar before serving.

Chapter 3 Vegetable

Chile Cornbread with Cheddar

Prep time: 10 minutes | Cook time: 15 minutes | Serves 6

Vegetable oil spray	diced mild green chiles, undrained
2 large eggs	½ cup grated Cheddar cheese
1 (8½-ounce / 241-g) package corn muffin mix	¼ cup whole milk
1 cup corn kernels	Parchment paper
1 (4-ounce / 113-g) can	

1. Whisk together the eggs and milk in a medium bowl. Add the muffin mix and stir until the batter is smooth. Stir in the cheese, corn and undrained chiles.
2. Spray a 3-cup Bundt pan lightly with vegetable oil spray. Line the pan with parchment paper. (To do this, cut a circle of parchment about 1 inch larger in diameter than the top of the pan. Gently fold the parchment in half and cut a hole in the middle to accommodate the center of the Bundt pan. Put the parchment in the pan and trim any excess parchment from around the top.)
3. Add the batter into the prepared pan. Arrange the pan in the air fryer basket. Air fry for about 15 minutes at 350ºF (180ºC).
4. Let the bread rest in the closed air fryer for 10 minutes before serving.

Cinnamon Butternut Squash

Prep time: 10 minutes | Cook time: 15 minutes | Serves 2 to 3

Olive oil, in a spray bottle	Pinch ground cinnamon
1 butternut squash, peeled	Pinch ground nutmeg
2 tbsps. butter, softened	Chopped fresh sage
2 tbsps. honey	Salt and freshly ground black pepper, to taste

1. Preheat the air fryer to 370ºF (188ºC).
2. Cut the neck of the butternut squash into disks about ½-inch thick. (Use the base of the butternut squash for another use.) Brush or spray the disks lightly with oil and season with salt and freshly ground black pepper to taste.
3. Take the butternut disks to the air fryer in one layer (or just ever so slightly overlapping). Air fry for 5 minutes at 370ºF (188ºC).
4. While the butternut squash is cooking, combine the butter, cinnamon, nutmeg and honey in a small bowl. Brush this mixture on the butternut squash, flip the disks over and brush the other side as well. Continue to air fry for another 5 minutes at 370ºF (188ºC). Flip the disks once more, brush with more of the honey butter and cook for 5 minutes more. The butternut should be browning nicely around the edges.
5. Take the butternut squash from the air-fryer and repeat with additional batches if necessary. Transfer to a serving platter, garnish with the fresh sage and serve warm.

Mashed Potato Tots with Bacon

Prep time: 10 minutes | Cook time: 40 minutes | Makes 18–24 tots

Oil for misting or cooking spray	onions, tops only
1 medium potato	2 tbsps. flour
1 egg white, beaten	1 tbsp. real bacon bits
½ cup panko breadcrumbs	1 tsp. dried chopped chives
2 tbsps. chopped green	¼ tsp. onion powder
	Salt, to taste

1. Peel potato and cut into ½-inch cubes. (Small pieces cook more quickly.) Put in a saucepan, pour water to cover, and heat to boil. Lower heat slightly and continue cooking just until tender, for about 10 minutes.
2. Drain potatoes and place in ice cold water. Let cool for a minute or two, then drain well and mash.
3. Preheat air fryer to 390ºF (200ºC).
4. Mix together the potatoes, bacon bits, onions, chives, onion powder, salt to taste, and flour in a large bowl. Add egg white and stir well.
5. Arrange panko crumbs on a sheet of wax paper.
6. For each tot, add about 2 tsps. of potato mixture. To shape, drop the measure of potato mixture onto panko crumbs and push crumbs up and around potatoes to coat edges. Then turn tot over to coat the other side with crumbs.
7. Mist tots with oil or cooking spray and spread in air fryer basket, crowded but not stacked.
8. Air fry for about 10 to 12 minutes at 390ºF (200ºC), until browned and crispy.
9. Repeat steps 8 and 9 to cook the remaining tots.

Tart and Spicy Potatoes

Prep time: 10 minutes | Cook time: 15 minutes | Serves 4

3 tbsps. vegetable oil	1 tsp. ground turmeric
4 cups quartered baby yellow potatoes	1 tsp. amchoor
¼ cup chopped fresh cilantro or parsley	¼ tsp. ground cumin
	¼ tsp. ground coriander
1 tbsp. fresh lime or lemon juice	¼ to ½ tsp. cayenne pepper
	1 tsp. kosher salt

1. In a large bowl, toss together the potatoes, vegetable oil, turmeric, amchoor, coriander, salt, cumin and cayenne until the potatoes are well coated.
2. Arrange the seasoned potatoes in the air fryer basket. Select the Root Vegetables function, adjust time to 15 minutes, then press Start/Pause. When the cooking is complete, the potatoes should be cooked through and tender when pierced with a fork.
3. Take the potatoes to a serving platter or bowl. Drizzle with the lime juice and sprinkle with the cilantro before serving.

Crispy Latkes with Sour Cream and Applesauce

Prep time: 10 minutes | Cook time: 12 minutes | Makes 12 latkes

Canola or vegetable oil, in a spray bottle	1 tsp. salt
1 russet potato	Freshly ground black pepper, to taste
2 eggs, lightly beaten	Chopped chives, for garnish
⅓ cup flour	
¼ onion	Apple sauce for serving
½ tsp. baking powder	Sour cream for serving

1. Use a coarse box grater or a food processor with a shredding blade to shred the potato and onion. Put the shredded vegetables into a colander or mesh strainer and squeeze or press down firmly to remove the excess water.
2. Take the onion and potato to a large bowl and add the flour, eggs, baking powder, salt and black pepper. Mix to combine well and then shape the mixture into patties, about ¼-cup of mixture each. Brush or spray both sides of the latkes lightly with oil.
3. Preheat the air fryer to 400ºF (205ºC).
4. Cook the latkes in batches. Transfer one layer of the latkes to the air fryer basket and air fry for 12 to 13 minutes at 400ºF (205ºC), flipping them over halfway through the cooking time. Take the finished latkes to a platter and cover with aluminum foil, or put them in a warm oven to keep warm.
5. Sprinkle the latkes with chopped chives and serve with sour cream and applesauce.

Green Tomatoes with Sriracha Mayo

Prep time: 15 minutes | Cook time: 13 minutes | Serves 4

Olive oil, in a spray bottle	chopped fresh chives
3 green tomatoes	Salt and freshly ground black pepper, to taste
1 cup panko breadcrumbs	**FOR THE SRIRACHA MAYO:**
1 cup cornmeal	½ cup mayonnaise
2 eggs	1 tbsp. milk
½ cup buttermilk	1 to 2 tbsps. sriracha hot sauce
⅓ cup all-purpose flour	
Fresh thyme sprigs or	

1. Cut the tomatoes in ¼-inch slices. Use a clean kitchen towel to pat them dry and season generously with salt and pepper.
2. Set up a dredging station using three shallow dishes. Put the flour in the first shallow dish, whisk the eggs and buttermilk together in the second dish, and mix the panko breadcrumbs and cornmeal in the third dish.
3. Preheat the air fryer to 400ºF (205ºC).
4. Dredge the tomato slices in flour to coat on all sides. Then dip them into the egg mixture and finally press them into the breadcrumbs to coat all sides of the tomato.
5. Spray or brush the air-fryer basket lightly with olive oil. Transfer 3 to 4 tomato slices into the basket and spray the top with olive oil. Air fry for 8 minutes at 400ºF (205ºC). Flip them over, spray the other side with oil and cook for another 4 minutes until golden brown.
6. While the tomatoes are cooking, make the sriracha mayo. In a small bowl, combine the mayonnaise, 1 tbsp. of the sriracha hot sauce and milk. Stir well until the mixture is smooth. Add more sriracha sauce to taste.
7. When the tomatoes are done, take them to a cooling rack or a platter lined with paper towels so the bottom does not get soggy. Before serving, carefully stack all the tomatoes into air fryer and air fry for 1 to 2 minutes at 350ºF (180ºC) to heat them back up.
8. Serve the fried green tomatoes warm with the sriracha mayo on the side. Season one last time with salt and freshly ground black pepper and sprinkle with sprigs of fresh thyme or chopped fresh chives.

Yuca Roots Fries

Prep time: 5 minutes | Cook time: 25 minutes | Serves 4

Vegetable oil for spraying
3 yuca roots
Toum, Chipotle Ketchup, or Mint Chimichurri for serving
1 tsp. kosher salt

1. Trim the ends off the yuca roots and chop each one into 2 or 3 pieces depending on the length. Have a bowl of water ready. Peel off the rough outer skin with a paring knife or sharp vegetable peeler. Halve each piece of yuca lengthwise. Put the peeled pieces in a bowl of water to prevent them from oxidizing and turning brown.
2. Fill a large pot with water and bring to a boil over high heat. Season with salt. Place the yuca pieces to the water and cook until they are tender enough to be pierced with a fork, but not falling apart, about 12 to 15 minutes. Drain. Some of the yuca pieces will have fibrous string running down the center. Remove it. Dice the yuca into 2 or 3 pieces to resemble thick-cut french fries.
3. Working in batches, spread the yuca fries in a rotisserie basket. Spray with oil. Select the French Fries function, adjust time to 10 minutes, then press Start/Pause. When the cooking is complete, the outside of the fries should be crisp and browned and the inside fluffy. Repeat with the remaining fries. Spray the cooked yuca with oil and toss with 1 tsp. salt.
4. Serve the yuca fries hot with Toum, Chipotle Ketchup, or Mint Chimichurri.

Bell Peppers Salad with Feta

Prep time: 5 minutes | Cook time: 54 minutes | Serves 4

1 tbsp. extra-virgin olive oil plus extra for drizzling
4 bell peppers, red, orange, or yellow or a combination thereof
2 ounces Greek Feta cheese in brine,
crumbled
1 sprig basil, leaves removed and cut into ribbons
2 tbsps. pine nuts
1 tsp. red wine vinegar

1. Lightly brush the outside of the peppers with the olive oil and put them in the air fryer basket. You will likely be able to fit 2 or 3 peppers at the most. Air fry for about 25 to 30 minutes at 400ºF (205ºC), turning several times, until blackened on all sides.
2. Put the cooked peppers in a bowl and cover with a clean towel. Let the peppers steam for 10 minutes. While the peppers are steaming, toast the pine nuts.

Place the pine nuts in the pizza pan insert for the air fryer. Put the pan in the air fryer basket. Air fry for 4 to 5 minutes at 325ºF (160ºC), until the pine nuts are lightly browned and smell toasty. Check frequently to make sure the pine nuts do not scorch. Remove from the pan and keep aside.

3. When the peppers are cool enough to handle, remove the skin from the peppers and, if necessary, the seeds and core. Tear whole peppers into 3 or 4 pieces.
4. Spread the peppers on a serving platter. Top with crumbled Feta and toasted pine nuts. Drizzle the peppers with additional olive oil and vinegar. Sprinkle basil over the peppers. Serve warm.

Hasselback with Sour Cream and Pesto

Prep time: 10 minutes | Cook time: 40 minutes | Serves 2

5 tbsps. olive oil
2 (8- to 10-ounce / 227- to 283-g) medium russet potatoes
¼ cup sour cream
¼ cup roughly chopped fresh chives
1 small garlic clove, peeled
2 tbsps. packed fresh flat-leaf parsley leaves
1 tbsp. grated Parmesan cheese
1 tbsp. chopped walnuts
1 tsp. fresh lemon juice
Kosher salt and freshly ground black pepper, to taste

1. Put the potatoes on a cutting board and lay a chopstick or thin-handled wooden spoon to the side of each potato. Thinly cut the potatoes crosswise, letting the chopstick or spoon handle stop the blade of your knife, and stop ½ inch short of each end of the potato. Rub the potatoes with 1 tbsp. of olive oil evenly and season with salt and black pepper.
2. Arrange the potatoes, cut-side up, in the air fryer and air fry for 40 minutes at 375ºF (190ºC), until golden brown and crisp on the outside and tender inside, drizzling the insides with 1 tbsp. more olive oil and seasoning with more salt and black pepper halfway through.
3. At the same time, combine the remaining 3 tbsps. olive oil, chives, parsley, walnuts, Parmesan, lemon juice and garlic in a small blender or food processor, and puree until smooth. Season the chive pesto with salt and pepper.
4. Remove the potatoes from the air fryer and transfer to plates. Drizzle the potatoes with the pesto, letting it drip down into the grooves, then dollop each with sour cream and serve warm.

Breaded Okra

Prep time: 5 minutes | Cook time: 12 minutes | Serves 4

Oil for misting or cooking spray
7- to 8-ounce (198- to 227-g) fresh okra
1 cup milk
1 cup breadcrumbs
1 egg
½ tsp. salt

1. Remove stem ends from okra and slice in ½-inch slices.
2. Beat together egg and milk in a medium bowl. Add okra slices and stir to coat well.
3. In a sealable plastic bag or container with lid, mix together the breadcrumbs and salt.
4. Remove okra from egg mixture, letting excess drip off, and transfer into the bag with breadcrumbs.
5. Shake okra in crumbs to coat well.
6. Put all of the coated okra into the air fryer basket and mist with oil or cooking spray. Okra doesn't need to cook in a single layer, nor is it necessary to spray all sides at this point. A good spritz on top will do.
7. Air fry for about 5 minutes at 390ºF (200ºC). Shake the basket to redistribute and give it another spritz as you shake.
8. Cook for another 5 minutes. Shake and spray again. Cook for 2 to 5 minutes longer or until golden brown and crispy.

Breaded Yellow Squash

Prep time: 5 minutes | Cook time: 11 minutes | Serves 4

Oil for misting or cooking spray
2 eggs
1½ cups large yellow squash
1 cup panko breadcrumbs
¼ cup white cornmeal
¼ cup buttermilk
½ tsp. salt

1. Preheat air fryer to 390ºF (200ºC).
2. Cut the squash into ¼-inch slices.
3. Beat together eggs and buttermilk in a shallow dish.
4. In sealable plastic bag or container with lid, mix ¼ cup panko crumbs, white cornmeal and salt. Shake to mix well.
5. Put the remaining ¾ cup panko crumbs in a separate shallow dish.
6. Dump all the squash slices into the egg/buttermilk mixture. Stir to coat well.
7. Remove squash from buttermilk mixture with a slotted spoon, letting excess drip off, and take to the panko/cornmeal mixture. Close bag or container and shake to well coat.
8. Remove squash from crumb mixture, letting excess

fall off. Return squash to egg/buttermilk mixture, stirring gently to coat. If you need more liquid to coat all the squash, add a little more buttermilk.
9. Take each squash slice from egg wash and dip in a dish of ¾ cup panko crumbs.
10. Mist squash slices with oil or cooking spray and arrange in air fryer basket. Squash should be in a single layer, but it's okay if the slices crowd together and overlap a little.
11. Air fry for about 5 minutes at 390ºF (200ºC). Shake the basket to break up any that have stuck together. Mist again with oil or spray.
12. Cook for 5 minutes longer and check. If necessary, mist again with oil and cook for another 1-2 minutes until squash slices are golden brown and crisp.

Fried Smashed Red Potatoes

Prep time: 10 minutes | Cook time: 18 minutes | Serves 3 to 4

Cooking spray oil
1½ pounds (680 g) baby red or baby Yukon gold potatoes
1 tsp. olive oil
¼ cup butter, melted
2 scallions, finely chopped
1 tsp. dried parsley
½ tsp. paprika
Salt and freshly ground black pepper, to taste

1. Bring a large pot of salted water to a boil. Place the potatoes and boil for about 18 minutes or until the potatoes are fork-tender.
2. Drain the potatoes and take them to a cutting board to cool slightly. Spray or brush the bottom of a drinking glass lightly with a little oil. Smash or flatten the potatoes by pressing the glass down on each potato slowly. Try not to completely flatten the potato or smash it so hard that it breaks apart.
3. Combine the melted butter, olive oil, parsley and paprika together.
4. Preheat the air fryer to 400ºF (205ºC).
5. Spray the bottom of the air fryer basket lightly with oil and transfer one layer of the smashed potatoes into the basket. Brush with some of the butter mixture and season generously with salt and black pepper.
6. Select the Root Vegetables function, adjust time to 10 minutes, then press Start/Pause. When the cooking is complete, carefully flip the potatoes over and air fry for another 8 minutes until crispy and lightly browned.
7. Keep the potatoes warm in a 170ºF (77ºC) oven or tent with aluminum foil while you cook the second batch. Scatter minced scallions over the potatoes and serve right away.

Blackened Zucchini with Kimchi Sauce

Prep time: 10 minutes | Cook time: 20 minutes | Serves 2

2 tbsps. olive oil
2 (6-ounce / 170-g) medium zucchinis, ends trimmed
½ cup kimchi, finely chopped
¼ cup finely chopped fresh flat-leaf parsley, plus more for garnish
¼ cup finely chopped fresh cilantro
2 tbsps. rice vinegar
2 tsps. Asian chili-garlic sauce
1 tsp. grated fresh ginger
Kosher salt and freshly ground black pepper, to taste

1. Brush the zucchinis lightly with half of the olive oil, place in the air fryer, and air fry at 400ºF (205ºC), turning halfway through, until lightly charred on the outside and soft, for about 15 minutes.
2. Meanwhile, combine the remaining 1 tbsp. olive oil, the kimchi, cilantro, parsley, vinegar, chili-garlic sauce and ginger in a small bowl.
3. Once the zucchinis are finished cooking, take them to a colander and let it cool for about 5 minutes. Using your fingers, pinch and break the zucchinis into bite-size pieces, allowing them to fall back into the colander. Season the zucchinis with salt and black pepper, toss to combine well, then let sit a further 5 minutes to allow some of its liquid to drain. Pile the zucchinis atop the kimchi sauce on a plate and scatter with more parsley to serve.

Mole-Braised Cauliflower with Sesame Seeds

Prep time: 15 minutes | Cook time: 18 minutes | Serves 2

1 tbsp. vegetable oil
8 ounces (227 g) medium cauliflower florets
1½ cups vegetable broth
2 tbsps. New Mexico chile powder (or regular chili powder)
2 tbsps. salted roasted peanuts
1 tbsp. toasted sesame seeds, plus more for garnish
1 tbsp. finely chopped golden raisins
1 tsp. dark brown sugar
1 tsp. kosher salt
½ tsp. dried oregano
¼ tsp. cayenne pepper
⅛ tsp. ground cinnamon
Kosher salt and freshly ground black pepper, to taste

1. In a large bowl, toss the cauliflower with the oil and season with salt and freshly ground black pepper. Transfer to a 7-inch round cake pan insert, metal cake pan, or foil pan. Put the pan in the air fryer and air fry for 10 minutes at 375ºF (190ºC), until the cauliflower is soft and lightly browned at the edges, stirring halfway through.
2. At the same time, combine the broth, chile powder, peanuts, sesame seeds, raisins, salt, brown sugar, oregano, cayenne and cinnamon in a small blender, and puree until smooth. Pour into a small saucepan or skillet and bring to a simmer over medium heat, then cook until reduced by half, for 3 to 5 minutes.
3. Add the hot mole sauce over the cauliflower in the pan, stir to coat, then cook until the sauce is thickened and lightly charred on the cauliflower, for about 5 minutes more. Garnish with more sesame seeds and serve warm.

Simple Caesar Whole Cauliflower

Prep time: 10 minutes | Cook time: 30 minutes | Serves 2 to 4

3 tbsps. olive oil
1 (1-pound / 454-g) small head cauliflower, green leaves trimmed and stem trimmed flush with the bottom of the head
4 oil-packed anchovy fillets, drained and finely minced
4 garlic cloves, minced
2 tbsps. red wine vinegar
2 tbsps. Worcestershire sauce
2 tbsps. grated Parmesan cheese
1 tbsp. Dijon mustard
1 tbsp. roughly chopped fresh flat-leaf parsley (optional)
Kosher salt and freshly ground black pepper, to taste

1. In a liquid measuring cup, whisk together the olive oil, vinegar, Worcestershire, mustard, garlic, Parmesan, anchovies, and salt and pepper to taste. Put the cauliflower head upside down on a cutting board and use a paring knife to make an "x" through the full length of the core. Take the cauliflower head to a large bowl and pour half the dressing over it. Turn the cauliflower head to coat it in the dressing, then let it rest, stem-side up, in the dressing for at least 10 minutes and up to 30 minutes to let the dressing seep into all its nooks and crannies.
2. Transfer the cauliflower head, stem-side down, to the air fryer and air fry for about 25 minutes at 340ºF (170ºC). Drizzle the remaining dressing over the cauliflower and cook for 5 minutes more at 400ºF (205ºC), until the top of the cauliflower is golden brown and the core is soft.
3. Remove the basket from the air fryer and transfer the cauliflower to a large plate. Garnish with the parsley, if you like, and serve warm.

Easy Asparagus with Tarragon

Prep time: 5 minutes | Cook time: 5 minutes | Serves 4

1 to 2 tsps. extra-light olive oil	washed and trimmed
1 (1-pound / 454-g) bunch asparagus,	⅛ tsp. dried tarragon, crushed
	Salt and pepper, to taste

1. Spread asparagus spears on cookie sheet or cutting board.
2. Scatter with tarragon, salt, and pepper.
3. Drizzle with 1 tsp. of oil and roll the spears or mix by hand. If needed, add up to 1 more tsp. of oil and mix again until all the spears are lightly coated.
4. Arrange spears in air fryer basket. If necessary, bend the longer spears to make them fit. It doesn't matter if they don't lie flat.
5. Air fry for about 5 minutes at 390ºF (200ºC). Shake air fryer basket or stir spears with a scoop.
6. Cook for another 4 to 5 minutes or just until crisp-tender.

Air-Fried Cauliflower with Tahini Sauce

Prep time: 10 minutes | Cook time: 20 minutes | Serves 4

FOR THE CAULIFLOWER:	½ tsp. kosher salt
3 tbsps. vegetable oil	**FOR THE SAUCE:**
5 cups cauliflower florets	2 tbsps. tahini (sesame paste)
6 garlic cloves, smashed and cut into thirds	1 tbsp. fresh lemon juice
½ tsp. ground coriander	2 tbsps. hot water
½ tsp. ground cumin	1 tsp. minced garlic
	½ tsp. kosher salt

MAKE THE CAULIFLOWER:
1. Combine the cauliflower florets and garlic in a large bowl. Drizzle with the vegetable oil. Sprinkle with the coriander, cumin, and salt. Toss until well coated.
2. Arrange the cauliflower in the air-fryer basket. Air fry for 20 minutes at 400ºF (205ºC), turning the cauliflower halfway through the cooking time.

MAKE THE SAUCE:
3. Combine the tahini, water, lemon juice, garlic and salt in a small bowl. (The sauce will appear curdled at first, but keep stirring until you have a thick, creamy, smooth mixture.)
4. Take the cauliflower to a large serving bowl. Pour the sauce over and toss gently to coat. Serve warm.

Fingerling Potatoes with Parsley

Prep time: 5 minutes | Cook time: 15 minutes | Serves 4

1 tbsp. light olive oil	½ tsp. lemon juice
1 pound (454 g) fingerling potatoes	½ tsp. dried parsley
	Coarsely ground sea salt

1. Slice potatoes in half lengthwise.
2. In a large bowl, combine potatoes, parsley, oil and lemon juice. Stir to coat potatoes well.
3. Spread potatoes in air fryer basket. Select the Root Vegetables function, adjust time to 17 minutes, then press Start/Pause.
4. Season with sea salt after cooking.

Spicy Turkish Leek Fritters

Prep time: 10 minutes | Cook time: 26 minutes | Serves 4

Vegetable oil for spraying	green parts only, sliced
2 tbsps. extra-virgin olive oil	3 tbsps. all-purpose flour
1 egg, beaten	2 tbsps. minced chives
¾ cup panko bread crumbs	Lemon wedges for serving
3 leeks, white and light	Kosher salt and pepper, to taste

1. In a large, deep skillet over medium heat, heat the olive oil. Sauté the sliced leeks until softened, for about 10 minutes. Lower the heat as necessary, so the leeks do not brown. Season the leeks well with salt and pepper.
2. Take the cooked leeks to a medium bowl. Add the beaten egg, flour, and chives and stir with a fork to combine. The mixture should start to thicken and become a bit pasty. Spread the panko on a plate. Divide the leek mixture into 4 equal quarters and form each quarter into a patty, squeezing as necessary to get the patty to stick together. Dredge the top and bottom of each patty in the panko. Take the breaded patties to a plate.
3. Spray the air fryer basket with oil. Gently transfer the patties to the basket, working in 2 batches if necessary to avoid overcrowding. Spray the tops of the patties lightly with oil. Air fry for 8 minutes at 375ºF (190ºC) until the tops of the patties are browned. Carefully flip the patties and spray the tops with oil. Cook for about 5 minutes until the second side is browned.
4. Remove the patties and transfer to a serving platter. Serve the leek patties hot with lemon wedges.

Cheesy Corn in a Cup

Prep time: 10 minutes | Cook time: 10 minutes | Serves 4

Vegetable oil spray
4 cups frozen corn kernels (do not thaw)
¼ cup sour cream
¼ cup mayonnaise
¼ cup grated Parmesan cheese (or Feta, cotija, or queso fresco)

2 tbsps. butter
2 tbsps. fresh lemon or lime juice
1 tsp. chili powder
Chopped fresh green onion (optional)
Chopped fresh cilantro (optional)

1. Put the corn in the bottom of the air fryer basket and lightly spray with vegetable oil spray. Air fry for about 10 minutes at 350ºF (180ºC).
2. Take the corn to a serving bowl. Add the butter and stir until melted. Place the sour cream, cheese, mayonnaise, lemon juice and chili powder and stir until well combined. Serve warm with green onion and cilantro (if using).

Cheddar Red Potato Pot

Prep time: 10 minutes | Cook time: 15 minutes | Serves 4

1 tbsp. oil
3 cups cubed red potatoes (unpeeled, cut into ½-inch cubes)
½ tsp. garlic powder
Salt and pepper, to taste
Chopped chives for

garnish (optional)
FOR THE SAUCE:
2 ounces (57 g) sharp Cheddar cheese, grated
2 tbsps. milk
1 tbsp. butter
1 tbsp. sour cream

1. In a large bowl, add potato cubes and sprinkle with garlic, salt and pepper. Pour the oil and stir to coat well.
2. Select the Root Vegetables function, adjust time to 15 minutes, then press Start/Pause. Stir every 4 or 5 minutes during cooking time.
3. While the potatoes are cooking, combine milk and butter in a small saucepan. Warm over medium-low heat to melt butter. Place cheese and stir until it melts. The melted cheese will remain separated from the milk mixture. Turn off the heat until potatoes are done.
4. When ready to serve, put sour cream to the cheese mixture and stir over medium-low heat just until warmed. Arrange cooked potatoes in serving bowl. Pour sauce over potatoes and stir to combine well.
5. Garnish with chives if desired.

Chiles Rellenos with Tomato Sauce

Prep time: 20 minutes | Cook time: 30 minutes | Serves 2

FOR THE PEPPERS:
2 poblano peppers, rinsed and dried
⅔ cup thawed frozen or drained canned corn kernels
⅔ cup grated Monterey Jack cheese
1 scallion, sliced
2 tbsps. chopped fresh cilantro
½ tsp. kosher salt
¼ tsp. black pepper
FOR THE SAUCE:
3 tbsps. extra-virgin olive

oil
1 (6-ounce / 170-g) can tomato paste
½ cup finely chopped yellow onion
2 cups chicken broth
2 tbsps. ancho chile powder
2 tbsps. fresh lemon juice
2 tsps. minced garlic
1 tsp. dried oregano
1 tsp. ground cumin
½ tsp. kosher salt
Mexican crema or sour cream, for serving

MAKE THE PEPPERS:
1. Put the peppers in the air-fryer basket. Air fry for 10 minutes at 400ºF (205ºC), turning the peppers halfway through the cooking time, until their skins are charred. Transfer the peppers to a resealable plastic bag, seal, and keep aside to steam for 5 minutes. Peel the peppers and discard the skins. Cut a slit down the center of each pepper, starting at the stem and continuing to the tip. Remove the seeds, being careful not to tear the chile.
2. In a medium bowl, combine the corn, cilantro, scallion, salt, black pepper, and cheese and keep aside.

MAKE THE SAUCE:
3. In a large skillet, heat the olive oil over medium-high heat. Add the onion and cook, stirring, until soft, for about 5 minutes. Add the garlic and cook, stirring, for 30 seconds. Stir in the tomato paste, chile powder, oregano, cumin and salt. Cook, stirring, for about 1 minute. Whisk in the broth and lemon juice. Bring to a simmer and cook, stirring occasionally, while the stuffed peppers finish cooking.
4. Cut a slit down the center of each poblano pepper, starting at the stem and continuing to the tip. Remove the seeds, being careful not to tear the chile.
5. Carefully stuff each pepper with half the corn mixture. Arrange the stuffed peppers in a 7-inch round baking pan with 4-inch sides. Put the pan in the air-fryer basket. Air fry for about 10 minutes at 400ºF (205ºC), or until the cheese has melted.
6. Take the stuffed peppers to a serving platter and drizzle with the sauce and some crema.

Breaded Okra, page 28

Onion Rings, page 33

Air-Fried Green Beans and Bacon, page 35

Sweet Butternut Squash, page 39

Button Mushrooms

Prep time: 10 minutes | Cook time: 10 minutes | Serves 4

Oil for misting or cooking spray	breadcrumbs
8 ounces (227 g) whole white button mushrooms	5 tbsps. potato starch
	¼ tsp. garlic powder
1 egg, beaten	¼ tsp. onion powder
¾ cup panko	½ tsp. salt
	⅛ tsp. pepper

1. Add mushrooms in a large bowl. Place the salt, pepper, onion powders and garlic, and stir well to distribute seasonings.
2. Put potato starch to mushrooms and toss in bowl until well coated.
3. Dip mushrooms in beaten egg, roll in panko crumbs, and mist with oil or cooking spray.
4. Arrange mushrooms in air fryer basket. You can cook them all at once, and it's okay if a few are stacked.
5. Air fry for about 5 minutes at 390ºF (200ºC). Shake the air fryer basket, then continue cooking for another 5 to 7 minutes, until golden brown and crispy.

Sweet Glazed Carrot

Prep time: 10 minutes | Cook time: 30 minutes | Serves 4

Vegetable oil spray	½ tsp. ground cinnamon
4 cups frozen sliced carrots (do not thaw)	½ tsp. ground cumin
	¼ tsp. kosher salt
2 tbsps. coconut oil	Chopped fresh parsley, for garnish
2 tbsps. brown sugar	
2 tbsps. water	

1. Spray a 6 × 4-inch round heatproof pan lightly with vegetable oil spray.
2. Combine the carrots, brown sugar, water, cumin, cinnamon and salt in a medium bowl. Toss to coat well. Transfer to the prepared pan. Dot the carrots with the coconut oil, distributing it evenly across the pan. Cover the pan with foil.
3. Arrange the pan in the air fryer basket. Select the Root Vegetables function, adjust time to 10 minutes, then press Start/Pause. Remove the foil and stir well when done. Put the uncovered pan back in the air fryer. Air fry for 20 minutes at 400ºF (205ºC), or until the glaze is bubbling and the carrots are cooked through.
4. Garnish with parsley and serve warm.

Onion Rings

Prep time: 5 minutes | Cook time: 12 minutes | Serves 4

Oil for misting or cooking spray	breadcrumbs
	½ cup flour, plus 2 tbsps.
1 large onion	½ cup beer, plus 2 tbsps.
1 cup crushed panko	½ tsp. salt

1. Peel onion, slice and separate into rings.
2. Mix together the flour and salt in a large bowl. Add beer and stir until it stops foaming and makes a thick batter.
3. Put onion rings in batter and stir to coat.
4. Place breadcrumbs in a sealable plastic bag or container with a lid.
5. Working with a few at a time, remove onion rings from the batter, shaking off excess, and drop into breadcrumbs. Shake to coat well, then spread onion rings on cookie sheet or wax paper.
6. When finished, spray onion rings lightly with oil or cooking spray and pile into air fryer basket.
7. Air fry for about 5 minutes at 390ºF (200ºC). Shake the basket and mist with oil. Cook for 5 minutes and mist again. Cook for an additional 2 to 4 minutes, until golden brown and crispy.

Potato Wedges

Prep time: 10 minutes | Cook time: 10 minutes | Serves 3 to 4

Oil for misting or cooking spray	½ tsp. thyme
	½ tsp. garlic powder
1 pound (454 g) medium Yukon gold potatoes	½ tsp. smoked paprika
	½ tsp. cayenne pepper
1 cup dry breadcrumbs	½ tsp. salt

1. Wash potatoes, cut into thick wedges and drop wedges into a bowl of water to prevent browning.
2. Mix together the cayenne pepper, garlic powder, thyme, salt, paprika and breadcrumbs and spread evenly on a sheet of wax paper.
3. Remove potatoes from water and, without drying them, roll in the breadcrumb mixture.
4. Spray air fryer basket lightly with oil or cooking spray and pile potato wedges into the basket. It's okay if they form more than a single layer.
5. Air fry for 8 minutes at 390ºF (200ºC). Shake the basket, then continue cooking for 2 to 7 minutes longer, until the coating is crisp and potato centers are tender. Total cooking time will vary, depending on the thickness of potato wedges.

Garlicky Baby Carrot with Sesame Seeds

Prep time: 5 minutes | Cook time: 16 minutes | Serves 4 to 6

1 tbsp. sesame oil
1 pound (454 g) baby carrots
6 cloves garlic, peeled
3 tbsps. sesame seeds

½ tsp. dried dill
Pinch salt
Freshly ground black pepper, to taste

1. Drizzle the baby carrots with the sesame oil in a medium bowl. Sprinkle with the dill, salt and pepper and toss to coat well.
2. Arrange the baby carrots in the air fryer basket. Select the Root Vegetables function, adjust time to 8 minutes, then press Start/Pause.
3. Remove the basket and stir in the garlic when done. Take the basket back to the air fryer and cook for another 8 minutes, or until the carrots are lightly browned.
4. Sprinkle with the sesame seeds and serve warm.

Spicy Indian Okra

Prep time: 15 minutes | Cook time: 15 minutes | Serves 4

2 tbsps. vegetable oil
1 pound (454 g) okra, sliced ¼ inch thick
1 cup coarsely chopped red onion
½ cup chopped fresh tomato
¼ cup chopped fresh cilantro or parsley

Juice of 1 lemon
1 tsp. ground cumin
1 tsp. ground coriander
1 tsp. ground turmeric
¼ to ½ tsp. cayenne pepper
¼ tsp. amchoor (optional)
1 tsp. kosher salt

1. Combine the okra and onion in a large bowl. Drizzle with the vegetable oil and sprinkle with the turmeric, salt, cumin, cayenne, coriander and amchoor (if using).
2. Spread the spiced vegetables evenly over the air-fryer basket, making as even and flat a layer as possible. Air fry for 15 minutes at 375ºF (190ºC), stirring halfway through the cooking time. (Don't panic if you see some stickiness in the okra. This will dissipate once it cooks.) After 10 minutes, put the tomato to the basket. Cook for the remaining 5 minutes, until the tomato is wilted and cooked through.
3. Drizzle the vegetables with the lemon juice and toss to combine well. Sprinkle with the cilantro and serve warm.

Bottom Rice with Pistachios

Prep time: 10 minutes | Cook time: 20 minutes | Serves 2

1 tbsp. olive oil
2 cups cooked white basmati, jasmine, or other long-grain rice
¼ cup dried currants
¼ cup roughly chopped pistachios

1 tbsp. thinly sliced fresh cilantro
¼ tsp. ground turmeric
Kosher salt and freshly ground black pepper, to taste

1. Combine the turmeric and olive oil in the bottom of a 7-inch round cake pan insert, metal cake pan, or foil pan.
2. Combine the rice, currants, and pistachios, season with salt and pepper in a bowl, then scoop the rice over the oil, making sure to not stir the oil into the rice. Very gently press the rice into an even layer.
3. Put the pan in the air fryer and air fry for 20 to 25 minutes at 300ºF (150ºC), until the rice is warmed through and the bottom is toasted and crispy.
4. Remove the pan from the air fryer and invert onto a serving plate. Break up the crust on the bottom of the rice, scatter with the cilantro, and serve hot.

Parmesan Broccoli Crust with Alfredo Sauce

Prep time: 5 minutes | Cook time: 28 minutes | Serves 1

3 cups broccoli rice, steamed
1 egg
½ cup Parmesan cheese, grated

½ cup Mozzarella cheese, grated
3 tbsps. low-carb Alfredo sauce

1. Drain the broccoli rice and combine with the egg and Parmesan cheese in a bowl, mixing well.
2. Slice a piece of parchment paper roughly the size of the base of the air fryer basket. Spoon four equal-sized amounts of the broccoli mixture onto the paper and press each portion into the shape of a pizza crust. You may have to complete this part in two batches. Take the parchment to the fryer.
3. Air fry for 5 minutes at 370ºF (188ºC). When the crust is firm, flip it over and cook for another 2 minutes.
4. Pour the Alfredo sauce and Mozzarella cheese on top of the crusts and cook for 7 minutes more. The crusts are ready when the sauce and cheese have melted. Serve warm.

Green Peas with Lettuce

Prep time: 5 minutes | Cook time: 5 minutes | Serves 4

1 tsp. melted butter
1 (10-ounce / 283-g) package frozen green peas, thawed

1 cup shredded lettuce
1 tbsp. fresh mint, shredded

1. Spread the shredded lettuce in the air fryer basket.
2. Toss together the mint, peas, and melted butter and scoop over the lettuce.
3. Air fry for about 5 minutes at 360ºF (180ºC), until peas are warm and lettuce wilts. Serve right away.

Pearl Onions with Rosemary

Prep time: 10 minutes | Cook time: 18 minutes | Serves 3

2 tbsps. extra-virgin olive oil
1 (14½-ounce / 411 g) package frozen pearl onions (do not thaw)

2 tbsps. balsamic vinegar
2 tsps. finely chopped fresh rosemary
½ tsp. kosher salt
¼ tsp. black pepper

1. In a medium bowl, combine the onions, rosemary, olive oil, vinegar, salt and pepper until well coated.
2. Transfer the onions to the air fryer basket. Air fry for 18 minutes at 400ºF (205ºC), or until the onions are soft and lightly charred, stirring once or twice during the cooking time.

Air-Fried Green Beans and Bacon

Prep time: 5 minutes | Cook time: 20 minutes | Serves 4

3 cups frozen cut green beans (do not thaw)
3 slices bacon, chopped
1 medium onion,

chopped
¼ cup water
Kosher salt and black pepper, to taste

1. In a 6 × 3-inch round heatproof pan, combine the frozen green beans, bacon, onion and water. Toss to combine well. Arrange the pan in the air fryer basket. Air fry for 15 minutes at 375ºF (190ºC).
2. Raise the air fryer temperature to 400ºF (205ºC), and set time to 5 minutes. Sprinkle the beans with salt and pepper to taste and toss well.
3. Take the pan from the air fryer basket and cover with foil. Allow the beans to rest for 5 minutes before serving.

Air-Fried Brussels Sprouts

Prep time: 5 minutes | Cook time: 5 minutes | Serves 3

2 tsps. olive oil
1 (10-ounce / 283-g) package frozen brussels

sprouts, thawed and halved
Salt and pepper, to taste

1. Toss the brussels sprouts and olive oil together.
2. Spread them in the air fryer basket and season with salt and pepper to taste.
3. Air fry for about 5 minutes at 360ºF (180ºC), until the edges begin to brown.

Broccoli Salad with Bacon

Prep time: 5 minutes | Cook time: 7 minutes | Serves 6

2 tbsps. coconut oil, melted
3 cups fresh broccoli

florets
¼ cup sliced bacons
½ medium lemon, juiced

1. Take a 6-inch baking dish and spread with the broccoli florets. Add the melted coconut oil over the broccoli and place in the sliced bacons. Toss together. Put the dish in the air fryer.
2. Air fry for 7 minutes at 380ºF (195ºC), stirring at the halfway point.
3. Put the broccoli in a bowl and drizzle the lemon juice over it.

Stuffed Eggplant Shell with Spinach

Prep time: 5 minutes | Cook time: 28 minutes | Serves 2

1 large eggplant
1 cup spinach
¼ cup artichoke hearts, chopped

¼ medium yellow onion, diced
2 tbsps. red bell pepper, diced

1. Slice the eggplant lengthwise into slices and scoop out the flesh, leaving a shell about a half-inch thick. Chop it up and keep aside.
2. Set a skillet over a medium heat and spritz with cooking spray. Cook the onions for 3 to 5 minutes to soften. Then place the pepper, spinach, artichokes and the flesh of the eggplant. Cook for another 5 minutes, then remove from the heat.
3. Spoon this mixture in equal parts into the eggplant shells and put each one in the fryer.
4. Air fry for 20 minutes at 320ºF (160ºC), until the eggplant shells are soft. Serve hot.

Air-Fried Corn on the Cob

Prep time: 5 minutes | Cook time: 12 minutes | Serves 4

2 large ears of corn   Salt (optional)
Olive oil for misting

1. Shuck corn, remove the silks and wash.
2. Cut or break each ear in half crosswise.
3. Spray corn lightly with olive oil.
4. Air fry for about 12 to 15 minutes at 390ºF (200ºC), or until browned as much as you like.
5. Serve plain or with salt.

Super Colorful Vegetable Rolls

Prep time: 20 minutes | Cook time: 10 minutes | Serves 6

1 packet spring roll   ½ cup bread crumbs
sheets   ¼ cup mashed carrots
2 potatoes, mashed   ¼ cup peas
1 small cabbage, sliced   ¼ cup beans
1 small onion, chopped   2 tbsps. sweetcorn
½ cup cornstarch slurry

1. Boil all the vegetables in water over a low heat. Rinse and allow them to dry.
2. Unroll the spring roll sheets and scoop equal amounts of vegetable onto the center of each one. Gently fold into spring rolls and coat each one with the slurry and bread crumbs.
3. Air fry for 10 minutes at 390ºF (200ºC).
4. Serve hot.

Maple Cheery Tomatoes with Thyme

Prep time: 10 minutes | Cook time: 20 minutes | Serves 2

1 tbsp. vegetable oil   stems removed
10 ounces (283 g) cherry   1 garlic clove, minced
tomatoes, halved   Kosher salt, to taste
2 tbsps. maple syrup   Freshly ground black
2 sprigs fresh thyme,   pepper, to taste

1. Put the tomatoes in a colander and sprinkle liberally with salt. Let stand for 10 minutes to drain.
2. Take the tomatoes cut-side up to a 7-inch round cake pan insert, metal cake pan, or foil pan, then drizzle with the maple syrup, followed by the oil. Scatter

with the thyme leaves and garlic and season with pepper. Put the pan in the air fryer and air fry for 20 minutes at 325ºF (160ºC) until the tomatoes are tender, collapsed, and lightly caramelized on top.
3. Serve straight from the pan or transfer the tomatoes to a plate and drizzle with the juices from the pan to serve.

Bella Mushrooms with Bacon

Prep time: 5 minutes | Cook time: 10 minutes | Serves 4

16 ounces (454 g)   ¼ cup chopped fresh
baby bella (cremini)   parsley, for garnish
mushrooms, halved   Kosher salt and black
4 slices bacon, each cut   pepper, to taste (optional)
into 8 pieces

1. Put the mushrooms in the air-fryer basket. Sprinkle the bacon over the mushrooms. Air fry for about 10 minutes at 375ºF (190ºC) and cook, very gently shaking the basket halfway through the cooking time—you still want the bacon slices mostly on top. (As the bacon cooks, it drips its luscious fat onto the mushrooms and flavors them with bacon-y goodness.)
2. Season with salt and pepper to taste, if necessary. You may not need any.
3. Garnish with the parsley and serve warm.

Fragrant Jerk Rubbed Corn on the Cob

Prep time: 10 minutes | Cook time: 6 minutes | Serves 4

2 tbsps. butter, melted   ½ tsp. ground ginger
4 ears of corn, husked   ¼ tsp. ground nutmeg
1 tsp. ground allspice   1 tsp. salt
1 tsp. dried thyme   ⅛ tsp. ground cayenne
½ tsp. ground cinnamon   pepper

1. Preheat the air fryer to 380ºF (195ºC).
2. Combine all the spices in a bowl. Brush the corn lightly with the melted butter and then scatter the spices generously on all sides of each ear of corn.
3. Take the ears of corn to the air fryer basket. It's ok if they are crisscrossed on top of each other. Air fry for 6 minutes at 380ºF (195ºC), rotating the ears as they cook.
4. Brush more butter on the end and scatter with any remaining spice mixture.

Quick Lemony Cauliflower

Prep time: 5 minutes | Cook time: 15 minutes | Serves 2

2 tbsps. salted butter, melted
1 medium head cauliflower

1 medium lemon
1 tsp. dried parsley
½ tsp. garlic powder

1. Having removed the leaves from the cauliflower head, brush it lightly with the melted butter. Grate the rind of the lemon over it and then drizzle some juice. Finally place the parsley and garlic powder on top.
2. Take the cauliflower to the air fryer basket.
3. Air fry for 15 minutes at 350ºF (180ºC), checking regularly to ensure it doesn't overcook. The cauliflower is ready when it is hot and fork tender.
4. Take care when taking it from the fryer, cut up and serve warm.

Sesame Broccoli Florets

Prep time: 10 minutes | Cook time: 15 minutes | Serves 4

3 tbsps. toasted sesame oil
1 (16-ounce / 454-g) package frozen broccoli florets (do not thaw)
1 tbsp. chili-garlic sauce

2 tsps. sesame seeds
2 tsps. minced fresh ginger
½ tsp. kosher salt
½ tsp. black pepper

1. Combine the sesame oil, sesame seeds, chili-garlic sauce, ginger, salt, and pepper in a large bowl. Stir until well combined. Place the broccoli and toss until well coated.
2. Spread the broccoli in the air fryer basket. Air fry for about 15 minutes at 325ºF (160ºC), or until the broccoli is crisp, tender, and the edges are lightly browned, carefully tossing halfway through the cooking time.

Easy Parmesan Coated Artichokes

Prep time: 5 minutes | Cook time: 10 minutes | Serves 4

2 tbsps. coconut oil, melted
2 medium artichokes, trimmed and quartered, with the centers removed

½ cup Parmesan cheese, grated
¼ cup blanched, finely ground flour
1 egg, beaten

1. Put the artichokes in a bowl with the coconut oil and toss to coat well, then dip the artichokes into a bowl of beaten egg.
2. Mix together the Parmesan cheese and the flour in a separate bowl. Combine with the pieces of artichoke, making sure to coat each piece well. Take the artichoke to the fryer.
3. Air fry for about 10 minutes at 400ºF (205ºC), shaking occasionally throughout the cooking time. Serve warm.

Parmesan Zucchini Gratin with Parsley

Prep time: 5 minutes | Cook time: 13 minutes | Serves 2

1 tsp. butter, melted
2 zucchinis
5 ounces (142 g) Parmesan cheese,

shredded
1 tbsp. coconut flour
1 tbsp. dried parsley

1. In a bowl, mix the Parmesan and coconut flour together, seasoning with parsley to taste.
2. Slice the zucchini in half lengthwise and chop the halves into four slices.
3. Preheat the fryer at 400ºF (205ºC).
4. Add the melted butter over the zucchini and then dip the zucchini into the Parmesan-flour mixture, coating it all over. Air fry for about 13 minutes at 400ºF (205ºC). Serve hot.

Fluffy Cheddar Mushroom Loaf

Prep time: 5 minutes | Cook time: 15 minutes | Serves 2

2 tbsps. butter, melted
2 cups mushrooms, chopped
¾ cup flour
½ cup Cheddar cheese,

shredded
2 eggs
salt and pepper to taste (optional)

1. In a food processor, pulse together the mushrooms, flour, cheese, melted butter and eggs, along with some salt and pepper if desired, until a uniform consistency is achieved.
2. Transfer into a silicone loaf pan, spreading and levelling with a palette knife.
3. Preheat the fryer at 375ºF (190ºC) and place the rack inside.
4. Air fry for 15 minutes at 375ºF (190ºC).
5. Take care when taking the pan from the fryer and leave it to cool. Then slice and serve warm.

Heirloom Carrots with Orange Zest

Prep time: 5 minutes | Cook time: 12 minutes | Serves 2

1 tsp. olive oil
10 to 12 (1-pound / 454-g) heirloom or rainbow carrots
1 tbsp. butter

1 tsp. fresh orange zest
1 tsp. chopped fresh thyme
Salt and freshly ground black pepper, to taste

1. Preheat the air fryer to 400ºF (205ºC).
2. Scrub the carrots and halve them lengthwise. Toss them in the olive oil, season with salt and black pepper and transfer to the air fryer.
3. Select the Root Vegetables function, adjust time to 12 minutes, then press Start/Pause, shaking the basket every once in a while to rotate the carrots as they cook.
4. Once the carrots have finished cooking, place the butter, orange zest and thyme and toss all the ingredients together in the air fryer basket to melt the butter and coat well. Serve hot.

Classic Gobi Manchurian

Prep time: 15 minutes | Cook time: 20 minutes | Serves 4

FOR THE CAULIFLOWER:
2 tbsps. vegetable oil
4 cups chopped cauliflower
1 cup chopped yellow onion
1 large bell pepper, chopped
1 tsp. ground turmeric

2 tsps. kosher salt
FOR THE SAUCE:
3 tbsps. ketchup
2 tbsps. soy sauce
1 tbsp. rice vinegar
1 tsp. sriracha or other hot sauce
1 tsp. minced garlic
1 tsp. minced fresh ginger

MAKE THE CAULIFLOWER:
1. Combine the cauliflower, onion and bell pepper in a large bowl. Drizzle with the vegetable oil and sprinkle with salt and turmeric. Stir until the cauliflower is well coated.
2. Arrange the cauliflower in the air-fryer basket. Air fry for 20 minutes at 400ºF (205ºC), stirring the cauliflower halfway through the cooking time.
MAKE THE SAUCE:
3. Combine the ketchup, soy sauce, vinegar, garlic, ginger and sriracha in a small bowl.
4. Transfer the cauliflower to a large bowl. Pour the sauce over and toss well to combine. Serve warm.

Mushroom and Carrot with Grated Eggs

Prep time: 5 minutes | Cook time: 12 minutes | Serves 4

2 tsps. melted butter
1 cup chopped mushrooms
1 carrot, chopped
2 hard-boiled eggs, grated
1 cup cooked rice

1 cup peas
1 red onion, chopped
1 garlic clove, minced
1 tbsp. soy sauce
Salt and black pepper, to taste

1. Coat a baking dish evenly with melted butter.
2. In a large bowl, stir together the mushrooms, carrot, peas, cooked rice, onion, garlic, salt and pepper until well mixed.
3. Pour the mixture into the prepared baking dish and take to the air fryer.
4. Air fry for 12 minutes at 380ºF (195ºC), until the vegetables are soft.
5. Divide the mixture evenly among four plates. Serve hot with a sprinkle of grated eggs and a drizzle of soy sauce.

Fried Shallots

Prep time: 5 minutes | Cook time: 35 minutes | Makes 2 cups fried shallots

Vegetable oil for spraying
12 ounces (340 g) shallots

1 tsp. kosher salt

1. Use a sharp knife, a mandoline, or a food processor outfitted with a slicing blade to peel the shallots and slice them as thinly as possible. Arrange the sliced shallots in the air fryer basket. Air fry for 5 minutes at 250ºF (120ºC), then open and shake the basket to toss the shallots. Repeat this process, air frying the shallots at 250ºF (120ºC) and shaking and tossing them every 5 minutes, until they become brown and crispy, about 35 to 40 minutes. Halfway through the cooking time, after 15 or 20 minutes, spray the shallots lightly with oil.
2. Once all of the shallots are browned, remove them from the air fryer. Do not let the shallots burn or they will become bitter. (Do not be dismayed if the browned shallots are soft immediately upon removal from the air fryer; they will crisp as they cool.)
3. Toss the crispy shallots with salt. Serve warm.

Sweet Butternut Squash

Prep time: 5 minutes | Cook time: 15 minutes | Serves 4

2 tbsps. vegetable oil
4 cups 1-inch-cubed butternut squash

1 to 2 tbsps. brown sugar
1 tsp. Chinese five-spice powder

1. Combine the squash, oil, sugar, and five-spice powder in a medium bowl. Toss to coat well.
2. Arrange the squash in the air fryer basket. Air fry for 15 minutes at 400ºF (205ºC) or until tender.

Spicy Green Beans

Prep time: 5 minutes | Cook time: 10 minutes | Serves 2

2 tbsps. vegetable oil
2 cups halved fresh green beans

1 tbsp. Lebanese Shawarma Spice Mix
½ tsp. kosher salt

1. Toss together the green beans, vegetable oil, spice mix, and salt until well coated in a medium bowl.
2. Put the seasoned green beans in the air-fryer basket. Air fry for 10 minutes at 375ºF (190ºC), shaking the basket halfway through the cooking time.

Chapter 4 Poultry

Garlic Chicken Tender

Prep time: 5 minutes | Cook time: 8 minutes | Makes 2½ cups

Cooking spray	boneless
1 pound (454 g) chicken tenders, skinless and	½ tsp. garlic powder
	½ tsp. ground cumin

1. Rub the raw chicken tenders with seasonings.
2. Lightly spray air fryer basket with cooking spray to prevent sticking.
3. Place the chicken in air fryer basket in single layer.
4. Select the Poultry function, adjust time to 4 minutes, then press Start/Pause. When the cooking is complete, turn chicken strips over, and cook for an additional 4 minutes.
5. Test for doneness. Thick tenders may require an additional minute or two.

Buttermilk-Fried Chicken Drumsticks

Prep time: 10 minutes | Cook time: 20 minutes | Serves 2

Oil for misting or cooking spray	breadcrumbs
4 chicken drumsticks, skin on	½ cup buttermilk
1 egg	1 tsp. salt
¾ cup self-rising flour	¼ tsp. ground black pepper (to mix into coating)
¾ cup seasoned panko	

1. In a shallow dish, beat together egg and buttermilk.
2. In a second shallow dish, combine the panko crumbs, flour, salt and pepper.
3. Season chicken legs with additional salt and pepper to taste.
4. Dip legs in buttermilk mixture, then roll in panko mixture, pressing in crumbs to make coating stick. Mist with oil or cooking spray.
5. Spray air fryer basket lightly with cooking spray.
6. Air fry the drumsticks for 10 minutes at 360ºF (180ºC). Turn pieces over and cook for an additional 10 minutes.
7. Turn pieces to check for browning. If you have any white spots that haven't begun to brown, spray them

with oil or cooking spray. Continue cooking for 5 more minutes or until the crust is golden brown and juices run clear. Larger, meatier drumsticks will take longer to cook than small ones.

Spicy Chicken Chimichangas

Prep time: 15 minutes | Cook time: 10 minutes | Serves 4

Oil for misting or cooking spray	Salt and pepper, to taste
8 (6- or 7-inch diameter) flour tortillas	**FOR THE CHIMICHANGA SAUCE:**
2 cups cooked chicken, shredded	2 tbsps. butter
2 tbsps. chopped green chiles	¼ cup light sour cream
½ tsp. onion powder	2 ounces (57 g) Pepper Jack or Monterey Jack cheese, shredded
½ tsp. oregano	1 cup chicken broth
½ tsp. cumin	2 tbsps. flour
¼ tsp. garlic powder	¼ tsp. salt

1. Make the sauce by melting butter in a saucepan over medium-low heat. Stir in flour until smooth and slightly bubbly. Gradually pour in the broth, stirring frequently until smooth. Cook and stir for 1 minute, until the mixture slightly thickens. Turn off the heat and stir in sour cream and salt. Keep aside.
2. Mix together the chicken, chiles, oregano, cumin, onion powder, garlic, salt, and pepper in a medium bowl. Stir in 3 to 4 tbsps. of the sauce, using just enough to make the filling moist but not soupy.
3. Divide filling evenly among the 8 tortillas. Put filling down the center of tortilla, stopping about 1 inch from edges. Gently fold one side of tortilla over filling, fold the two sides in, and then roll up. Mist all sides with oil or cooking spray.
4. Put chimichangas in air fryer basket seam side down. To fit more into the basket, you can stand them on their sides with the seams against the sides of the basket.
5. Air fry for 8 to 10 minutes at 360ºF (180ºC), or until heated through and crispy brown outside.
6. Place the shredded cheese to the remaining sauce. Stir over low heat, warming just until the cheese melts. Don't boil or sour cream may curdle.
7. Pour the sauce over the chimichangas and serve warm.

Simple Chicken Hand Pies

Prep time: 10 minutes | Cook time: 15 minutes | Makes 8 pies

Oil for misting or cooking spray
1 cup cooked chicken, chopped
1 can organic flaky biscuits
¾ cup frozen mixed peas and carrots
¾ cup chicken broth
1 tbsp. cornstarch
1 tbsp. milk
Salt and pepper, to taste

1. Bring chicken broth to a boil in a medium saucepan. Stir in the frozen peas and carrots and cook for about 5 minutes over medium heat. Stir in chicken.
2. Combine the cornstarch into the milk until it dissolves. Stir it into the simmering chicken broth mixture and cook just until thickened.
3. Turn off the heat, season with salt and pepper to taste, and allow to cool slightly.
4. Lay the biscuits out on wax paper. Peel each biscuit apart in the middle to make 2 rounds so you have 16 rounds total. Using your hands or a rolling pin, flatten each biscuit round slightly to make it larger and thinner.
5. Divide chicken filling evenly among 8 of the biscuit rounds. Put the remaining biscuit rounds on top and press edges all around. Crimp biscuit edges with the tines of a fork and make sure they are sealed well.
6. Lightly spray both sides with oil or cooking spray.
7. Air fry for 10 minutes in a single layer, 4 at a time, at 330ºF (165ºC), or until the biscuit dough is cooked through and golden brown.

Fiesta Chicken Plate with Refried Beans

Prep time: 15 minutes | Cook time: 15 minutes | Serves 4

1 pound (454 g) boneless, skinless chicken breasts (2 large breasts)
1 (16-ounce / 454-g) can refried beans
2 cups shredded lettuce
1 medium tomato, chopped
2 avocados, peeled and sliced
½ cup grated Pepper Jack cheese
½ cup salsa
1 small onion, sliced into thin rings
2 tbsps. lime juice
1 tsp. cumin
½ tsp. salt
Sour cream
Tortilla chips (optional)

1. Split each chicken breast in half lengthwise.
2. Mix lime juice, salt and cumin together and brush on all surfaces of chicken breasts.
3. Place in air fryer basket and air fry for 12 to 15 minutes at 390ºF (200ºC), until well done.
4. Divide the cheese evenly over chicken breasts and cook for an additional minute to melt the cheese.
5. While the chicken is cooking, heat refried beans on stovetop or in microwave.
6. When ready to serve, divide the beans evenly among 4 plates. Put chicken breasts on top of beans and spoon salsa over. Arrange the lettuce, tomatoes, and avocados artfully on each plate and sprinkle with the onion rings.
7. Take sour cream to the table and serve warm with tortilla chips if desired.

Breaded Chicken with Spaghetti and Marinara Sauce

Prep time: 10 minutes | Cook time: 10 minutes | Serves 4

Oil for misting or cooking spray
4 chicken tenders
8 ounces (227 g) spaghetti, cooked
1 (24-ounce / 680-g) jar marinara sauce
½ cup Italian salad dressing
¼ cup cornstarch
¼ cup panko breadcrumbs
¼ cup grated Parmesan cheese, plus more for serving
Italian seasoning, to taste
Salt, to taste

1. Use meat mallet or rolling pin to pound chicken tenders until about ¼-inch thick.
2. Season both sides with Italian seasoning and salt to taste.
3. Put the cornstarch and salad dressing in 2 separate shallow dishes.
4. Mix together the panko crumbs and Parmesan cheese in a third shallow dish.
5. Dip flattened chicken in cornstarch, then salad dressing. Dip in the panko mixture, pressing into the chicken so the coating sticks well.
6. Spray both sides lightly with oil or cooking spray. Place in air fryer basket in single layer.
7. Air fry for 5 minutes at 390ºF (200ºC). Spray with oil again, turning chicken to coat both sides.
8. Air fry for another 4 to 6 minutes or until chicken juices run clear and the outside is browned.
9. While the chicken is cooking, heat marinara sauce and stir into cooked spaghetti.
10. To serve, divide spaghetti with sauce among 4 dinner plates evenly, and top each with a fried chicken tender.

Chicken Cordon Bleu with Ham

Prep time: 10 minutes | Cook time: 16 minutes | Serves 4

2 tbsps. olive oil	4 slices deli ham
4 small boneless, skinless chicken breasts	2 tsps. marjoram
	¼ tsp. paprika
4 (3- to 4-inch square) slices deli Swiss cheese	Salt and pepper, to taste

1. Split each chicken breast horizontally almost in two, leaving one edge intact.
2. Lay the breasts open flat and season with salt and pepper to taste.
3. Put a ham slice on top of each chicken breast.
4. Slice cheese slices in half and place one half atop each breast. Keep aside remaining halves of cheese slices.
5. Roll up chicken breasts to enclose cheese and ham and secure with toothpicks.
6. Mix together the olive oil, paprika, and marjoram. Rub all over the outsides of chicken breasts.
7. Put chicken in air fryer basket. Select the Poultry function, adjust time to 18 minutes, then press Start/Pause. When the cooking is complete, the juices should run clear.
8. Remove all toothpicks. To avoid burns, arrange chicken breasts on a plate to remove toothpicks, then quickly return them to the air fryer basket.
9. Add a half cheese slice on top of each chicken breast and cook for a minute or so just to melt the cheese.

Golden Panko-Crusted Chicken Nuggets

Prep time: 10 minutes | Cook time: 26 minutes | Makes 20 to 24 nuggets

Oil for misting or cooking spray	½ cup panko breadcrumbs
1 pound (454 g) boneless, skinless chicken thighs, cut into 1-inch chunks	3 tbsps. plain breadcrumbs
	½ tsp. garlic powder
	½ tsp. onion powder
2 eggs, beaten	¾ tsp. salt
½ cup flour	½ tsp. black pepper

1. In the bowl of a food processor, combine chicken, garlic powder, ½ tsp. salt, pepper and onion powder. Process in short pulses until chicken is very finely chopped and well blended.
2. Put the flour in one shallow dish and beaten eggs in another. In a third dish or plastic bag, mix together the plain breadcrumbs, panko crumbs, and ¼ tsp. salt.
3. Form the chicken mixture into small nuggets. Dip nuggets in flour, then eggs, then panko crumb mixture.
4. Spray nuggets on both sides lightly with oil or cooking spray and place in air fryer basket in a single layer, close but not overlapping.
5. Air fry for 10 minutes at 360ºF (180ºC). Spray with oil and cook 3 to 4 minutes, until chicken is done and the coating is golden brown.
6. Repeat step 5 to cook the remaining nuggets. Serve warm.

Coconut Chicken Tender with Apricot-Ginger Sauce

Prep time: 15 minutes | Cook time: 14 minutes | Serves 4

Oil for misting or cooking spray	**FOR THE APRICOT-GINGER SAUCE:**
1½ pounds (680 g) boneless, skinless chicken tenders, cut in large chunks (1¼ inches)	½ cup apricot preserves
	2 tbsps. white vinegar
	2 tsps. white or yellow onion, grated or finely minced
3 cups shredded coconut	
½ cup cornstarch	¼ tsp. ground ginger
2 eggs	¼ tsp. low-sodium soy sauce
1 tbsp. milk	
Salt and pepper, to taste	

1. Mix all the ingredients for the Apricot-Ginger Sauce well and allow to sit for flavors to blend while you cook the chicken.
2. Sprinkle the chicken chunks with salt and pepper to taste.
3. Put the cornstarch in a shallow dish.
4. Beat together eggs and milk in another shallow dish.
5. Place the coconut in a third shallow dish.
6. Spray air fryer basket lightly with oil or cooking spray.
7. Dip each chicken chunk into cornstarch, shake off the excess, and dip in the egg mixture.
8. Shake off excess egg mixture and roll lightly in coconut or coconut mixture. Spray with oil.
9. Arrange the coated chicken chunks in air fryer basket in a single layer, close together but without sides touching.
10. Air fry for 4 minutes to 360ºF (180ºC), stop, and turn chunks over.
11. Cook for 3 to 4 minutes more or until chicken is done inside and the coating is crispy brown.
12. Repeat steps 9 through 11 to cook the remaining chicken chunks.

Black Bean and Turkey Burgers with Cumin-Avocado Spread

Prep time: 15 minutes | Cook time: 21 minutes | Serves 2

Olive or vegetable oil
¾ pound (340 g) lean ground turkey
2 slices pepper jack cheese
1 cup canned black beans, drained and rinsed
1 Jalapeño pepper, seeded and minced
2 tbsps. minced red onion
2 tbsps. plain breadcrumbs
½ tsp. chili powder
¼ tsp. cayenne pepper

Toasted burger rolls, sliced tomatoes and lettuce leaves
sweet potato fries for serving
Salt, to taste
FOR THE CUMIN-AVOCADO SPREAD:
1 ripe avocado
Juice of 1 lime
1 tbsp. chopped fresh cilantro
1 tsp. ground cumin
½ tsp. salt
Freshly ground black pepper, to taste

1. In a large bowl, place the black beans and smash them slightly with the back of a fork. Add the ground turkey, Jalapeño pepper, red onion, breadcrumbs, chili powder and cayenne pepper. Season with salt to taste. Mix with your hands to combine all the ingredients and then shape them into 2 patties. Brush both sides of the burger patties lightly with a little olive or vegetable oil.
2. Preheat the air fryer to 380ºF (195ºC).
3. Take the burgers to the air fryer basket and air fry for 20 minutes at 380ºF (195ºC), flipping them over halfway through the cooking process. Top the burgers with the pepper jack cheese (securing the slices to the burgers with a toothpick) for the last 2 minutes of the cooking process.
4. While the burgers are cooking, prepare the cumin avocado spread. Add the avocado, cumin, lime juice and salt in food processor and process until smooth. (For a chunkier spread, you can mash this by hand in a bowl.) Stir in the cilantro and season with black pepper. Chill the spread until you are ready to serve.
5. When the burgers have finished cooking, take them from the air fryer and let them rest on a plate, covered gently with aluminum foil. Brush a little olive oil on the insides of the burger rolls. Arrange the rolls, cut side up, into the air fryer basket and air-fry at 400ºF (205ºC), and set time to 1 minute to air fry and warm them.
6. Rub the cumin-avocado spread on the rolls and build your burgers with sliced tomatoes and lettuce leaves and any other ingredients you like. Serve with a side of sweet potato fries.

General Tso's Chicken

Prep time: 15 minutes | Cook time: 25 minutes | Serves 4

2 tbsps. vegetable or canola oil plus additional oil for spraying
2 pounds (907 g) boneless, skinless chicken breast, cut into bite-size cubes
12 dried red chiles
½ cup soy sauce, divided
½ cup mirin or rice wine, divided
½ cup plus ½ tbsp.

cornstarch
¼ cup rice vinegar
¼ cup granulated sugar
2 scallions, white and light green part only, sliced
2 cloves garlic, minced
1 tbsp. grated fresh ginger
2 tsps. hoisin sauce (optional)
1 tsp. sesame seeds

1. In a glass bowl or baking dish, toss the chicken with ¼ cup of the soy sauce and ¼ cup of the mirin. Cover and refrigerate for at least 15 and up to 30 minutes.
2. Spread ½ cup of cornstarch on a plate. Take 2 pieces of chicken and dredge them in the cornstarch, then tap them against each other to remove any excess. Repeat this until you have dredged one-third of the chicken in the cornstarch. Spray the air fryer basket lightly with oil. Place the dredged chicken pieces in the basket in a single layer. Spray with oil. Air fry for 8 minutes at 400ºF (205ºC), turning once, spraying with additional oil if there are dry patches of cornstarch. Set aside.
3. When the first batch of chicken is cooking, dredge the second third of the chicken in the cornstarch. Spray the air fryer basket lightly with oil and cook the second batch of chicken in the same manner. When the second batch is cooking, dredge the remaining chicken in the cornstarch. Cook the last third of the chicken in the same manner as the others. Keep the cooked chicken aside.
4. Whisk together the remaining ½ tbsp. of cornstarch with ½ tbsp. of water to create a slurry and keep aside. Heat the 2 tbsps. of oil in a large, deep skillet over medium heat. Add the ginger, garlic and dried red chiles and sauté for 1 minute until fragrant but not browned. Place the remaining soy sauce, mirin, sugar, rice vinegar and hoisin sauce, if using, and bring to a boil, stirring to dissolve the sugar. Pour the cornstarch slurry and cook until the mixture begins to thicken, for 1 to 2 minutes.
5. Put the chicken to the sauce in the pan and toss to coat well. Cook until the chicken is heated through. Remove the chicken and sauce to a platter and sprinkle with scallions and sesame seeds. Serve hot.

Fried Chicken Breast with Buttermilk Waffles

Prep time: 20 minutes | Cook time: 32 minutes | Serves 4

FOR THE FRIED CHICKEN:
Vegetable oil for spraying
4 (2-pound / 907-g) small boneless, skinless chicken breasts
1½ cups panko bread crumbs
½ cup all-purpose flour
1 egg
2 tbsps. buttermilk
Dash hot sauce
1 tsp. kosher salt
½ tsp. cayenne pepper

FOR THE BUTTERMILK WAFFLES:
1¾ cups all-purpose flour
1¾ cups buttermilk
2 eggs
½ cup unsalted butter, melted and cooled
2 tsps. baking powder
1 tsp. granulated sugar
1 tsp. baking soda
Maple syrup or honey to serve
1 tsp. kosher salt

MAKE THE CHICKEN:

1. To make the chicken, slice each chicken breast in half lengthwise to make 2 long chicken tenders. Whisk together the flour, salt and cayenne pepper on a large plate. In a large, shallow bowl, beat the egg with the buttermilk and hot sauce. Put the panko in a separate shallow bowl or pie plate.
2. Dredge the chicken tenders in the flour, shaking off any excess, then dip them in the egg mixture. Dredge the chicken tenders in the panko, making sure to coat them entirely. Shake off any excess panko. Put the battered chicken tenders on a plate.
3. Preheat the air fryer to 375ºF (190ºC). Lightly spray the basket with oil. Place half the chicken tenders in the air fryer basket and spray the tops with oil. Air fry for about 8 to 10 minutes at 375ºF (190ºC) until the top side of the tenders is browned and crispy. Gently flip the tenders and spray the second side with oil. Cook until the second side is browned and crispy and the internal temperature reaches 165ºF (74ºC), another 8 to 10 minutes. Remove the first batch of tenders and keep it warm. Cook the second batch in the same manner.

MAKF THF WAFFLES:

4. While the tenders are cooking, make the waffles. Whisk together the flour, baking powder, sugar, baking soda and salt in a large bowl. In a separate bowl, whisk together the eggs, buttermilk and melted butter, reserving a small amount of butter to brush on the waffle iron. Place the wet ingredients to the dry ingredients and stir with a fork until just combined. Let the batter rest for at least 5 minutes. Brush the waffle iron with reserved melted butter and preheat according to the manufacturer's instructions. Spoon ⅓ to ½ cup of batter into each grid of the waffle iron and cook according to your waffle iron's instructions. (You should be able to make 8 waffles.)
5. To serve, put 2 chicken tenders on top of 1 or 2 waffles, depending on the person's appetite. Serve warm with maple syrup or honey and additional hot sauce.

Buffalo Egg Rolls with Blue Cheese Dip

Prep time: 15 minutes | Cook time: 18 minutes | Makes 8 egg rolls

Oil for misting or cooking spray
8 egg roll wraps
2½ cups cooked chicken, diced or shredded
1 egg
⅓ cup chopped green onion
⅓ cup diced celery
⅓ cup buffalo wing sauce
1 tbsp. cornstarch
1 tsp. water

FOR THE BLUE CHEESE DIP:
3 ounces (85 g) cream cheese, softened
⅓ cup blue cheese, crumbled
¼ cup buttermilk (or sour cream)
1 tsp. Worcestershire sauce
¼ tsp. garlic powder

1. In a small bowl, mix water and cornstarch until dissolved. Add egg, beat well, and keep aside.
2. Mix together chicken, green onion, celery, and buffalo wing sauce in a medium size bowl.
3. Divide chicken mixture evenly among 8 egg roll wraps, scooping ½ inch from one edge.
4. Moisten all edges of each wrap with beaten egg wash.
5. Gently fold the short ends over filling, then roll up tightly and press to seal the edges.
6. Brush outside of wraps lightly with egg wash, then spray with oil or cooking spray.
7. Put 4 egg rolls in air fryer basket.
8. Air fry for 9 minutes at 390ºF (200ºC), or until outside is brown and crispy.
9. While the rolls are cooking, prepare the Blue Cheese Dip. Mash together cream cheese and blue cheese with a fork.
10. Stir in the remaining ingredients.
11. Dip should be just thick enough to slightly cling to egg rolls. If too thick, stir in buttermilk or milk 1 tbsp. at a time until you reach the desired consistency.
12. Cook the remaining 4 egg rolls as in steps 7 and 8.
13. Serve while hot with blue cheese dip, more buffalo wing sauce, or both.

Herbed Turkey Breast

Prep time: 10 minutes | Cook time: 50 minutes | Serves 4

1 tbsp. olive oil
1 (3½-pound / 1.6-kg) boneless turkey breast
2 tbsps. unsalted butter
1 tsp. dried thyme
1 tsp. dried oregano
1 tsp. salt
½ tsp. freshly ground black pepper

1. Melt the butter in a small microwave-safe bowl on low for 45 seconds.
2. Add the salt, pepper, oregano and thyme to the melted butter. Allow the butter to cool until you can handle it without burning yourself.
3. Rub the butter mixture all over the turkey breast, then rub on the olive oil, over the butter.
4. Put the turkey breast in the air fryer basket, skin-side down.
5. Select the Poultry function, adjust time to 20 minutes, then press Start/Pause.
6. Flip the turkey with tongs.
7. Reset the timer and cook the turkey breast for another 30 minutes. Check that it has reached an internal temperature of 165ºF (74ºC). Add cooking time if needed.
8. Remove the turkey from the air fryer with tongs and let rest for 10 minutes before carving.

Lemony Chicken Souvlaki

Prep time: 10 minutes | Cook time: 15 minutes | Serves 3 or 4

FOR THE CHICKEN:
Vegetable oil spray
2 tbsps. extra-virgin olive oil
1 pound (454 g) boneless, skinless chicken breast, cut into 2-inch chunks
Grated zest and juice of
1 lemon
1 tbsp. Greek souvlaki seasoning
FOR SERVING:
Warm pita bread or hot cooked rice
Thinly sliced red onion
Sliced cucumbers
Tzatziki

1. In a small bowl, combine the lemon zest, lemon juice, olive oil, and souvlaki seasoning. Put the chicken in a gallon-size resealable plastic bag. Pour the marinade over the chicken. Seal bag and massage to coat well. Place the bag in a large bowl and marinate for about 30 minutes, or cover and refrigerate up to 24 hours, turning the bag occasionally.
2. Arrange the chicken in a single layer in the air-fryer basket. Select the Poultry function, adjust time to

10 minutes, then press Start/Pause, turning the chicken and spraying with a little vegetable oil spray halfway through the cooking time. Increase the air-fryer temperature to 400ºF (205ºC), and cook for 5 minutes more to allow the chicken to crisp and brown a little.
3. Take the chicken to a serving platter and serve warm with pita bread or rice, cucumbers, onion and tzatziki.

Herbed Turkey Breast with Cherry Glaze

Prep time: 10 minutes | Cook time: 42 minutes | Serves 6 to 8

2 tsps. olive oil
1 (5-pound / 2.3-kg) turkey breast
½ cup cherry preserves
1 tbsp. chopped fresh thyme leaves
1 tsp. salt
½ tsp. freshly ground black pepper
1 tsp. dried thyme
½ tsp. dried sage
1 tsp. soy sauce
Freshly ground black pepper, to taste

1. All turkeys are built differently, so depending on the turkey breast and how your butcher has prepared it, you may need to trim the bottom of the ribs in order to get the turkey to sit upright in the air fryer basket without touching the heating element. The key to this recipe is getting the right size turkey breast. When you've managed that, the rest is easy, so make sure your turkey breast fits into the air fryer basket before you preheat the air fryer.
2. Preheat the air fryer to 350ºF (180ºC).
3. Brush the turkey breast all over with the olive oil. Mix the dried sage, dried thyme, salt and pepper and rub the outside of the turkey breast with the spice mixture.
4. Take the seasoned turkey breast to the air fryer basket, breast side up, and select the Poultry function, adjust time to 25 minutes, then press Start/Pause. Turn the turkey breast on its side and air-fry for another 12 minutes. Turn the turkey breast on the opposite side and air-fry for 12 more minutes. The internal temperature of the turkey breast should reach 165ºF (74ºC) when completely cooked.
5. While the turkey is air-frying, make the glaze by mixing the cherry preserves, fresh thyme, pepper and soy sauce in a small bowl. When the cooking time is up, take the turkey breast back to an upright position and brush the glaze all over the turkey. Air-fry for a final 5 minutes, until the skin is nicely browned and crispy. Allow the turkey to rest, loosely tented with foil, for at least 5 minutes before slicing and serving.

Butter Coated Chicken Breast

Prep time: 5 minutes | Cook time: 14 minutes | Serves 2

olive oil or cooking spray
4 tbsps. cold unsalted butter, cut into 1-tbsp. slices

2 (8-ounce / 227-g) boneless, skinless chicken breasts
1 sleeve Ritz crackers

1. Spray the air fryer basket lightly with olive oil, or spray an air fryer–size baking sheet with olive oil or cooking spray.
2. Dip the chicken breasts in water.
3. Place the crackers in a resealable plastic bag. Crush the crackers with a mallet or your hands.
4. Put the chicken breasts inside the bag one at a time and coat them with the cracker crumbs.
5. Place the chicken in the greased air fryer basket, or on the greased baking sheet set into the air fryer basket.
6. Add 1 to 2 dabs of butter onto each piece of chicken.
7. Select the Poultry function, adjust time to 7 minutes, then press Start/Pause.
8. Flip the chicken with tongs. Spray the chicken generously with olive oil to avoid uncooked breading.
9. Reset the timer and cook for 7 minutes more.
10. Check that the chicken has reached an internal temperature of 165ºF (74ºC). Add cooking time if needed.
11. Remove the chicken from the air fryer with tongs and serve warm.

Peanut Butter-BBQ Chicken

Prep time: 10 minutes | Cook time: 20 minutes | Serves 4

Cooking spray
1 pound (454 g) boneless, skinless chicken thighs
1 large orange
½ cup barbecue sauce

2 tbsps. smooth peanut butter
2 tbsps. chopped peanuts for garnish (optional)
Salt and pepper, to taste

1. Season the chicken to taste with salt and pepper. Place in a shallow dish or plastic bag.
2. Grate orange peel, squeeze orange and reserve 1 tbsp. of juice for the sauce.
3. Pour the remaining juice over chicken and marinate for about 30 minutes.
4. Mix together the reserved 1 tbsp. of orange juice, peanut butter, barbecue sauce and 1 tsp. grated orange peel.
5. Put ¼ cup of sauce mixture in a small bowl for basting. Keep the remaining sauce aside to serve with cooked chicken.
6. Preheat air fryer to 360ºF (180ºC). Spray air fryer basket lightly with nonstick cooking spray.
7. Remove chicken from marinade, letting excess drip off. Place in air fryer basket and cook for about 5 minutes. Turn chicken over and cook for 5 minutes longer.
8. Brush both sides of chicken lightly with sauce.
9. Air fry the chicken for 5 minutes, then turn thighs one more time, again brushing both sides lightly with sauce. Cook for another 5 minutes or until chicken is done and juices run clear.
10. Serve chicken warm with the remaining sauce on the side and sprinkle with chopped peanuts if you like.

Authentic Taquitos

Prep time: 15 minutes | Cook time: 10 minutes | Makes 12 taquitos

Oil for misting or cooking spray
1 tsp. butter
12 corn tortillas
1 cup cooked chicken, shredded
2 ounces (57 g) Pepper Jack cheese, shredded
4 tbsps. salsa
2 tbsps. chopped green

onions
2 tbsps. chopped green chiles
½ tsp. lime juice
½ tsp. chile powder
¼ tsp. cumin
⅛ tsp. garlic powder
guacamole or sour cream for serving

1. In a saucepan over medium heat, melt butter. Add green onions and sauté for a minute or two, until tender.
2. Remove from heat and stir in the chicken, cheese, green chiles, salsa, lime juice and seasonings.
3. Preheat air fryer to 390ºF (200ºC).
4. To soften refrigerated tortillas, wrap in damp paper towels and microwave for 30 to 60 seconds, until slightly warmed.
5. Take one tortilla at a time, keeping others covered with damp paper towels. Put a heaping tbsp. of filling into tortilla, roll up and secure with toothpick. Spray all sides lightly with oil or cooking spray.
6. Arrange taquitos in air fryer basket, either in a single layer or stacked. To stack, leave plenty of space between taquitos and alternate the direction of the layers, 4 on the bottom lengthwise, then 4 more on top crosswise.
7. Air fry for about 4 to 6 minutes or until brown and crispy.
8. Repeat steps 6 and 7 to cook remaining taquitos.
9. Serve warm with guacamole or sour cream.

Quick Marinaded Chicken Strips

Prep time: 10 minutes | Cook time: 12 minutes | Serves 4

1 pound (454 g) chicken tenders	1 tsp. garlic powder
FOR THE MARINADE:	1 tsp. onion powder
¼ cup olive oil	½ tsp. paprika
2 tbsps. honey	½ tsp. salt
2 tbsps. white vinegar	½ tsp. crushed red
2 tbsps. water	pepper

1. Combine all the marinade ingredients and mix well.
2. Add chicken and stir to coat well. Cover tightly and allow to marinate in refrigerator for 30 minutes.
3. Remove tenders from the marinade and put them in a single layer in the air fryer basket.
4. Select the Poultry function, adjust time to 3 minutes, then press Start/Pause. When the cooking is complete, turn tenders over and cook for 3 to 5 minutes longer or until chicken is done and juices run clear.
5. Repeat step 4 to cook the remaining tenders.

Poblano Pepper with Turkey

Prep time: 10 minutes | Cook time: 12 minutes | Serves 4

2 large poblano peppers (approx. 5½ inches long excluding stem)	1 (8-ounce / 227-g) jar salsa, warmed
¾ pound (340 g) ground turkey, raw	¾ cup cooked brown rice
	1 tsp. chile powder
4 ounces (113 g) sharp Cheddar cheese, grated	½ tsp. garlic powder
	½ tsp. ground cumin

1. Cut each pepper in half lengthwise so that you have four wide, flat pepper halves.
2. Remove the seeds and membrane and discard. Rinse inside and out.
3. Combine turkey, rice, chile powder, cumin and garlic powder in a large bowl. Mix well.
4. Divide turkey filling evenly into 4 portions and stuff one into each of the 4 pepper halves. Press lightly to pack down.
5. Place 2 pepper halves in air fryer basket and air fry for 10 minutes at 390ºF (200ºC), or until turkey is well done.
6. Top each pepper half with ¼ of the grated cheese. Cook for about 1 minute or just until the cheese melts.
7. Repeat steps 5 and 6 to cook the remaining pepper halves.
8. To serve, place each pepper half on a plate and add ¼ cup warm salsa on top.

Lime Curried Chicken with Coconut Rice

Prep time: 15 minutes | Cook time: 1¼ hours | Serves 4

Vegetable or olive oil	1 tsp. ground cumin
1 (3- to 4-pound / 1.4- to 1.8-kg) chicken, cut into 8 pieces	Fresh cilantro leaves
	Salt and freshly ground black pepper, to taste
1 (14-ounce / 397-g) can coconut milk	**FOR THE RICE:**
Zest and juice of one lime	1 cup basmati or jasmine rice
1 clove garlic, minced	1 cup coconut milk
2 tbsps. green or red curry paste	1 cup water
	½ tsp. salt
1 tbsp. grated fresh ginger	Freshly ground black pepper, to taste

1. Make the marinade by mixing the coconut milk, curry paste, lime zest and juice, ginger, garlic and cumin. Coat the chicken on all sides with the marinade and marinate the chicken for about 1 hour to overnight in the refrigerator.
2. Preheat the air fryer to 380ºF (195ºC).
3. Brush the bottom of the air fryer basket lightly with oil. Take the chicken thighs and drumsticks from the marinade to the air fryer basket, letting most of the marinade drip off. Season with salt and freshly ground black pepper to taste.
4. Select the Poultry function, adjust time to 12 minutes, then press Start/Pause. Flip the chicken over and continue to air-fry for another 12 minutes. Set aside and air-fry the chicken breast pieces at 380ºF (195ºC), and set time to 15 minutes. Turn the chicken breast pieces over and air-fry for another 12 minutes. Take the chicken thighs and drumsticks back to the air fryer and air-fry for an additional 5 minutes.
5. While the chicken is cooking, make the coconut rice. Rinse the rice kernels with water and drain well. Add the rice in a medium saucepan with a tight fitting lid, along with the coconut milk, water, salt and freshly ground black pepper. Bring the mixture to a boil and then cover, lower the heat and let it cook gently for 20 minutes without lifting the lid. When the time is up, lift the lid, fluff with a fork and keep aside.
6. Transfer the chicken to a platter and serve warm with the coconut rice and fresh cilantro scattered around.

Chicken Breast with Dark Cherries

Prep time: 10 minutes | Cook time: 14 minutes | Serves 4

Oil for misting or cooking spray	unsweetened dark cherries, thawed and drained
1 tsp. light olive oil	⅓ cup peach preserves
1 pound (454 g) boneless chicken breasts, cut in 1½-inch chunks	1 tsp. ground rosemary
	½ tsp. marjoram
10 ounces (283 g) package frozen	½ tsp. salt
	½ tsp. black pepper

1. Mix together peach preserves, rosemary, pepper, salt, marjoram and olive oil in a medium bowl.
2. Stir in chicken chunks and toss to coat well with the preserved mixture.
3. Spray air fryer basket lightly with oil or cooking spray and lay the chicken chunks in the basket.
4. Air fry for 7 minutes at 390ºF (200ºC). Stir and cook for 6 to 8 more minutes or until chicken juices run clear.
5. When the chicken has cooked through, scatter the cherries over and cook for another minute to heat the cherries.

Simple Spicy Chicken Thighs

Prep time: 10 minutes | Cook time: 10 minutes | Serves 4

2 tbsps. olive oil	½ tsp. ground cinnamon
1 pound (454 g) boneless, skinless chicken thighs, cut crosswise into thirds	½ tsp. cayenne pepper
	¼ tsp. ground cloves
	¼ tsp. kosher salt
1 tbsp. cider vinegar	Zoodles, steamed rice, naan bread or a mixed salad, for serving
1 tsp. ground turmeric	

1. Combine the turmeric, cayenne, cinnamon, cloves, salt, vinegar, and oil in a small bowl. Stir to form a thick paste.
2. Put the chicken in a resealable plastic bag and add the marinade. Seal the bag and massage until the chicken is well coated. Marinate at room temperature for about 30 minutes or in the refrigerator for up to 24 hours.
3. Put the chicken in the air fryer basket. Select the Poultry function, adjust time to 10 minutes, then press Start/Pause, turning the chicken halfway through the cooking time. Use a meat thermometer to ensure that the chicken has reached an internal temperature of 165ºF (74ºC).

4. Serve warm with steamed rice or naan, over zoodles or with a mixed salad.

Chicken and Dill Pickle with Nashville Hot Sauce

Prep time: 15 minutes | Cook time: 47 minutes | Serves 4

Vegetable oil, in a spray bottle	2 tbsps. paprika
	1 tsp. onion powder
1 (4-pound / 1.8-kg) chicken, cut into 6 pieces (2 breasts, 2 thighs and 2 drumsticks)	1 tsp. garlic powder
	2 tsps. salt
	1 tsp. freshly ground black pepper
2 eggs	**FOR THE NASHVILLE HOT SAUCE:**
2 cups all-purpose flour	
1 cup buttermilk	¼ cup vegetable oil
4 slices white bread	1 tbsp. cayenne pepper
Dill pickle slices	1 tsp. salt

1. Cut the chicken breasts into 2 pieces so that you have a total of 8 pieces of chicken.
2. Set up a two-stage dredging station. In a bowl, whisk the eggs and buttermilk together. Mix the flour, paprika, garlic powder, onion powder, salt and black pepper in a zipper-sealable plastic bag. Dip the chicken pieces into the egg-buttermilk mixture, then toss them in the seasoned flour, coating all sides. Repeat this procedure (egg mixture and then flour mixture) one more time. This can be a little messy, but make sure all sides of the chicken are completely covered. Spray the chicken with vegetable oil and set aside.
3. Preheat the air fryer to 370ºF (188ºC). Spray or brush the bottom of the air-fryer basket lightly with a little vegetable oil.
4. Air fry for 20 minutes at 370ºF (188ºC). Cook the chicken in two batches, flipping the pieces over halfway through the cooking process. Take the chicken to a plate, but do not cover. Repeat with the second batch of chicken.
5. Lower the temperature of the air fryer to 340ºF (170ºC). Gently flip the chicken back over and put the first batch of chicken on top of the second batch already in the basket. Air-fry for 7 minutes more.
6. While the chicken is air-frying, mix the cayenne pepper and salt in a bowl. In a small saucepan, heat the vegetable oil and when it is very hot, add it to the spice mix, whisking until smooth. It will sizzle briefly when you add it to the spices. Put the fried chicken on top of the white bread slices and brush the hot sauce all over the chicken. Put the pickle slices on top and serve warm. Enjoy the heat and the flavor!

Airy Breaded Chicken

Prep time: 5 minutes | Cook time: 14 minutes | Serves 2

4 to 5 tbsps. vegetable oil
2 (8-ounce / 227-g) boneless, skinless chicken breasts

2 large eggs
1 cup bread crumbs or panko bread crumbs
1 tsp. Italian seasoning

1. Preheat the air fryer to 370ºF (188ºC). Spray the air fryer basket (or an air fryer–size baking sheet) lightly with olive oil or cooking spray.
2. Beat the eggs until frothy in a small mixing bowl.
3. Mix together the bread crumbs, Italian seasoning and vegetable oil in a separate small mixing bowl.
4. Dip the chicken in the egg mixture, then in the bread crumb mixture.
5. Put the chicken directly into the greased air fryer basket, or on the greased baking sheet set into the basket.
6. Spray the chicken generously and thoroughly with olive oil to avoid powdery, uncooked breading.
7. Air fry for 7 minutes at 370ºF (188ºC).
8. Flip the chicken with tongs and generously spray it with olive oil.
9. Reset the timer and air fry for 7 minutes more.
10. Check that the chicken has reached an internal temperature of 165ºF (74ºC). Add cooking time if needed.
11. Once the chicken is completely cooked, remove it from the air fryer with tongs and serve warm.

Chili Peanut Chicken

Prep time: 15 minutes | Cook time: 20 minutes | Serves 4

1 pound (454 g) bone-in chicken thighs
¼ cup creamy peanut butter
¼ cup chopped green onions, for garnish
½ cup hot water
1 clove garlic, minced
2 tbsps. sweet chili sauce
2 tbsps. fresh lime juice

2 tbsps. chopped fresh cilantro, for garnish
2 to 3 tbsps. crushed roasted and salted peanuts, for garnish
1 tbsp. sriracha
1 tbsp. soy sauce
1 tsp. minced fresh ginger
½ tsp. kosher salt

1. Combine the peanut butter, sweet chili sauce, lime juice, sriracha, soy sauce, ginger, garlic and salt in a small bowl. Add the hot water and whisk until smooth.
2. Put the chicken in a resealable plastic bag and pour in half of the sauce. (Reserve the remaining sauce for serving.) Seal the bag and massage until all of the chicken is well coated. Marinate at room temperature for about 30 minutes or in the refrigerator for up to 24 hours.
3. Take the chicken from the bag and discard the marinade. Place the chicken in the air fryer basket. Select the Poultry function, adjust time to 20 minutes, then press Start/Pause. Use a meat thermometer to ensure the chicken has reached an internal temperature of 165ºF (74ºC) when done.
4. Transfer the chicken to a serving platter. Garnish with the cilantro, green onions and peanuts. Serve warm with the reserved sauce for dipping.

Buttermilk-Fried Chicken

Prep time: 10 minutes | Cook time: 26 minutes | Serves 4

olive oil
1 pound (454 g) chicken thighs and drumsticks
1 cup all-purpose flour
½ cup buttermilk
2 tsps. onion powder

2 tsps. garlic powder
½ tsp. sweet paprika
2 tsps. salt, plus 1 tbsp.
1 tsp. freshly ground black pepper

1. Whisk together the buttermilk, 2 tsps. of salt, and pepper in a large mixing bowl.
2. Add the chicken pieces to the bowl, and allow the chicken to marinate for at least an hour, covered, in the refrigerator.
3. About 5 minutes before the chicken is done marinating, prepare the dredging mixture. Combine the flour, 1 tbsp. of salt, onion powder, garlic powder and paprika in a large mixing bowl.
4. Spray the air fryer basket with olive oil.
5. Remove the chicken from the buttermilk mixture and dredge it in the flour mixture. Shake off any excess flour.
6. Put the chicken pieces into the greased air fryer basket in a single layer, leaving space between each piece. (You may have to fry the chicken in more than one batch.) Spray the chicken generously with olive oil.
7. Air fry for 13 minutes at 390ºF (200ºC).
8. Flip the chicken with tongs. Spray generously with olive oil.
9. Reset the timer and fry for 13 minutes more.
10. Check that the chicken has reached an internal temperature of 165ºF (74ºC). Add cooking time if needed.
11. When the chicken is fully cooked, plate, serve warm and enjoy!

Simple Seasoned Cornish Hen, page 57

Italian Lemony Chicken Thighs, page 54

Airy Breaded Chicken, page 50

Poblano Pepper with Turkey, page 48

Marinara Chicken Breast Parmesan

Prep time: 10 minutes | Cook time: 12 minutes | Serves 4

Vegetable oil for spraying
1 pound (454 g) boneless, skinless hand-filleted chicken breasts or regular breasts sliced in half crosswise to create 4 thin breasts
1 egg
1 cup panko bread crumbs
¼ cup Marinara Sauce
½ cup freshly grated Parmesan cheese
6 tbsps. grated Mozzarella cheese
1 tbsp. mayonnaise
1 tsp. Italian seasoning
pasta for serving

1. In a shallow bowl, mix the egg and mayonnaise until smooth. In another bowl, combine the Parmesan cheese, panko, and Italian seasoning. Dip each piece of chicken in the mayonnaise mixture, shaking off any excess, then dredge in the panko mixture until both sides are coated. Put the breaded chicken on a plate or rack.
2. Preheat the air fryer to 350ºF (180ºC), and set time to 3 minutes. Spray the air fryer basket lightly with oil and place 2 pieces of chicken in the basket. Spray the chicken cutlets with oil. Air fry for 6 minutes at 350ºF (180ºC), then turn them over. Add 1 tbsp. of marinara sauce and 1½ tbsps. of grated Mozzarella cheese on top of each piece of chicken. Cook the chicken until the cheese is melted, for about 3 additional minutes.
3. Transfer the cooked chicken to a serving dish and keep warm. Cook the remaining pieces of chicken in the same manner. Serve with pasta on the side.

Turkey and Zucchini Meatballs with Chili Sauce

Prep time: 15 minutes | Cook time: 10 minutes | Serves 4 to 6

1½ pounds (680 g) ground turkey (a mix of light and dark meat)
1½ cups grated zucchini, squeezed dry in a clean kitchen towel
2 eggs, lightly beaten
1 cup Thai sweet chili sauce (spring roll sauce)
3 scallions, finely chopped
Zest of 1 lime
2 cloves garlic, minced
1 tbsp. finely chopped fresh cilantro
1 tbsp. grated fresh ginger
rice noodles or white rice, for serving
Lime wedges, for serving
1 tsp. salt
Freshly ground black pepper, to taste

1. In a bowl, combine the zucchini, scallions, ginger, garlic, cilantro, lime zest, salt, pepper, ground turkey and eggs and mix the ingredients together. Gently shape the mixture into 24 balls, about the size of golf balls.
2. Preheat the air fryer to 380ºF (195ºC).
3. Working in batches, Air fry for about 10 to 12 minutes at 380ºF (195ºC), turning the meatballs over halfway through the cooking time. When the meatballs have finished cooking, toss them in a bowl with the Thai sweet chili sauce to coat.
4. Serve the meatballs warm over rice noodles or white rice with the remaining Thai sweet chili sauce and lime wedges to squeeze over the top.

Lemony Chicken with Sage

Prep time: 5 minutes | Cook time: 1 hour | Serves 4

1 (4-pound / 1.8-kg) chicken
1 lemon, zest and juice
1 bunch sage, divided
Salt and freshly ground black pepper, to taste

1. Preheat the air fryer to 350ºF (180ºC) and add a little water into the bottom of the air fryer drawer. (This will help prevent the grease that drips into the bottom drawer from burning and smoking.)
2. Run your fingers between the skin and flesh of the chicken breasts and thighs. Push a couple of sage leaves up underneath the skin of the chicken on each breast and each thigh.
3. Push some of the lemon zest up under the skin of the chicken next to the sage. Scatter some of the zest inside the chicken cavity, and reserve any leftover zest. Squeeze the lemon juice all over the chicken and in the cavity as well.
4. Season the chicken, inside and out, with salt and black pepper. Set a few sage leaves aside for the final garnish. Crumple up the remaining sage leaves and push them into the cavity of the chicken, along with one of the squeezed lemon halves.
5. Put the chicken breast side up into the air fryer basket and air fry for about 20 minutes at 350ºF (180ºC). Gently flip the chicken over so that it is breast side down and continue to air-fry for another 20 minutes. Return the chicken to breast side up and finish air-frying for 20 more minutes. The internal temperature of the chicken should register 165ºF (74ºC) in the thickest part of the thigh when completely cooked. Take the chicken from the air fryer and allow it to rest on a cutting board for at least 5 minutes.
6. Dice the rested chicken into pieces, sprinkle with the reserved lemon zest and sage leaves.

Sweet Chicken Drumsticks

Prep time: 10 minutes | Cook time: 20 minutes | Serves 4

2 tbsps. olive oil
4 to 6 chicken drumsticks
¼ cup brown sugar
1 tsp. smoked paprika
1 tsp. chili powder
1 tsp. dry mustard
1 tsp. garlic powder
1 tsp. onion powder
1 tbsp. salt
½ tsp. freshly ground black pepper

1. Combine the brown sugar, salt, pepper, chili powder, paprika, mustard, garlic powder and onion powder in a small mixing bowl.
2. Wipe any moisture off the chicken by using a paper towel.
3. Put the chicken drumsticks into a large resealable plastic bag, then pour in the dry rub. Seal the bag.
4. Shake the bag to coat the chicken.
5. Arrange the drumsticks in the air fryer basket. Brush the drumsticks with olive oil.
6. Select the Poultry function, adjust time to 10 minutes, then press Start/Pause.
7. Flip the drumsticks with tongs, and brush them with olive oil.
8. Reset the timer and cook for 10 minutes more.
9. Check that the chicken has reached an internal temperature of 165ºF (74ºC). Add cooking time if needed.
10. Once the chicken is completely cooked, transfer it to a platter and serve warm.

Cheesy Chicken Breast

Prep time: 10 minutes | Cook time: 14 minutes | Serves 4

olive oil or cooking spray
2 (8-ounce / 227-g) boneless, skinless chicken breasts
2 large eggs
1 cup Italian-style bread crumbs
½ cup marinara sauce
½ cup shredded Mozzarella cheese
¼ cup shredded Parmesan cheese

1. Preheat the air fryer to 360ºF (180ºC). Spray an air fryer–size baking sheet lightly with olive oil or cooking spray.
2. Flatten the chicken breasts to about ¼ inch thick with a mallet or rolling pin.
3. Beat the eggs until frothy in a small mixing bowl. Mix together the bread crumbs and Parmesan cheese in another small mixing bowl.
4. Dip the chicken in the egg, then in the bread crumb mixture.
5. Put the chicken on the greased baking sheet. Set the baking sheet into the air fryer basket.
6. Spray the chicken generously with olive oil to avoid powdery, uncooked breading.
7. Air fry for 7 minutes at 360ºF (180ºC), or until cooked through and the juices run clear.
8. Gently flip the chicken and pour the marinara sauce over the chicken. Sprinkle with the Mozzarella cheese. Cook for another 7 minutes.
9. Once the chicken Parmesan is completely cooked, remove it from the air fryer with tongs and serve.

Paprika Fried Chicken

Prep time: 10 minutes | Cook time: 47 minutes | Serves 4

Vegetable oil, in a spray bottle
1 (4-pound / 1.8-kg) chicken, cut into 8 pieces
2 eggs, lightly beaten
2 cups buttermilk
1½ cups flour
2 tsps. paprika
Hot sauce (optional)
1 tsp. salt
Freshly ground black pepper, to taste

1. Cut the chicken into 8 pieces and submerge them in the buttermilk and hot sauce, if using. A zipper-sealable plastic bag works well for this. Allow the chicken to soak in the buttermilk for at least one hour or even overnight in the refrigerator.
2. Set up a dredging station. Mix the paprika, flour, salt and black pepper in a clean zipper-sealable plastic bag. Whisk the eggs and place them in a shallow dish. Remove four pieces of chicken from the buttermilk and take them to the bag with the flour. Shake them around to coat on all sides. Remove the chicken from the flour, shaking off any excess flour, and dip them into the beaten egg. Take the chicken back to the bag of seasoned flour and shake again. Keep the coated chicken aside and repeat with the remaining four pieces of chicken.
3. Preheat the air fryer to 370ºF (188ºC).
4. Spray the chicken on all sides lightly with the vegetable oil and then transfer one batch to the air fryer basket. Air fry for 20 minutes at 370ºF (188ºC), flipping the pieces over halfway through the cooking process, taking care not to knock off the breading. Transfer the chicken to a plate, but do not cover. Repeat with the second batch of chicken.
5. Reduce the temperature of the air fryer to 340ºF (170ºC). Gently flip the chicken back over and place the first batch of chicken on top of the second batch already in the basket. Air-fry for another 7 minutes and serve hot.

Italian Lemony Chicken Thighs

Prep time: 10 minutes | Cook time: 20 minutes | Serves 4

2 tbsps. olive oil	lemon juice
4 to 6 chicken thighs	1 tsp. salt
1 lemon, sliced	1 tsp. freshly ground
2 tbsps. Italian seasoning	black pepper
2 tbsps. freshly squeezed	

1. In a medium mixing bowl, place the chicken thighs and season them with salt and pepper to taste.
2. Add the olive oil, lemon juice and Italian seasoning and toss until the chicken thighs are thoroughly coated with oil.
3. Place the sliced lemons.
4. Put the chicken thighs into the air fryer basket in a single layer.
5. Select the Poultry function, adjust time to 10 minutes, then press Start/Pause.
6. Flip the chicken with tongs.
7. Reset the timer and cook for about 10 minutes more.
8. Check that the chicken has reached an internal temperature of 165ºF (74ºC). Add cooking time if needed.
9. When the chicken is fully cooked, transfer to plate. Serve warm and enjoy!

Sweet Gochujang Chicken Wings

Prep time: 15 minutes | Cook time: 25 minutes | Serves 4

FOR THE WINGS:

2 pounds (907 g) chicken wings	oil
	1 tbsp. mayonnaise
1 tsp. kosher salt	1 tbsp. minced garlic
1 tsp. black pepper or gochugaru (Korean red pepper)	1 tbsp. minced fresh ginger
	1 tsp. agave nectar or honey
FOR THE SAUCE:	1 tsp. sugar
2 tbsps. gochujang (Korean chile paste)	**FOR SERVING:**
1 tbsp. toasted sesame	¼ cup chopped scallions
	1 tsp. sesame seeds

MAKE THE WINGS:
1. Season the wings with salt and pepper to taste and put in the air-fryer basket. Air fry for about 20 minutes at 400ºF (205ºC), turning the wings halfway through the cooking time.

MAKE THE SAUCE:
2. Combine the gochujang, mayonnaise, sesame oil, ginger, garlic, sugar and agave in a small bowl and set aside.
3. As you near the 20-minute mark, use a meat thermometer to check the meat. When the wings reach 160ºF (71ºC), transfer them to a large bowl. Add about half the sauce on the wings and toss to coat well (serve the remaining sauce as a dip).
4. Take the wings back to the air-fryer basket and cook for about 5 minutes, until the sauce has glazed.
5. Transfer the wings to a serving platter. Scatter with the sesame seeds and scallions. Serve warm with the reserved sauce on the side for dipping.

Garlic Cream Chicken Thighs

Prep time: 10 minutes | Cook time: 27 minutes | Serves 4

2 tbsps. extra-virgin olive oil	3 cloves garlic, minced
	8 cloves garlic, chopped
2 tbsps. butter	1 tbsp. Dijon mustard
1 pound (454 g) boneless, skinless chicken thighs, halved crosswise	1 tbsp. apple cider vinegar
	2 tsps. herbes de Provence
¼ cup heavy whipping cream	½ tsp. kosher salt
	1 tsp. black pepper

1. Combine the olive oil, mustard, vinegar, minced garlic, herbes de Provence, salt and pepper in a small bowl. Use a wire whisk to emulsify the mixture.
2. Pierce the chicken all over with a fork to let the marinade penetrate better. Put the chicken in a resealable plastic bag, pour the marinade over, and seal. Massage until the chicken is well coated. Marinate at room temperature for 30 minutes or in the refrigerator for up to 24 hours.
3. When you are ready to cook, add the butter and chopped garlic in a 7 × 3-inch round heatproof pan and place it in the air fryer basket. Select the Poultry function, adjust time to 5 minutes, then press Start/Pause. When the cooking is complete, the butter is melted and the garlic is sizzling.
4. Add the chicken and the marinade to the seasoned butter. Air fry for 15 minutes at 350ºF (180ºC). Use a meat thermometer to ensure the chicken has reached an internal temperature of 165ºF (74ºC). Take the chicken to a plate and cover lightly with foil to keep warm.
5. Place the cream to the pan, stirring to combine with the butter, garlic and cooking juices. Put the pan in the air fryer basket. Air fry for another 7 minutes at 350ºF (180ºC).
6. Add the thickened sauce over the chicken and serve warm.

Chicken and Onion with Pineapple

Prep time: 10 minutes | Cook time: 11 minutes | Serves 4

1 tbsp. olive or peanut oil
2 boneless, skinless chicken breasts
1 (8-ounce / 227-g) can pineapple tidbits, drained, juice reserved
1 onion, sliced
1 red bell pepper, chopped
1 egg white, lightly beaten
2 tbsps. cornstarch
2 tbsps. reduced-sodium soy sauce

1. Dice the chicken breasts into cubes and put into a medium bowl. Place the cornstarch and egg white and mix together thoroughly. Keep aside.
2. Combine the oil and the onion in a 6-inch metal bowl. Air fry for 2 to 3 minutes or until the onion is crisp and tender.
3. Drain the chicken and add to the bowl with the onions; stir well. Cook for 7 to 9 minutes or until the chicken is thoroughly cooked to 165ºF (74ºC).
4. Stir the chicken mixture, then put the pepper, pineapple tidbits, 3 tbsps. of the reserved pineapple liquid, and the soy sauce, and stir again. Cook for another 2 to 3 minutes or until the food is cooked and the sauce is slightly thickened. Serve warm.

Spicy Chicken Fries

Prep time: 10 minutes | Cook time: 12 minutes | Serves 4 to 6

Oil for misting or cooking spray
1 pound (454 g) chicken tenders
2 eggs
¾ cup panko breadcrumbs
¾ cup crushed organic nacho cheese tortilla
chips
¼ cup flour
Salt, to taste
FOR THE SEASONING MIX:
1 tbsp. chili powder
1 tsp. ground cumin
½ tsp. onion powder
½ tsp. garlic powder

1. In a small cup, stir together all seasonings and set aside.
2. Slice chicken tenders in half crosswise, then cut into strips no wider than about ½ inch.
3. Preheat air fryer to 390ºF (200ºC).
4. Season chicken with salt to taste. Arrange strips in a large bowl and sprinkle with 1 tbsp. of the seasoning mix. Stir well to distribute seasonings.
5. Add flour to chicken and stir well to coat all sides.
6. In a shallow dish, beat eggs together.
7. Combine the panko, crushed chips, and the remaining 2 tsps. of seasoning mix in a second

shallow dish.
8. Dip chicken strips in eggs, then roll in crumbs. Mist with oil or cooking spray.
9. Chicken strips will cook best if done in two batches. They can be crowded and overlapping a little but not stacked in double or triple layers.
10. Air fry for about 4 minutes. Shake the basket, mist with oil, and air fry for 2 to 3 more minutes, until the chicken juices run clear and the outside is crispy.
11. Repeat step 10 to cook the remaining chicken fries.

Peruvian-Style Chicken with Herb-Mayonnaise

Prep time: 15 minutes | Cook time: 15 minutes | Serves 4

FOR THE CHICKEN:
1 tbsp. extra-virgin olive oil
1½ pounds (680 g) boneless, skinless chicken thighs
1 serrano chile, seeded and minced
2 tbsps. fresh lemon juice
2 tsps. grated lemon zest
1 tsp. ground cumin
½ tsp. dried oregano, crushed
½ tsp. kosher salt
FOR THE SAUCE:
1 tbsp. extra-virgin olive oil
1 jalapeño, seeded and coarsely chopped
1 cup fresh cilantro leaves
⅓ cup mayonnaise
1 garlic clove, minced
2½ tsps. fresh lime juice
¼ tsp. kosher salt

MAKE THE CHICKEN:
1. Use a fork to pierce the chicken all over to let the marinade penetrate better. Combine the lemon zest, lemon juice, olive oil, serrano, cumin, oregano and salt in a small bowl. Put the chicken in a large bowl or large resealable plastic bag. Add the marinade over the chicken. Toss to coat well. Marinate at room temperature for 30 minutes, or cover and refrigerate for up to 24 hours.
2. Put the chicken in the air-fryer basket. (Discard the remaining marinade.) Air fry for 15 minutes at 350ºF (180ºC), turning halfway through the cooking time.
MAKE THE SAUCE:
3. At the same time, combine the cilantro, olive oil, jalapeño, garlic, lime juice and salt in a blender. Blend until combined well. Add the mayonnaise and blend until pureed. Transfer to a small bowl. Cover and chill until ready to serve.
4. At the end of the cooking time, use a meat thermometer to ensure the chicken has reached an internal temperature of 165ºF (74ºC). Serve the chicken warm with the sauce.

Super Cheesy Chicken

Prep time: 10 minutes | Cook time: 9 minutes | Serves 4

olive oil
2 (8-ounce / 227-g) chicken breasts
½ cup keto marinara
6 tbsps. gluten-free seasoned breadcrumbs
6 tbsps. Mozzarella cheese
2 tbsps. grated Parmesan cheese
1 tbsp. melted ghee

1. Ensure air fryer is preheated to 360ºF (180ºC). Spray the basket lightly with olive oil.
2. Mix Parmesan cheese and breadcrumbs together.
3. Brush melted ghee onto the chicken and dip into the breadcrumb mixture.
4. Put coated chicken in the air fryer and top with olive oil.
5. Select the Poultry function, adjust time to 6 minutes, then press Start/Pause. Add a tbsp. of sauce and 1½ tbsps. of Mozzarella cheese on top of each breast. Air fry for another 3 minutes to melt the cheese.
6. Keep the cooked pieces warm as you repeat the process with remaining breasts.

Mozzarella Chicken Fritters with Garlic Dip

Prep time: 15 minutes | Cook time: 20 minutes | Makes 16 to 18 fritters

FOR THE CHICKEN FRITTERS:
1½ pounds (680 g) chicken breasts
2 eggs
1⅓ cups shredded Mozzarella cheese
⅓ cup coconut flour
⅓ cup vegan mayo
1½ tbsps. fresh dill
½ tsp. salt
⅛ tsp. pepper
FOR THE GARLIC DIP:
⅓ cup vegan mayo
1 pressed garlic cloves
½ tbsp. lemon juice
¼ tsp. salt
⅛ tsp. pepper

1. Cut chicken breasts into ⅓" pieces and place in a bowl. Place all remaining fritter ingredients to the bowl and stir well. Cover and chill for 2 hours or overnight.
2. Ensure your air fryer is preheated to 350ºF (180ºC). Spray the basket lightly with a bit of olive oil.
3. Add the marinated chicken to air fryer and air fry for 20 minutes, making sure to turn halfway through the cooking process.
4. Combine all the dip ingredients until smooth to make the dipping sauce.
5. Serve with the dipping sauce.

Quick Buffalo Chicken Wings

Prep time: 5 minutes | Cook time: 30 minutes | Serves 6 to 8

4 pounds (1.8 kg) chicken wings
½ cup vegan butter
½ cup cayenne pepper sauce
1 to 2 tbsps. brown sugar
1 tbsp. Worcestershire sauce
1 tsp. salt
celery sticks for serving

1. Whisk salt, brown sugar, butter, Worcestershire sauce and hot sauce together and set aside.
2. Dry wings and add to air fryer basket.
3. Air fry for 25 minutes at 380ºF (195ºC), tossing halfway through.
4. When the timer sounds, shake wings and bump up the temperature to 400ºF (205ºC) and cook for another 5 minutes.
5. Take out wings and put into a big bowl. Add the sauce and toss well.
6. Serve warm alongside celery sticks!

Chicken and Bell Peppers Fajita Roll-Ups

Prep time: 10 minutes | Cook time: 24 minutes | Serves 6 to 8

3 chicken breasts
½ yellow bell pepper, sliced into strips
½ green bell pepper, sliced into strips
½ red bell pepper, sliced into strips
½ sliced red onion
2 tsps. paprika
1 tsp. cumin
1 tsp. garlic powder
½ tsp. oregano
a pinch or two of pepper and salt
½ tsp. cayenne pepper

1. Mix oregano, cayenne pepper, cumin, garlic powder and paprika along with a pinch or two of pepper and salt. Set aside.
2. Cut chicken breasts lengthwise into 2 slices.
3. Between two pieces of parchment paper, put breast slices and pound till they are ¼-inch thick. Liberally season both sides of chicken slices with seasoning.
4. Place 2 strips of each color of bell pepper and a few onion slices onto chicken pieces.
5. Roll up tightly and secure with toothpicks.
6. Repeat with remaining ingredients and scatter and rub mixture that is left over the chicken rolls.
7. Grease your air fryer basket lightly and place 3 rollups into the fryer. Air fry for 12 minutes at 400ºF (205ºC).
8. Repeat with the remaining rollups.

Easy Turkey Wings

Prep time: 5 minutes | Cook time: 26 minutes | Serves 4

3 tbsps. olive oil or sesame oil	wings
2 pounds (907 g) turkey	3 to 4 tbsps. chicken rub (any type)

1. Place the turkey wings in a large mixing bowl.
2. Add the olive oil and rub in the bowl.
3. Rub the oil mixture over the turkey wings with your hands.
4. Put the turkey wings in the air fryer basket.
5. Air fry for 13 minutes at 380ºF (195ºC).
6. Flip the wings with tongs.
7. Reset the timer and cook for 13 minutes more.
8. Take the turkey wings from the air fryer, transfer to a plate and serve warm.

Simple Seasoned Cornish Hen

Prep time: 5 minutes | Cook time: 30 minutes | Serves 2

1 (1½- to 2-pound / 680- to 907-g) Cornish hen	2 tbsps. Montreal chicken seasoning

1. Preheat the air fryer to 390ºF (200ºC).
2. Gently rub the seasoning over the chicken, coating it thoroughly.
3. Put the chicken in the Rotisserie Spit. Select the Poultry function, adjust time to 15 minutes, then press Start/Pause.
4. Flip the chicken with tongs and cook for another 15 minutes.
5. Check that the chicken has reached an internal temperature of 165ºF (74ºC). Add cooking time if needed. Serve warm.

Greek Chicken Salad with Kalamata Olives

Prep time: 10 minutes | Cook time: 12 minutes | Serves 4

1 pound (454 g) chicken breasts, boneless, skinless	1 red onion, thinly sliced
4 Kalamata olives, pitted and minced	1 bell pepper, sliced
1 small Greek cucumber, grated and squeezed	4 tbsps. Greek yogurt
	4 tbsps. mayonnaise
	1 tbsp. fresh lemon juice
	Coarse sea salt and red pepper flakes, to taste

1. Use paper towels to pat the chicken dry. Put the chicken breasts in a lightly oiled air fryer basket.
2. Select the Poultry function, adjust time to 12 minutes, then press Start/Pause, turning them over halfway through the cooking time.
3. Dice the chicken breasts and take them to a salad bowl, place the remaining ingredients and toss to combine well.
4. Serve well-chilled and enjoy!

Garlic Breaded Chicken Breast

Prep time: 10 minutes | Cook time: 12 minutes | Serves 4

1 tbsp. butter, room temperature	1 egg, whisked
1 pound (454 g) chicken breasts, boneless and skinless	1 tsp. garlic powder
½ cup breadcrumbs	1 tsp. cayenne pepper
	Kosher salt and ground black pepper, to taste

1. Pat the chicken dry with paper towels.
2. Thoroughly combine the butter, egg, cayenne pepper, garlic powder, kosher salt, black pepper in a bowl.
3. Dip the chicken breasts into the egg mixture. Then roll the chicken breasts over the breadcrumbs.
4. Air fry for 12 minutes at 380ºF (195ºC), turning them over halfway through the cooking time.
5. Serve warm!

Honey Glazed Cornish Hens

Prep time: 5 minutes | Cook time: 25 minutes | Serves 2 to 3

Cooking spray	hen
1 tbsp. honey	1 tbsp. lime juice
1 (1½- to 2-pound / 680- to 907-g) Cornish game	1 tsp. poultry seasoning
	Salt and pepper, to taste

1. Cut through breastbone and down one side of the backbone to split the hen into halves.
2. Mix the lime juice, honey and poultry seasoning together and brush or rub onto all sides of the hen evenly. Season with salt and pepper to taste.
3. Spray air fryer basket with cooking spray and put the hen halves in the basket, skin-side down.
4. Select the Poultry function, adjust time to 30 minutes, then press Start/Pause. Hen will be done when juices run clear when pierced at leg joint with a fork. Allow hen to rest for 5 to 10 minutes.

Simple Mustard Chicken Tenders

Prep time: 5 minutes | Cook time: 10 minutes | Serves 4 to 6

1 pound (454 g) of chicken tenders	1 tbsp. spicy brown mustard
2 beaten eggs	pepper and salt to taste
½ cup coconut flour	

1. Season tenders with pepper and salt to taste.
2. Put a thin layer of mustard onto tenders and then dredge in flour and dip in egg.
3. Place to air fryer and air fry for 10 to 15 minutes at 390ºF (200ºC), or till crispy. Serve warm.

Teriyaki Paprika Chicken Legs

Prep time: 5 minutes | Cook time: 18 minutes | Serves 2

Cooking spray	1 tbsp. orange juice
4 chicken legs	1 tsp. smoked paprika
4 tbsps. teriyaki sauce	

1. Mix together the teriyaki sauce, smoked paprika and orange juice. Brush on all sides of chicken legs.
2. Spray air fryer basket lightly with nonstick cooking spray and place the chicken in the basket.
3. Select the Poultry function, adjust time to 6 minutes, then press Start/Pause. Turn and baste with sauce when done. Cook for 6 minutes more, turn and baste. Cook for 6 to 8 minutes more, until juices run clear when chicken is pierced with a fork.

Spicy Chicken and Corn Stir-Fry

Prep time: 10 minutes | Cook time: 13 minutes | Serves 4

2 tbsps. peanut oil	1 red bell pepper, chopped
2 boneless, skinless chicken breasts	1 jalapeño pepper, sliced
1 cup frozen corn	2 tbsps. cornstarch
½ cup salsa	hot rice for serving
1 onion, sliced	

1. Dice the chicken breasts into 1-inch cubes. Place the cornstarch on a shallow plate and toss the chicken to coat well. Keep the chicken aside.
2. Combine the oil and onion in a 6-inch metal bowl. Cook for 2 to 3 minutes or until crisp and tender.
3. Add the chicken to the bowl. Cook for about 7 to 8 minutes or until almost cooked. Stir in the red bell pepper, jalapeño pepper, corn and salsa.
4. Air fry for 4 to 5 minutes or until the chicken is cooked to 165ºF (74ºC) and the vegetables are crisp and soft. Serve over hot rice.

Easy Turkey Burgers

Prep time: 10 minutes | Cook time: 10 minutes | Serves 4

1 pound (454 g) ground turkey	seasoning
4 whole-grain sandwich buns	½ tsp. dried parsley
4 slices provolone cheese	½ tsp. salt
¼ cup diced red onion	**SUGGESTED TOPPINGS:**
1 tbsp. grilled chicken	lettuce, sliced tomatoes, dill pickles and mustard

1. Combine the turkey, chicken seasoning, onion, parsley and salt and mix well.
2. Shape the turkey mixture into 4 patties.
3. Air fry for 9 to 11 minutes at 360ºF (180ºC), or until turkey is well done and juices run clear.
4. Place a slice of cheese on top of each burger and cook for 1 to 2 minutes to melt.
5. Serve warm on sandwich buns with your favorite toppings.

Spinach and Cheese Stuffed Chicken

Prep time: 10 minutes | Cook time: 20 minutes | Serves 4

2 tbsps. olive oil	2 ounces (57 g) Feta cheese
1 pound (454 g) chicken breasts, skinless, boneless and cut into pieces	1 garlic clove, minced
	2 tbsps. olives, chopped
2 cups spinach, torn into pieces	Sea salt and ground black pepper, to taste

1. Use a mallet to flatten the chicken breasts.
2. Stuff each piece of chicken with garlic, olives, spinach and cheese. Roll them up and secure with toothpicks.
3. Season the chicken with the salt, black pepper and olive oil.
4. Put the stuffed chicken breasts in the air fryer basket. Air fry for about 20 minutes at 400ºF (205ºC), turning them over halfway through the cooking time.
5. Serve warm!

Simple Herbed Turkey Breasts

Prep time: 5 minutes | Cook time: 1 hour | Serves 4

1 tbsp. butter, room temperature
1 pound (454 g) turkey breast, bone-in
1 tsp. Italian herb mix
1 tsp. cayenne pepper
Kosher salt and ground black pepper, to taste

1. Thoroughly combine the butter, salt, black pepper, cayenne pepper and herb mix in a mixing bowl.
2. Rub the mixture all over the turkey breast.
3. Air fry for 1 hour at 350ºF (180ºC), turning them over every 20 minutes.
4. Serve warm!

BBQ Chicken Thighs

Prep time: 5 minutes | Cook time: 15 minutes | Serves 4

¼ cup gluten-free barbecue sauce
6 boneless, skinless
chicken thighs
2 tbsps. lemon juice
2 cloves garlic, minced

1. Combine the chicken, barbecue sauce, cloves, and lemon juice in a medium bowl, and mix well. Let marinate for 10 minutes.
2. Take the chicken thighs from the bowl and shake off excess sauce. Place the chicken pieces in the air fryer, leaving a bit of space between each one.
3. Air fry for about 15 to 18 minutes or until the chicken is 165ºF (74ºC) on an instant-read meat thermometer. Serve warm.

Hoisin Duck Breast

Prep time: 5 minutes | Cook time: 30 minutes | Serves 3

1 pound (454 g) duck breast
1 tbsp. Hoisin sauce
1 tbsp. Five-spice powder
¼ tsp. ground cinnamon
Sea salt and black pepper, to taste

1. Use paper towels to pat the duck breasts dry. Toss the duck breast with the remaining ingredients.
2. Select the Poultry function, adjust time to 15 minutes, then press Start/Pause, turning them over halfway through the cooking time.
3. Turn the heat to 350ºF (180ºC) and continue to cook for about 15 minutes or until cooked through.
4. Allow it to rest for 10 minutes before carving and serving. Bon appétit!

Smoked Paprika Chicken Breasts

Prep time: 5 minutes | Cook time: 12 minutes | Serves 4

1 tbsp. butter, melted
1 pound (454 g) chicken breasts, boneless, skinless, cut into 4 pieces
1 tsp. smoked paprika
1 tsp. garlic powder
Kosher salt and ground black pepper, to taste

1. Flatten the chicken breasts to ¼-inch thickness.
2. Toss the chicken breasts evenly with the remaining ingredients.
3. Select the Poultry function, adjust time to 12 minutes, then press Start/Pause, turning them over halfway through the cooking time.
4. Serve warm!

BBQ Chicken Burgers

Prep time: 10 minutes | Cook time: 17 minutes | Serves 3

¾ pound (340 g) chicken, ground
1 egg, beaten
¼ cup Parmesan cheese, grated
¼ cup tortilla chips, crushed
2 garlic cloves, minced
2 tbsps. onion, minced
1 tbsp. BBQ sauce

1. Mix all the ingredients until everything is well combined. Shape the mixture into three patties.
2. Air fry for about 17 minutes at 380ºF (195ºC), or until cooked through, making sure to turn them over halfway through the cooking time.
3. Serve warm!

Mayo Chicken and Carrot Salad

Prep time: 5 minutes | Cook time: 12 minutes | Serves 3

1 pound (454 g) chicken breast
1 carrot, shredded
½ cup mayonnaise
2 tbsps. scallions,
chopped
1 tbsp. mustard
Sea salt and ground black pepper, to taste

1. Use kitchen towels to pat the chicken dry. Put the chicken in a lightly oiled air fryer basket.
2. Select the Poultry function, adjust time to 12 minutes, then press Start/Pause, turning them over halfway through the cooking time.
3. Cut the chicken breasts and transfer them to a salad bowl, place the remaining ingredients and toss to combine well. Bon appétit!

Chinese Chicken Patties

Prep time: 5 minutes | Cook time: 17 minutes | Serves 4

1 tbsp. olive oil
1 pound (454 g) ground chicken
1 small onion, chopped
1 tbsp. chili sauce
1 tsp. garlic, minced
Kosher salt and ground black pepper, to taste

1. Mix all the ingredients until everything is well combined. Shape the mixture into four patties.
2. Air fry for about 17 minutes at 380ºF (195ºC), or until cooked through, making sure to turn them over halfway through the cooking time.
3. Serve warm!

Five-Spice Chicken Drumsticks

Prep time: 5 minutes | Cook time: 22 minutes | Serves 3

2 tbsps. sesame oil
3 chicken drumsticks
1 tbsp. soy sauce
1 tsp. Five-spice powder
Kosher salt and ground black pepper, to taste

1. Use paper towels to pat the chicken drumsticks dry. Toss the chicken drumsticks with the remaining ingredients.
2. Select the Poultry function, adjust time to 22 minutes, then press Start/Pause, turning them over halfway through the cooking time.
3. Serve warm!

Garlic Honey Chicken Wings

Prep time: 10 minutes | Cook time: 55 minutes | Serves 8

olive oil
16 chicken wings
¾ cup almond flour
¼ cup vegan butter
¼ cup raw honey
4 tbsps. minced garlic
⅛ cup water
½ tsp. salt

1. Rinse off and dry chicken wings well.
2. Spray air fryer basket lightly with olive oil.
3. Coat chicken wings with almond flour and add the coated wings to air fryer. Air fry for 25 minutes at 380ºF (195ºC), shaking every 5 minutes.
4. When the timer goes off, cook for about 5 to 10 minutes at 400ºF (205ºC) till the skin becomes crispy and dry.
5. As chicken cooks, melt butter in a saucepan and place garlic. Sauté the garlic for 5 minutes. Add salt and honey, simmering for about 20 minutes. Make sure to stir every so often, so the sauce does not burn. Pour a bit of water after 15 minutes to ensure the sauce does not harden.
6. Remove chicken wings from the air fryer and coat in sauce. Enjoy!

Garlic Chicken Breasts

Prep time: 5 minutes | Cook time: 14 minutes | Serves 4

2 tbsps. olive oil, divided
4 boneless, skinless chicken breasts
½ tsp. garlic powder
1 tsp. dried parsley
1 tsp. salt
½ tsp. freshly ground black pepper

1. Mix together the garlic powder, salt, pepper, and parsley in a small mixing bowl.
2. Using 1 tbsp. of olive oil and half of the seasoning mix, rub each chicken breast evenly with oil and seasonings.
3. Put the chicken breast in the air fryer basket.
4. Select the Poultry function, adjust time to 7 minutes, then press Start/Pause.
5. Flip the chicken with tongs and brush the remaining olive oil and spices onto the chicken.
6. Reset the timer and cook for 7 minutes more.
7. Check that the chicken has reached an internal temperature of 165ºF (74ºC). Add cooking time if needed.
8. Once the chicken is completely cooked, transfer it to a platter and serve warm.

Breaded Fried Chicken Drumsticks

Prep time: 10 minutes | Cook time: 25 minutes | Serves 4

8 chicken drumsticks
1 beaten egg
¼ cup cauliflower
¼ cup gluten-free oats
3 tbsps. coconut milk

2 tbsps. mustard powder
2 tbsps. oregano
2 tbsps. thyme
1 tsp. cayenne pepper
pepper and salt to taste

1. Ensure air fryer is preheated to 350ºF (180ºC).
2. Lay out chicken and season with pepper and salt to taste on all sides.
3. Add all other ingredients except for egg to a blender, blending till a smooth-like breadcrumb mixture is created. Put in a bowl and add a beaten egg to another bowl.
4. Dip chicken into breadcrumbs, then into egg, and breadcrumbs once more.
5. Put the coated drumsticks into air fryer and air fry for 20 minutes at 350ºF (180ºC). Bump up the temperature to 390ºF (200ºC) and cook for another 5 minutes till crispy. Serve warm.

Quick Panko-Crusted Chicken Chunks

Prep time: 5 minutes | Cook time: 16 minutes | Serves 4

Oil for misting or cooking spray
1 pound (454 g) chicken tenders cut in large chunks, about 1½ inches
2 eggs, beaten

1 cup panko breadcrumbs
½ cup cornstarch
Salt and pepper, to taste

1. Season chicken chunks with salt and pepper to taste.
2. Dip chicken chunks in cornstarch. Then dip in the egg and shake off excess. Then roll in panko crumbs to coat well.
3. Spray all sides of chicken chunks lightly with oil or cooking spray.
4. Put chicken in air fryer basket in single layer and air fry for 5 minutes at 390ºF (200ºC). Spray with oil, turn chunks over, and spray the other side.
5. Air fry for another 3 to 5 minutes or until the chicken juices run clear and the outside is golden brown.
6. Repeat steps 4 and 5 to cook the remaining chicken. Serve warm.

Chapter 5 Pork

Lemony Breaded Schnitzel

Prep time: 10 minutes | Cook time: 14 minutes | Serves 4

Oil for misting or cooking spray
4 thin boneless pork loin chops
2 eggs, beaten
1 cup plain breadcrumbs
½ cup flour
2 tbsps. lemon juice
¼ tsp. marjoram
1 tsp. salt
lemon wedges for serving

1. Rub the lemon juice into all sides of pork chops.
2. Mix together the flour, marjoram and salt.
3. Put the flour mixture on a sheet of wax paper.
4. Place breadcrumbs on another sheet of wax paper.
5. Roll pork chops in flour, dip in beaten eggs, then roll in breadcrumbs. Mist all sides with oil or cooking spray.
6. Spray air fryer basket lightly with nonstick cooking spray and put pork chops in the basket.
7. Air fry for 7 minutes at 390ºF (200ºC). Turn, mist again, and cook for 7 or 8 minutes more, until well done. Serve warm with lemon wedges.

Spicy Vietnamese Pork Sausages

Prep time: 15 minutes | Cook time: 15 minutes | Serves 4

FOR THE SAUSAGES:
1 pound (454 g) finely ground pork
1 heaping tbsp. jasmine rice
2 garlic cloves, minced
2 tbsps. fish sauce
1 tbsp. sugar
½ tsp. baking powder
½ tsp. kosher salt
½ tsp. black pepper
FOR SERVING:
Hot cooked rice or rice noodles
Shredded lettuce
Sliced cucumber
Fresh mint and basil leaves
Sliced scallions

MAKE THE SAUSAGES:
1. Put the rice in a small heavy-bottomed skillet. Toast over medium heat, stirring continuously, until it turns a deep golden yellow color, 5 to 8 minutes. Pour the rice onto a plate to cool completely. Grind in a spice or coffee grinder to a fine powder.
2. Stir together the rice powder, fish sauce, garlic, sugar, pepper, salt, and baking powder in a large bowl, until thoroughly combined. Add the pork and mix gently until the seasonings are incorporated.
3. Divide the meat mixture evenly into eight equal pieces. Roll each into a 3-inch-long log. Cover lightly with plastic wrap. Refrigerate for at least 30 minutes or up to 24 hours.
4. Place the sausages in the air-fryer basket, in multiple batches if necessary. Air fry 15 minutes for at 375ºF (190ºC). Use a meat thermometer to ensure the sausages have reached an internal temperature of 160ºF (71ºC).
5. Place the sausages, lettuce, mint, basil, cucumbers and scallions on top of the rice.

Thin Pork Cutlets with Aloha Salsa

Prep time: 15 minutes | Cook time: 7 minutes | Serves 4

Oil for misting or cooking spray
1 pound (454 g) boneless, thin pork cutlets (⅜- to ½-inch thick)
2 eggs
¼ cup cornstarch
¼ cup flour
¼ cup panko breadcrumbs
2 tbsps. milk
4 tsps. sesame seeds
Lemon pepper and salt
FOR THE ALOHA
SALSA:
1 cup fresh pineapple, chopped into small pieces
¼ cup green or red bell pepper, chopped
¼ cup red onion, finely chopped
1 tsp. low-sodium soy sauce
½ tsp. ground cinnamon
⅛ tsp. crushed red pepper
⅛ tsp. ground black pepper

1. Stir together all the ingredients for salsa in a medium bowl. Cover and refrigerate while cooking pork.
2. Preheat air fryer to 390ºF (200ºC).
3. In a shallow dish, beat together eggs and milk.
4. Mix together the flour, panko and sesame seeds in another shallow dish.
5. Sprinkle pork cutlets to taste with lemon pepper and salt. Most lemon pepper seasoning contains salt, so go easy adding extra.
6. Dip pork cutlets in cornstarch, egg mixture, and then panko coating. Spray both sides lightly with oil or cooking spray.
7. Air fry for 3 minutes at 390ºF (200ºC). Turn cutlets over, spraying both sides, and continue cooking for about 4 to 6 minutes or until well done.
8. Serve the fried cutlets with salsa on the side.

Air-Fried Pork and Creamer Potatoes

Prep time: 10 minutes | Cook time: 25 minutes | Serves 4

2 tsps. olive oil
1 (1-pound / 454-g) pork tenderloin, cut into 1-inch cubes
2 cups creamer potatoes, rinsed and dried
1 red bell pepper, chopped
1 onion, chopped
2 garlic cloves, minced
2 tbsps. low-sodium chicken broth
½ tsp. dried oregano

1. Toss the potatoes and olive oil to coat in a medium bowl.
2. Take the potatoes to the air fryer basket. Air fry for about 15 minutes.
3. Mix the potatoes, pork, onion, red bell pepper, garlic and oregano in a medium metal bowl.
4. Drizzle with the chicken broth. Place the bowl in the air fryer basket. Air fry for 10 minutes more, shaking the basket once during cooking, until the pork reaches at least 145ºF (63ºC) on a meat thermometer and the potatoes are tender. Serve hot.

Vietnamese Pork Shoulder with Roasted Peanuts

Prep time: 10 minutes | Cook time: 20 minutes | Serves 6

2 tbsps. vegetable oil
1½ pounds (680 g) boneless pork shoulder, cut into ½-inch-thick slices
¼ cup chopped salted roasted peanuts
¼ cup minced yellow onion
2 tbsps. chopped fresh cilantro or parsley
2 tbsps. sugar
1 tbsp. fish sauce
1 tbsp. minced garlic
1 tbsp. minced fresh lemongrass
2 tsps. dark soy sauce
½ tsp. black pepper

1. Combine the onion, sugar, vegetable oil, garlic, fish sauce, lemongrass, soy sauce and pepper in a large bowl. Add the pork and toss to coat well. Marinate at room temperature for about 30 minutes, or cover and refrigerate for up to 24 hours.
2. Place the pork slices in the air-fryer basket and discard the marinade. Air fry for 20 minutes at 400ºF (205ºC), turning the pork halfway through the cooking time.
3. Take the pork to a serving platter. Scatter with the peanuts and cilantro and serve warm.

Pork Tenderloin, Plum and Apricot Kebabs

Prep time: 10 minutes | Cook time: 10 minutes | Serves 4

2 tsps. olive oil
1 (1-pound / 454-g) pork tenderloin, cut into 1-inch cubes
4 plums, pitted and quartered
4 small apricots, pitted and halved
⅓ cup apricot jam
2 tbsps. freshly squeezed lemon juice
½ tsp. dried tarragon

1. Mix the jam, lemon juice, olive oil and tarragon in a large bowl.
2. Add the pork and stir to coat well. Allow to stand for 10 minutes at room temperature.
3. Alternating the items, thread the pork, plums, and apricots onto 4 metal skewers that fit into the air fryer. Brush with any remaining jam mixture. Discard any remaining marinade.
4. Air fry for about 9 to 12 minutes, or until the pork reaches 145ºF (63ºC) on a meat thermometer and the fruits are soft. Serve hot.

Sweet-Sour Pork Chunks

Prep time: 15 minutes | Cook time: 10 minutes | Serves 4 to 6

1 tsp. pure sesame oil
2 pounds (907 g) pork, sliced into chunks
2 eggs
1 cup almond flour
1/16 tsp. Chinese Five Spice
½ tsp. sea salt
¼ tsp. pepper
FOR THE SWEET AND

SOUR SAUCE:
½ cup sweetener of choice
½ cup rice vinegar
5 tbsps. tomato paste
1 tbsp. low-sodium soy sauce
½ tsp. garlic powder
¼ tsp. sea salt
⅛ tsp. water

1. To prepare the dipping sauce, whisk all sauce ingredients together over medium heat, stirring 5 minutes. Simmer uncovered for 5 minutes till thickened.
2. At the same time, combine almond flour, five spice, salt and pepper.
3. Mix eggs with sesame oil in another bowl.
4. Dredge pork in flour mixture and then in egg mixture. Shake any excess off before adding to the air fryer basket.
5. Air fry for 8 to 12 minutes at 340ºF (170ºC).
6. Serve warm with sweet and sour dipping sauce!

Bacon Lettuce Salad with Croutons

Prep time: 10 minutes | Cook time: 16 minutes | Serves 5

1 pound (454 g) bacon, cut into thick slices	1 tbsp. fresh tarragon, chopped
1 head lettuce, torn into leaves	1 tbsp. fresh parsley, chopped
2 cups bread cubes	1 tsp. red pepper flakes, crushed
2 garlic cloves, minced	Coarse sea salt and ground black pepper, to taste
2 tbsps. freshly squeezed lemon juice	
1 tbsp. fresh chive, chopped	

1. Put the bacon in the air fryer basket. Then cook the bacon at 400ºF (205ºC), and set time to approximately 10 minutes, tossing the basket halfway through the cooking time; reserve.
2. Air fry for about 6 minutes at 390ºF (200ºC), or until the bread is toasted.
3. In a salad bowl, toss the remaining ingredients and top your salad with the bacon and croutons. Bon appétit!

Tasty Pork Bulgogi

Prep time: 15 minutes | Cook time: 15 minutes | Serves 4

1 tbsp. toasted sesame oil	1 tbsp. minced garlic
1 pound (454 g) boneless pork shoulder, cut into ½-inch-thick slices	1 tbsp. soy sauce
	1 tbsp. Shaoxing wine (rice cooking wine)
1 onion, thinly sliced	1 tbsp. sesame seeds
¼ cup sliced scallions	1 tsp. sugar
2 tbsps. gochujang (Korean red chile paste)	¼ to 1 tsp. cayenne pepper or gochugaru (Korean ground red pepper)
1 tbsp. minced fresh ginger	

1. Combine the onion, gochujang, ginger, garlic, soy sauce, wine, sesame oil, sugar and cayenne in a large bowl. Place the pork and toss to coat well. Marinate at room temperature for about 30 minutes, or cover and refrigerate for up to 24 hours.
2. Place the pork and onion slices in the air-fryer basket and discard the marinade. Air fry for 15 minutes at 400ºF (205ºC), turning the pork halfway through the cooking time.
3. Put the pork on a serving platter. Garnish with the sesame seeds and scallions and serve warm.

Caribbean-Style Pork Patties with Brioche Hamburger Buns

Prep time: 10 minutes | Cook time: 15 minutes | Serves 4

1 pound (454 g) ground pork	chopped
4 brioche hamburger buns, lightly toasted	1 tbsp. fresh coriander, chopped
1 small onion, chopped	1 tsp. habanero pepper, sliced
1 clove garlic, minced	Kosher salt and ground black pepper, to taste
1 tbsp. teriyaki sauce	
1 tbsp. fresh parsley,	

1. Thoroughly combine the pork, spices, habanero pepper, teriyaki sauce, onion and garlic in a mixing bowl. Then roll the mixture into four patties.
2. Air fry for about 15 minutes at 380ºF (195ºC), or until cooked through, making sure to turn them over halfway through the cooking time.
3. Serve the patties warm with the brioche hamburger buns. Enjoy!

Chili Breaded Pork Chops

Prep time: 10 minutes | Cook time: 24 minutes | Serves 8

olive oil	2 tbsps. grated Parmesan cheese
6 center-cut boneless pork chops	1¼ tsps. sweet paprika
1 beaten egg	½ tsp. onion powder
½ cup panko breadcrumbs	½ tsp. garlic powder
⅓ cup crushed cornflake crumbs	¼ tsp. chili powder
	½ tsp. salt
	⅛ tsp. pepper

1. Ensure that your air fryer is preheated to 400ºF (205ºC). Spray the basket with olive oil.
2. Season both sides of pork chops with ½ tsp. salt and pepper.
3. Combine ¾ tsp. salt with pepper, chili powder, garlic powder, onion powder, paprika, cornflake crumbs, panko breadcrumbs and Parmesan cheese.
4. In another bowl, beat the egg.
5. Dip pork chops into the egg and then the crumb mixture.
6. Place pork chops to air fryer and spritz with olive oil. Air fry for 12 minutes, making sure to flip over halfway through the cooking process.
7. Only put 3 chops in at a time and repeat the process with remaining pork chops. Serve warm.

Pork Butt with Fresh Rosemary

Prep time: 5 minutes | Cook time: 55 minutes | Serves 4

1 tsp. butter, melted
1½ pounds (680 g) pork butt
2 tbsps. fresh rosemary, chopped

2 garlic cloves, pressed
Coarse sea salt and freshly ground black pepper, to taste

1. Toss all the ingredients in a lightly greased air fryer basket.
2. Air fry for about 55 minutes at 360ºF (180ºC), turning it over halfway through the cooking time.
3. Serve hot!

Paprika Pork Loin Roast

Prep time: 5 minutes | Cook time: 15 minutes | Serves 4

2 tbsps. olive oil
1½ pounds (680 g) top loin roasts, sliced into four pieces
1 tbsp. Dijon mustard

1 tsp. hot paprika
1 tsp. garlic, pressed
Sea salt and ground black pepper

1. Add all the ingredients in a lightly greased air fryer basket.
2. Air fry for 15 minutes at 400ºF (205ºC), turning it over halfway through the cooking time.
3. Serve warm!

Hot Center Cut Pork Roast

Prep time: 10 minutes | Cook time: 55 minutes | Serves 4

1 tbsp. olive oil
1½ pounds (680 g) center-cut pork roast
1 tsp. hot paprika
1 tsp. garlic powder
½ tsp. dried parsley

flakes
½ tsp. dried rosemary
Sea salt and freshly ground black pepper, to taste

1. Toss all the ingredients in a lightly greased air fryer basket.
2. Air fry for 55 minutes at 360ºF (180ºC), turning it over halfway through the cooking time.
3. Serve hot!

Pork Loin with Dijon Mustard

Prep time: 10 minutes | Cook time: 55 minutes | Serves 4

1 tbsp. olive oil
1½ pounds (680 g) pork top loin
2 cloves garlic, crushed
1 tbsp. Dijon mustard
1 tbsp. coriander

1 tbsp. parsley
½ tsp. red pepper flakes, crushed
Kosher salt and ground black pepper, to taste

1. Place all the ingredients in a lightly greased air fryer basket.
2. Air fry for 55 minutes at 360ºF (180ºC), turning it over halfway through the cooking time.
3. Serve hot and enjoy!

Picnic Ham with Tamari Sauce

Prep time: 5 minutes | Cook time: 45 minutes | Serves 4

2 tbsps. olive oil
1½ pounds (680 g) picnic ham

2 garlic cloves, minced
2 tbsps. rice vinegar
1 tbsp. tamari sauce

1. Start by preheating your Air Fryer to 400ºF (205ºC), and set time to about 13 minutes.
2. Toss the ham with the remaining ingredients, then wrap the ham in a piece of aluminum foil and place it into the air fryer basket.
3. Turn the temperature to 375ºF (191ºC) and air fry for 30 minutes.
4. Remove the foil, increase the temperature to 400ºF (205ºC), and continue to cook for an additional 15 minutes or until cooked through.
5. Serve warm!

Pork Dinner Rolls

Prep time: 10 minutes | Cook time: 15 minutes | Serves 4

1 tbsp. olive oil
1 pound (454 g) ground pork
8 dinner rolls, split
½ cup scallions, chopped
2 garlic cloves, minced

1 tbsp. soy sauce
1 tsp. red pepper flakes, crushed
Sea salt and freshly ground black pepper, to taste

1. Thoroughly combine the pork, spices, scallions, garlic, olive oil and soy sauce in a mixing bowl. Shape the mixture into four patties.
2. Air fry for about 15 minutes at 380ºF (195ºC), or until cooked through, making sure to turn them over halfway through the cooking time.
3. Serve the patties in dinner rolls warm and enjoy!

Orange Glazed Pork Chops

Prep time: 5 minutes | Cook time: 15 minutes | Serves 3

1½ tbsps. butter, melted
1 pound (454 g) rib pork chops
2 tbsps. orange juice,

freshly squeezed
1 tsp. rosemary, chopped
Sea salt and cayenne pepper, to taste

1. Place all the ingredients in a lightly greased air fryer basket.
2. Air fry for 15 minutes at 400ºF (205ºC), turning them over halfway through the cooking time.
3. Serve warm!

Garlic St. Louis-Style Ribs

Prep time: 5 minutes | Cook time: 35 minutes | Serves 4

1 tbsp. canola oil
1½ pounds (680 g) St. Louis-style ribs
2 garlic cloves, minced

1 tsp. hot sauce
Kosher salt and ground black pepper, to taste

1. Add all the ingredients in a lightly greased air fryer basket.
2. Air fry for 35 minutes at 350ºF (180ºC), turning them over halfway through the cooking time.
3. Serve warm!

Mexican-Style Pork and Chile Tacos

Prep time: 10 minutes | Cook time: 55 minutes | Serves 4

1 tbsp. olive oil
1½ pounds (680 g) pork butt
4 corn tortillas, warmed
2 ancho chiles, seeded and minced

2 garlic cloves, chopped
1 tsp. dried Mexican oregano
Kosher salt and freshly ground black pepper, to season

1. Add all the ingredients, except for the tortillas, in a lightly greased air fryer basket.
2. Air fry for 55 minutes at 360ºF (180ºC), turning it over halfway through the cooking time.
3. Shred the pork with two forks and serve in tortillas with toppings of choice. Serve warm!

Tasty Souvlaki

Prep time: 10 minutes | Cook time: 15 minutes | Serves 4

1 tbsp. olive oil
1 pound (454 g) pork tenderloin, cubed
½ pound (227 g) fennel, diced

1 eggplant, diced
2 bell peppers, diced
1 small lemon, freshly juiced
½ tsp. sweet paprika

1. In a mixing bowl, toss all the ingredients until well coated on all sides.
2. Thread the ingredients onto skewers and put them in the air fryer basket.
3. Then air fry for about 15 minutes at 400ºF (205ºC), turning them over halfway through the cooking time.
4. Serve warm!

Coconut Pork Chops with Salad

Prep time: 5 minutes | Cook time: 15 minutes | Serves 4

1 tbsp. coconut oil
4 pork chops
1 tbsp. coconut butter
2 tsps. parsley

2 tsps. grated garlic cloves
a green salad for serving

1. Ensure your air fryer is preheated to 350ºF (180ºC).
2. Mix coconut oil, coconut butter and all seasoning together. Then rub seasoning mixture over all sides of pork chops. Place in foil, seal, and chill for about 1 hour.
3. Take pork chops from foil and place into air fryer.
4. Air fry for 7 minutes on one side and 8 minutes on the other.
5. Spritz with olive oil and serve alongside a green salad.

Spicy Pork Gyros

Prep time: 10 minutes | Cook time: 55 minutes | Serves 4

1 pound (454 g) pork shoulder
4 pitta bread, warmed
1 tsp. smoked paprika
1 tsp. garlic powder

½ tsp. ground bay leaf
½ tsp. onion powder
½ tsp. ground cumin
Sea salt and ground black pepper, to taste

1. Toss the pork on all sides, top and bottom, with the spices. Put the pork in a lightly greased air fryer basket.
2. Air fry for 55 minutes at 360ºF (180ºC), turning it over halfway through the cooking time.
3. Use two forks to shred the pork and serve on warmed pitta bread and some extra toppings of choice. Enjoy!

Garlic Rosemary Pork Loin Roast

Prep time: 5 minutes | Cook time: 55 minutes | Serves 4

1½ pounds (680 g) pork loin roast
2 tbsps. butter, melted
1 tsp. garlic, pressed

1 tsp. cayenne pepper
1 tsp. dried rosemary
Sea salt and ground black pepper, to taste

1. Place all the ingredients in a lightly greased air fryer basket.
2. Air fry for 55 minutes at 360ºF (180ºC), turning it over halfway through the cooking time.
3. Serve hot and enjoy!

Sweet Pork Spareribs

Prep time: 10 minutes | Cook time: 35 minutes | Serves 4

2 pounds (907 g) pork spareribs
1 tbsp. brown sugar
1 tsp. cayenne pepper
1 tsp. mustard powder

1 tsp. garlic powder
1 tsp. coarse sea salt
⅓ tsp. freshly ground black pepper

1. Toss all the ingredients in a lightly greased air fryer basket.
2. Air fry for 35 minutes at 350ºF (180ºC), turning them over halfway through the cooking time.
3. Serve warm!

Breaded Pork Sirloin Chops

Prep time: 10 minutes | Cook time: 15 minutes | Serves 3

1 pound (454 g) sirloin chops
½ cup breadcrumbs
1 egg
3 tbsps. Pecorino cheese, grated

2 tbsps. butter, at room temperature
1 tsp. paprika
1 tsp. garlic powder
Sea salt and ground black pepper, to taste

1. Use kitchen towels to pat the pork sirloin chops dry.
2. Whisk the egg until pale and frothy in a shallow bowl.
3. Thoroughly combine the remaining ingredients in another shallow bowl. Dip the pork chops into the egg, then the cheese and crumb mixture.
4. Put the pork sirloin chops in a lightly oiled air fryer basket.
5. Air fry for 15 minutes at 400ºF (205ºC), turning them over halfway through the cooking time.
6. Serve warm!

BBQ Pork Butt

Prep time: 5 minutes | Cook time: 55 minutes | Serves 5

1 tbsp. olive oil
2 pounds (907 g) pork butt
½ cup BBQ sauce

1 tsp. ground cumin
Kosher salt and ground black pepper, to taste

1. Add all the ingredients in a lightly greased air fryer basket.
2. Air fry for 55 minutes at 360ºF (180ºC), turning it over halfway through the cooking time.
3. Serve hot and enjoy!

Hot Pork Rib Roast

Prep time: 10 minutes | Cook time: 55 minutes | Serves 4

2 tsps. butter, melted
1½ pounds (680 g) pork center cut rib roast
2 tbsps. tamari sauce
1 tsp. paprika

1 tsp. red chili powder
1 tsp. garlic powder
½ tsp. onion powder
Sea salt and ground black pepper, to taste

1. Add all the ingredients in a lightly greased air fryer basket.
2. Air fry for 55 minutes at 360ºF (180ºC), turning it over halfway through the cooking time.
3. Serve hot!

Cuban Cheesy Pork Sandwich

Prep time: 10 minutes | Cook time: 55 minutes | Serves 4

1½ pounds (680 g) pork butt
16 ounces (454 g) Cuban bread loaf, sliced
2 ounces Swiss cheese, sliced
2 cloves garlic, crushed
2 tbsps. fresh pineapple

juice
1 tsp. stone-ground mustard
½ tsp. ground allspice
½ tsp. ground cumin
Kosher salt and freshly ground black pepper, to season

1. Add all the ingredients, except for the cheese and bread, in a lightly greased air fryer basket.
2. Air fry for 55 minutes at 360ºF (180ºC), turning it over halfway through the cooking time.
3. Shred the pork with two forks. Assemble your sandwiches with cheese and bread. Serve warm and enjoy!

Hot Pork Rib Roast, page 68

Mexican-Style Pork and Chile Tacos, page 67

Orange Glazed Pork Chops, page 67

Mustard Breaded Pork Tenderloin, page 71

Easy Beer Pork Loin

Prep time: 5 minutes | Cook time: 55 minutes | Serves 5

2 pounds (907 g) pork loin
4 tbsps. beer
1 tbsp. garlic, crushed
1 tsp. paprika
Sea salt and ground black pepper, to taste

1. Place all the ingredients in a lightly greased air fryer basket.
2. Air fry for about 55 minutes at 360ºF (180ºC), turning it over halfway through the cooking time.
3. Serve hot and enjoy!

Chinese Pork Back Ribs

Prep time: 10 minutes | Cook time: 35 minutes | Serves 4

1 tbsp. sesame oil
1½ pounds (680 g) back ribs
½ cup tomato sauce
2 tbsps. agave syrup
2 tbsps. rice wine
1 tbsp. soy sauce

1. Add all the ingredients in a lightly greased air fryer basket.
2. Air fry for 35 minutes at 350ºF (180ºC), turning them over halfway through the cooking time.
3. Serve warm!

Dijon Pork Burgers

Prep time: 10 minutes | Cook time: 15 minutes | Serves 4

1 pound (454 g) ground pork
4 hamburger buns
1 egg
¼ cup Parmesan cheese, grated
¼ cup seasoned breadcrumbs
1 small onion, chopped
4 tbsps. mayonnaise
1 tbsp. Italian herb mix
4 tsps. Dijon mustard
1 tsp. garlic, minced
Sea salt and ground black pepper, to taste

1. Thoroughly combine the pork, spices, onion, garlic, Parmesan, breadcrumbs and egg in a mixing bowl. Shape the mixture into four patties.
2. Air fry for about 15 minutes at 380ºF (195ºC), or until cooked through, making sure to turn them over halfway through the cooking time.
3. Serve your burgers warm with hamburger buns, Dijon mustard and mayonnaise. Enjoy!

Pork Sausage and Fennel

Prep time: 5 minutes | Cook time: 15 minutes | Serves 4

1 pound (454 g) pork sausage
1 pound (454 g) fennel, quartered
2 tsps. mustard
1 tsp. garlic powder
½ tsp. onion powder

1. Toss all the ingredients in a lightly greased air fryer basket.
2. Air fry for about 15 minutes at 370ºF (188ºC), tossing the basket halfway through the cooking time.
3. Serve warm!

Pork Center Cut with Red Pepper

Prep time: 5 minutes | Cook time: 55 minutes | Serves 5

2 tbsps. olive oil
2 pounds (907 g) pork center cut
1 tsp. red pepper flakes, crushed
1 tbsp. Italian herb mix
Sea salt and freshly ground black pepper, to taste

1. Add all the ingredients in a lightly greased air fryer basket.
2. Air fry for 55 minutes at 360ºF (180ºC), turning it over halfway through the cooking time.
3. Serve hot and enjoy!

Chinese Slab Baby Back Ribs

Prep time: 10 minutes | Cook time: 30 minutes | Serves 4

1 tbsp. toasted sesame oil
1 (1½-pound / 680-g) slab baby back ribs, cut into individual ribs
1 tbsp. fermented black bean paste
1 tbsp. agave nectar or
honey
1 tbsp. dark soy sauce
1 tbsp. Shaoxing wine (rice cooking wine)
1 tsp. minced fresh ginger
1 tsp. minced garlic

1. Stir together the sesame oil, black bean paste, wine, soy sauce, agave, garlic and ginger in a large bowl. Add the ribs and toss to coat well. Marinate at room temperature for about 30 minutes, or cover and refrigerate for up to 24 hours.
2. Put the ribs in the air-fryer basket and discard the marinade. Air fry for 30 minutes at 350ºF (180ºC).
3. Serve hot.

Spareribs with Sriracha Sauce

Prep time: 5 minutes | Cook time: 35 minutes | Serves 5

¼ cup Sriracha sauce	1 tsp. paprika
2 pounds (907 g) spareribs	Sea salt and ground black pepper, to taste

1. Place all the ingredients in a lightly greased air fryer basket.
2. Air fry for 35 minutes at 350ºF (180ºC), turning them over halfway through the cooking time.
3. Serve warm!

Herbed Pork Belly

Prep time: 5 minutes | Cook time: 20 minutes | Serves 5

1 pound (454 g) pork belly	1 tbsp. tomato sauce
2 tbsps. rice vinegar	1 tsp. dried thyme
	1 tsp. dried rosemary

1. Place all the ingredients in a lightly greased air fryer basket.
2. Air fry for 20 minutes at 320ºF (160ºC). Now, turn it over and continue cooking for a further 25 minutes.
3. Serve hot and enjoy!

Herbed Pork Butt

Prep time: 10 minutes | Cook time: 55 minutes | Serves 4

1 tsp. olive oil	1 tsp. dried rosemary
1½ pounds (680 g) pork butt	1 tsp. dried basil
1 tsp. cayenne pepper	1 tsp. dried oregano
1 tsp. dried thyme	Sea salt and ground black pepper, to taste

1. Add all the ingredients in a lightly greased air fryer basket.
2. Air fry for 55 minutes at 360ºF (180ºC), turning it over halfway through the cooking time.
3. Serve hot and enjoy!

Country-Style Ribs with Red Wine

Prep time: 10 minutes | Cook time: 35 minutes | Serves 5

2 pounds (907 g) Country-style ribs	1 tsp. mustard powder
1 tbsp. butter, melted	1 tsp. chili sauce
4 tbsps. dry red wine	Coarse sea salt and ground black pepper, to taste
1 tsp. smoked paprika	

1. Add all the ingredients in a lightly greased air fryer basket.
2. Air fry for 35 minutes at 350ºF (180ºC), turning them over halfway through the cooking time.
3. Serve warm!

Honey-Lemon Pork Tenderloin

Prep time: 10 minutes | Cook time: 10 minutes | Serves 4

2 tsps. olive oil	1 tbsp. packed brown sugar
1 (1-pound / 454-g) pork tenderloin	2 tsps. espresso powder
1 tbsp. honey	1 tsp. ground paprika
1 tbsp. freshly squeezed lemon juice	½ tsp. dried marjoram

1. Mix the brown sugar, espresso powder, paprika, and marjoram in a small bowl.
2. Stir in the honey, lemon juice and olive oil until well mixed.
3. Spread the honey mixture evenly over the pork and allow to stand for 10 minutes at room temperature.
4. Air fry the tenderloin in the air fryer basket for 9 to 11 minutes, or until the pork registers at least 145ºF (63ºC) on a meat thermometer. Slice the pork to serve.

Mustard Breaded Pork Tenderloin

Prep time: 10 minutes | Cook time: 14 minutes | Serves 4

2 tsps. olive oil	crumbled
1 (1-pound / 454-g) pork tenderloin, silverskin and excess fat trimmed and discarded	¼ cup ground walnuts
	3 tbsps. low-sodium grainy mustard
2 slices low-sodium whole-wheat bread,	2 tbsps. cornstarch
	¼ tsp. dry mustard powder

1. Stir together the mustard, olive oil and mustard powder in a small bowl. Spread this mixture over the pork.
2. Mix the bread crumbs, walnuts and cornstarch on a plate. Dip the mustard-coated pork into the crumb mixture to coat.
3. Air fry the pork for about 12 to 16 minutes, or until it registers at least 145ºF (63ºC) on a meat thermometer. Slice to serve.

Paprika Pork Loin Chops

Prep time: 5 minutes | Cook time: 15 minutes | Serves 4

1 tbsp. olive oil
1 pound (454 g) pork loin chops

1 tbsp. smoked paprika
Sea salt and ground black pepper, to taste

1. Put all the ingredients in a lightly greased air fryer basket.
2. Air fry for 15 minutes at 400ºF (205ºC), turning them over halfway through the cooking time.
3. Serve warm!

Pulled Pork Sliders with Fish Sauce

Prep time: 10 minutes | Cook time: 55 minutes | Serves 4

1 tbsp. olive oil
1 pound (454 g) pork shoulder
8 dinner rolls
2 cloves garlic, minced
2 tbsps. fish sauce
1 tbsp. brown sugar

1 tbsp. fresh sage, chopped
1 tbsp. fresh thyme, chopped
1 tsp. cayenne pepper
Kosher salt and freshly ground pepper, to taste

1. Place all the ingredients, except for the dinner rolls, in a lightly greased air fryer basket.
2. Air fry for 55 minutes at 360ºF (180ºC), turning it over halfway through the cooking time.
3. Serve warm on dinner rolls and enjoy!

Pork Loin Ribs with Zucchini

Prep time: 10 minutes | Cook time: 37 minutes | Serves 4

1 tbsp. olive oil
1½ pounds (680 g) pork loin ribs
½ pound (227 g) zucchini, sliced

4 tbsps. whiskey
2 cloves garlic, minced
1 tsp. onion powder
Sea salt and ground black pepper, to taste

1. Toss the pork ribs with the olive oil, garlic, whiskey and spices. Put the ingredients in a lightly greased air fryer basket.
2. Air fry for 25 minutes at 350ºF (180ºC), turning them over halfway through the cooking time.
3. Add the sliced zucchini on top of the pork ribs and continue cooking for an additional 12 minutes. Serve warm.
4. Bon appétit!

Country-Style Ribs with Sriracha

Prep time: 5 minutes | Cook time: 35 minutes | Serves 5

1 tbsp. honey
2 pounds (907 g) Country-style ribs
¼ cup Sriracha sauce

2 tbsps. bourbon
1 tsp. stone-ground mustard

1. Place all the ingredients in a lightly greased air fryer basket.
2. Air fry for 35 minutes at 350ºF (180ºC), turning them over halfway through the cooking time.
3. Serve warm!

Pork Chops and Bell Peppers

Prep time: 10 minutes | Cook time: 15 minutes | Serves 4

2 tbsps. olive oil
1½ pounds (680 g) center-cut rib chops
2 bell peppers, seeded and sliced
1 tsp. fresh rosemary, chopped

1 tsp. fresh basil, chopped
½ tsp. mustard powder
Kosher salt and freshly ground black pepper, to taste

1. Place all the ingredients in a lightly greased air fryer basket.
2. Air fry for about 15 minutes at 400ºF (205ºC), turning them over halfway through the cooking time.
3. Serve warm!

Cheesy Pork Taquitos

Prep time: 5 minutes | Cook time: 10 minutes | Serves 8

olive oil
30 ounces (850 g) of cooked and shredded pork tenderloin

10 whole wheat tortillas
2½ cups shredded Mozzarella cheese
1 juiced lime

1. Ensure your air fryer is preheated to 380ºF (195ºC).
2. Pour lime juice over pork and gently mix.
3. Heat up tortillas in the microwave with a dampened paper towel to soften.
4. Place about 3 ounces of pork and ¼ cup of shredded cheese to each tortilla. Tightly roll them up.
5. Spray the air fryer basket lightly with a bit of olive oil.
6. Air fry for about 7 to 10 minutes till the tortillas turn a slight golden color, making sure to flip halfway through the cooking process.

Pepper Pork Loin Chops with Onions

Prep time: 5 minutes | Cook time: 15 minutes | Serves 4

2 tbsps. olive oil
1½ pounds (680 g) pork loin chops, boneless
1 onion, cut into wedges
1 tsp. garlic powder
½ tsp. cayenne pepper
Sea salt and ground black pepper, to taste

1. Toss all the ingredients in a lightly greased air fryer basket.
2. Air fry for 15 minutes at 400ºF (205ºC), turning them over halfway through the cooking time.
3. Serve warm!

Chinese-Style Pork Loin Porterhouse

Prep time: 10 minutes | Cook time: 15 minutes | Serves 4

1½ tbsps. sesame oil
1½ pounds (680 g) pork loin porterhouse, cut into four slices
2 garlic cloves, crushed
2 tbsps. Shaoxing wine
1 tbsp. soy sauce
1 tbsp. hoisin sauce
½ tsp. Five-spice powder

1. Toss all the ingredients in a lightly greased air fryer basket.
2. Air fry for 15 minutes at 400ºF (205ºC), turning them over halfway through the cooking time.
3. Serve warm!

Worcestershire Center-Cut Pork Chops

Prep time: 5 minutes | Cook time: 16 minutes | Serves 2

Cooking spray
2 (10-ounce / 283-g) bone-in, center-cut pork chops, 1-inch thick
2 tsps. Worcestershire sauce
Salt and pepper, to taste

1. Rub the Worcestershire sauce into both sides of pork chops.
2. Season to taste with salt and pepper.
3. Spray air fryer basket lightly with cooking spray and put the chops in the basket side by side.
4. Air fry for 16 to 20 minutes at 360ºF (180ºC), or until well done. Allow to rest for 5 minutes before serving.

Pork Shoulder Chops with Rosemary

Prep time: 5 minutes | Cook time: 15 minutes | Serves 4

2 tbsps. olive oil
1½ pounds (680 g) pork shoulder chops
2 sprigs rosemary, leaves
picked and chopped
1 tsp. garlic, pressed
Kosher salt and ground black pepper, to taste

1. Add all the ingredients in a lightly greased air fryer basket.
2. Air fry for 15 minutes at 400ºF (205ºC), turning them over halfway through the cooking time.
3. Serve warm!

Tasty Tortilla Chips Coated Pork Cutlets

Prep time: 5 minutes | Cook time: 15 minutes | Serves 4

2 tbsps. olive oil
1½ pounds (680 g) pork cutlets
1 cup tortilla chips,
crushed
½ tsp. cayenne pepper
Salt and ground black pepper, to taste

1. Toss the pork cutlets with the remaining ingredients. Put them in a lightly oiled air fryer basket.
2. Air fry for 15 minutes at 400ºF (205ºC), turning them over halfway through the cooking time.
3. Serve warm!

Pork Loin Fillets and Mushroom with Blue Cheese

Prep time: 5 minutes | Cook time: 15 minutes | Serves 4

2 tbsps. olive oil
1½ pounds (680 g) pork loin fillets
1 pound (454 g) mushrooms, sliced
2 ounces (57 g) blue cheese
Sea salt and ground black pepper, to taste

1. Put the pork, olive oil, salt and black pepper in a lightly greased air fryer basket.
2. Air fry for 10 minutes at 400ºF (205ºC), turning them over halfway through the cooking time.
3. Add the mushrooms on top of the pork loin fillets. Continue to cook for about 5 minutes longer. Top the warm pork with blue cheese.
4. Serve warm!

Honey Bratwurst and Brussels Sprouts

Prep time: 10 minutes | Cook time: 15 minutes | Serves 4

1 pound (454 g) bratwurst
1 pound (454 g) Brussels sprouts
1 large onion, cut into

wedges
2 tbsps. honey
1 tbsp. mustard
1 tsp. garlic, minced

1. Place all the ingredients in a lightly greased air fryer basket.
2. Air fry for about 15 minutes at 380ºF (195ºC), tossing the basket halfway through the cooking time.
3. Serve warm!

Pork, Eggplant and Bell Pepper Skewers

Prep time: 10 minutes | Cook time: 15 minutes | Serves 4

1 tbsp. olive oil
1 pound (454 g) pork tenderloin, cubed
1 pound (454 g) eggplant, diced
1 pound (454 g) bell

peppers, diced
1 tbsp. parsley, chopped
1 tbsp. cilantro, chopped
Sea salt and ground black pepper, to taste

1. In a mixing bowl, toss all the ingredients until well coated on all sides.
2. Thread the ingredients onto skewers and put them in the air fryer basket.
3. Then air fry for about 15 minutes at 400ºF (205ºC), turning them over halfway through the cooking time.
4. Serve warm!

Pork Tenderloin with Apple

Prep time: 10 minutes | Cook time: 15 minutes | Serves 4

2 tsps. olive oil
1 tbsp. apple butter
1 (1-pound / 454-g) pork tenderloin, cut into 4 pieces
2 Granny Smith apples or

Jonagold apples, sliced
3 celery stalks, sliced
1 onion, sliced
⅓ cup apple juice
½ tsp. dried marjoram

1. Rub each piece of pork evenly with apple butter and olive oil.

2. Mix the pork, apples, celery, onion, marjoram and apple juice in a medium metal bowl.
3. Put the bowl into the air fryer and air fry for 14 to 19 minutes, or until the pork reaches at least 145ºF (63ºC) on a meat thermometer and the apples and vegetables are tender. Stir once during cooking. Serve hot.

Balsamic Pork Loin with Red Pepper

Prep time: 10 minutes | Cook time: 25 minutes | Serves 6 to 8

2 pounds (907 g) pork loin
Balsamic vinegar
1 tsp. parsley

½ tsp. red pepper flakes
½ tsp. garlic powder
1 tsp. salt
1 tsp. pepper

1. Sprinkle pork loin with seasonings and brush with vinegar.
2. Put the pork in your air fryer. Air fry for 25 minutes at 340ºF (170ºC).
3. Remove the pork from air fryer and allow to rest for 10 minutes before slicing.

Sliced Pork Tenderloin and Mixed Greens Salad

Prep time: 10 minutes | Cook time: 5 minutes | Serves 4

1 tsp. olive oil
2 pounds (907 g) pork tenderloin, cut into 1-inch slices
6 cups mixed salad greens
1 (8-ounce / 227-g) package button

mushrooms, sliced
1 red bell pepper, sliced
⅓ cup low-sodium low-fat vinaigrette dressing
1 tsp. dried marjoram
⅛ tsp. freshly ground black pepper

1. Mix the pork slices and olive oil in a medium bowl. Toss to coat well.
2. Sprinkle with the marjoram and pepper and rub these into the pork.
3. Air fry the pork in the air fryer, in batches, for 4 to 6 minutes, or until the pork reaches at least 145ºF (63ºC) on a meat thermometer.
4. Meanwhile, mix the salad greens, red bell pepper and mushrooms in a serving bowl. Toss gently.
5. When the pork is cooked, place the pork slices to the salad. Drizzle with the vinaigrette and toss gently. Serve warm.

Smoked Pork Sausage with Onions Rings

Prep time: 5 minutes | Cook time: 15 minutes | Serves 4

1 pound (454 g) pork sausage, smoked

4 ounces (113 g) onion rings

1. Put the sausage in a lightly greased Air fryer basket.
2. Air fry for about 7 minutes at 370ºF (188ºC), tossing the basket halfway through the cooking time.
3. Place the onion rings and continue to cook for 8 minutes more. Serve warm!

Country-Style Pork Belly with Tomato Sauce

Prep time: 10 minutes | Cook time: 17 minutes | Serves 6

1½ pounds (680 g) pork belly, cut into pieces
¼ cup tomato sauce
2 tbsps. dark brown sugar

1 tbsp. tamari sauce
1 tsp. garlic, minced
Sea salt and ground black pepper, to taste

1. Toss all the ingredients in your air fryer basket.
2. Air fry for about 17 minutes at 400ºF (205ºC), shaking the basket halfway through the cooking time.
3. Serve warm!

Paprika Baby Back Ribs

Prep time: 10 minutes | Cook time: 35 minutes | Serves 4

2 tbsps. olive oil
1½ pounds (680 g) baby back ribs
1 tsp. garlic powder
1 tsp. onion powder
1 tsp. smoked paprika

1 tsp. mustard powder
1 tsp. dried thyme
½ tsp. ground cumin
Coarse sea salt and freshly cracked black pepper, to season

1. Place all the ingredients in a lightly greased air fryer basket.
2. Air fry for 35 minutes at 350ºF (180ºC), turning them over halfway through the cooking time.
3. Serve warm!

Chapter 6 Beef

Beef Satay with Cilantro

Prep time: 15 minutes | Cook time: 8 minutes | Serves 4

2 tbsps. vegetable oil
1 pound (454 g) beef flank steak, thinly sliced into long strips
½ cup chopped fresh cilantro
¼ cup chopped roasted peanuts
1 tbsp. soy sauce

1 tbsp. fish sauce
1 tbsp. minced garlic
1 tbsp. minced fresh ginger
1 tbsp. sugar
1 tsp. ground coriander
1 tsp. sriracha or other hot sauce
Peanut sauce, for serving

1. Put the beef strips in a large bowl or resealable plastic bag. Add the vegetable oil, ginger, garlic, fish sauce, soy sauce, sugar, sriracha, coriander and ¼ cup cilantro to the bag. Seal and massage the bag to thoroughly coat and combine. Marinate at room temperature for about 30 minutes, or cover and refrigerate for up to 24 hours.
2. Remove the beef strips from the bag with tongs and lay them flat in the air-fryer basket, minimizing overlap as much as possible; discard the marinade. Air fry for about 8 minutes at 400ºF (205ºC), turning the beef strips halfway through the cooking time.
3. Take the meat to a serving platter. Garnish with the remaining ¼ cup cilantro and the peanuts. Serve warm with peanut sauce.

Authentic Carne Asada

Prep time: 15 minutes | Cook time: 16 minutes | Serves 4

2 tbsps. vegetable oil
1½ pounds (680 g) skirt steak, cut into 3 pieces
1 cup fresh cilantro leaves
1 jalapeño, diced
1 orange, peeled and seeded
Juice of 2 limes

2 tbsps. apple cider vinegar
2 tsps. ancho chile powder
2 tsps. sugar
1 tsp. cumin seeds
1 tsp. coriander seeds
1 tsp. kosher salt

1. Combine the lime juice, orange, cilantro, jalapeño, vegetable oil, vinegar, chile powder, sugar, salt, cumin and coriander in a blender. Blend until smooth.
2. Put the steak in a resealable plastic bag. Pour the

marinade over the steak and seal the bag. Allow to stand at room temperature for 30 minutes or cover and refrigerate for up to 24 hours.
3. Arrange the steak pieces in the air-fryer basket (depending on the size of your air fryer, you may have to do this in two batches). Remove and discard marinade. Air fry for 8 minutes at 400ºF (205ºC). Use a meat thermometer to ensure the steak has reached an internal temperature of 145ºF (63ºC). (It is critical to not overcook skirt steak to avoid toughening the meat.)
4. Take the steak to a cutting board and allow to rest for 10 minutes. Slice across the grain and serve warm.

Ritzy Beef Steak with Mushroom Gravy

Prep time: 20 minutes | Cook time: 33 minutes | Serves 2

FOR THE MUSHROOM GRAVY:
¾ cup sliced button mushrooms
¼ cup unsalted butter, melted
¼ cup thinly sliced onions
¼ cup beef broth
½ tsp. fine sea salt
FOR THE STEAKS:
½ pound (227 g) ground

beef (85% lean)
2 tbsps. tomato paste
1 tbsp. dry mustard
½ tsp. onion powder
¼ tsp. garlic powder
Chopped fresh thyme leaves, for garnish
½ tsp. fine sea salt
¼ tsp. ground black pepper

1. In a baking pan, toss the mushrooms and onions with butter to coat well, then season with salt.
2. Put the baking pan in the air fryer and air fry for 8 minutes at 390ºF (200ºC), or until the mushrooms are tender. Stir the mixture halfway through.
3. Add the broth in the baking pan and cook for 10 more minutes to make the gravy.
4. Meanwhile, in a large bowl, combine all the ingredients for the steaks, except for the thyme leaves. Stir to mix well. Shape the mixture into two oval steaks.
5. Place the steaks over the gravy and cook for 15 minutes or until the patties are browned. Gently flip the steaks halfway through.
6. Take the steaks onto a plate and pour the gravy over. Garnish with fresh thyme and serve hot.

Beef, Mushroom and Broccoli

Prep time: 10 minutes | Cook time: 15 minutes | Serves 4

12 ounces (340 g) sirloin strip steak, cut into 1-inch cubes
2½ cups broccoli florets
1 cup sliced cremini mushrooms
1 onion, chopped
½ cup low-sodium beef broth
2 tbsps. cornstarch
1 tbsp. grated fresh ginger
1 tsp. low-sodium soy sauce
Brown rice, cooked (optional)

1. Stir together the cornstarch, beef broth and soy sauce in a medium bowl.
2. Add the beef and toss to coat well. Let stand for about 5 minutes at room temperature.
3. Transfer the beef from the broth mixture into a medium metal bowl by using a slotted spoon. Reserve the broth.
4. Add the broccoli, mushrooms, onion and ginger to the beef. Put the bowl into the air fryer and air fry for 12 to 15 minutes, or until the beef reaches at least 145ºF (63ºC) on a meat thermometer and the vegetables are soft.
5. Pour the reserved broth and cook for 2 to 3 minutes more, or until the sauce boils.
6. Serve right away over hot cooked brown rice, if desired.

Beef, Orange and Pineapple Stir-Fry

Prep time: 10 minutes | Cook time: 8 minutes | Serves 4

1 tsp. olive oil
12 ounces (340 g) sirloin tip steak, thinly sliced
1 cup canned mandarin orange segments, drained, juice reserved
1 cup canned pineapple chunks, drained, juice reserved
2 scallions, white and green parts, sliced
1 tbsp. cornstarch
1 tbsp. freshly squeezed lime juice
1 tsp. low-sodium soy sauce
Brown rice, cooked (optional)

1. Mix the steak with the lime juice in a medium bowl. Set aside.
2. Thoroughly mix 3 tbsps. of reserved mandarin orange juice, 3 tbsps. of reserved pineapple juice, the soy sauce and cornstarch in a small bowl.
3. Drain the beef and take it to a medium metal bowl, reserving the juice. Stir the reserved juice into the mandarin-pineapple juice mixture. Keep aside.
4. Place the olive oil and scallions to the steak. Put the metal bowl in the air fryer and air fry for 3 to 4 minutes, or until the steak is almost cooked, shaking the basket once during cooking.
5. Toss in the mandarin oranges, pineapple and juice mixture. Cook for another 3 to 7 minutes, or until the sauce is bubbling and the beef is tender and reaches at least 145ºF (63ºC) on a meat thermometer.
6. Stir and serve right away over hot cooked brown rice, if desired.

Cheesy Lasagna

Prep time: 15 minutes | Cook time: 20 minutes | Serves 4

FOR THE MEAT LAYER:
Extra-virgin olive oil
1 pound (454 g) 85% lean ground beef
1 cup prepared marinara sauce
¼ cup diced red onion
¼ cup diced celery
½ tsp. minced garlic
Kosher salt and black pepper, to taste
FOR THE CHEESE LAYER:
2 large eggs
1 cup shredded Mozzarella cheese
8 ounces (227 g) Ricotta cheese
½ cup grated Parmesan cheese
1 tsp. dried Italian seasoning, crushed
½ tsp. each minced garlic, garlic powder and black pepper

MAKE THE MEAT LAYER:
1. Grease a 7½-inch barrel cake pan lightly with 1 tsp. olive oil.
2. Combine the ground beef, marinara, celery, onion, garlic, salt and pepper in a large bowl. Place the seasoned meat in the pan.
3. Put the pan in the air-fryer basket. Air fry for 10 minutes at 375ºF (190ºC).
MAKE THE CHEESE LAYER:
4. Meanwhile, combine the ricotta, half the Mozzarella, the Parmesan, lightly beaten eggs, Italian seasoning, minced garlic, garlic powder and pepper in a medium bowl. Stir until well blended.
5. At the end of the cooking time, evenly spread the cheese mixture over the meat mixture. Scatter with the remaining ½ cup Mozzarella. Air fry for 10 minutes at 375ºF (190ºC), or until the cheese is browned and bubbling.
6. At the end of the cooking time, ensure the meat has reached an internal temperature of 160ºF (71ºC) by using a meat thermometer.
7. Drain the fat and liquid from the pan. Allow to stand for 5 minutes before serving.

Glazed Beef Cheese Cups

Prep time: 10 minutes | Cook time: 25 minutes | Serves 4

FOR THE MEATLOAVES:
1 pound (454 g) ground beef
¼ cup seasoned breadcrumbs
¼ cup Parmesan cheese, grated
1 small onion, minced
2 garlic cloves, pressed
1 egg, beaten
Sea salt and ground black pepper, to taste

FOR THE GLAZE:
4 tbsps. tomato sauce
1 tbsp. Dijon mustard
1 tbsp. brown sugar

1. Thoroughly mix all the ingredients for the meatloaves until everything is well combined.
2. Scrape the beef mixture into lightly oiled silicone cups and take them to the air fryer basket.
3. Air fry for about 20 minutes at 380ºF (195ºC).
4. Meanwhile, mix the rest of ingredients for the glaze. Then, evenly spread the glaze on top of each muffin and continue to cook for 5 minutes more.
5. Bon appétit!

Cheddar Roasted Stuffed Bell Peppers

Prep time: 10 minutes | Cook time: 18 minutes | Serves 4

1 tsp. olive oil
8 ounces (227 g) lean ground beef
2 green bell peppers
4 ounces (113 g) shredded Cheddar cheese
½ cup tomato sauce
½ chopped onion
1 minced garlic clove
1 tsp. Worcestershire sauce
½ tsp. salt
½ tsp. pepper

1. Ensure your air fryer is preheated to 390ºF (200ºC). Spray with olive oil.
2. Cut stems off bell peppers and remove the seeds. Cook in boiling salted water for about 3 minutes.
3. In a skillet, sauté garlic and onion together until golden in color.
4. Take skillet off the heat. Mix salt, pepper, Worcestershire sauce, ¼ cup of tomato sauce, half of cheese and beef together.
5. Distribute meat mixture evenly into pepper halves. Top filled peppers with remaining cheese and tomato sauce.
6. Put the filled peppers in air fryer and air fry for 15 to 20 minutes. Serve warm.

Light Herbed Beef Meatballs

Prep time: 10 minutes | Cook time: 15 minutes | Makes 24 meatballs

1 tsp. olive oil
1 pound (454 g) 96 percent lean ground beef
1 slice low-sodium whole-wheat bread, crumbled
1 medium onion, minced
2 garlic cloves, minced
3 tbsps. 1 percent milk
1 tsp. dried marjoram
1 tsp. dried basil

1. Combine the onion, garlic and olive oil in a 6-by-2-inch pan. Air-fry for 2 to 4 minutes, or until the vegetables are crisp-tender.
2. Take the vegetables to a medium bowl, and add the bread crumbs, milk, basil and marjoram. Mix well.
3. Add the ground beef. With your hands, work the mixture carefully but thoroughly until combined. Shape the meat mixture into about 24 (1-inch) meatballs.
4. Air fry the meatballs, in batches, in the air fryer basket for about 12 to 17 minutes, or until they reach 160ºF (71ºC) on a meat thermometer. Serve hot.

Spicy Beef with Fajita Veggie

Prep time: 10 minutes | Cook time: 18 minutes | Serves 4 to 6

FOR THE BEEF:
olive oil
2 pounds (907 g) beef flap meat
⅛ cup carne asada seasoning
Diet 7-Up

FOR THE FAJITA VEGGIES:
2 bell peppers, your choice of color
1 onion
1 tsp. chili powder
1 to 2 tsps. salt
1 to 2 tsps. pepper
wheat tortillas for serving
favorite keto fillings for serving

1. Cut flap meat into manageable pieces and put into a bowl. Season meat with carne seasoning and add diet soda over the meat. Cover and chill overnight.
2. Ensure your air fryer is preheated to 380ºF (195ºC).
3. Put a parchment liner into air fryer basket and spray lightly with olive oil. Place beef in layers into the basket.
4. Cook for about 8 to 10 minutes, making sure to flip halfway through. Remove and set aside.
5. Slice up veggies and spray air fryer basket with olive oil. Add veggies and spices to the fryer and spray with olive oil. Air fry for 10 minutes at 400ºF (205ºC), shaking 1 to 2 times during the cooking process.
6. Serve meat and veggies on wheat tortillas and add favorite keto fillings on top!

Saucy Mongolian Beef

Prep time: 15 minutes | Cook time: 12 minutes | Serves 6 to 10

Olive oil
2 pounds (907 g) beef tenderloin or beef chuck, sliced into strips
½ cup almond flour
cauliflower rice for serving
FOR THE SAUCE:
2 tbsps. olive oil
½ cup chopped green onion

½ cup low-sodium soy sauce
½ cup brown sugar
½ cup rice vinegar
½ cup water
1 tbsp. chopped garlic
1 tbsp. finely chopped ginger
1 tsp. red chili flakes
1 tsp. almond flour
1 tsp. hoisin sauce

1. Toss the beef strips in almond flour, ensuring they are coated well.
2. Air fry for 10 minutes at 300ºF (150ºC).
3. At the same time, place all sauce ingredients to the pan and bring to a boil. Mix well.
4. Put beef strips to the sauce and cook for 2 minutes.
5. Serve hot over cauliflower rice!

Salsa Sirloin Tip Steak

Prep time: 10 minutes | Cook time: 12 minutes | Serves 4

¾ pound (340 g) sirloin tip steak, cut into 4 pieces and gently pounded to about ⅓ inch thick
2 tbsps. low-sodium salsa
1 tbsp. apple cider

vinegar
1 tbsp. minced chipotle pepper
1 tsp. ground cumin
⅛ tsp. red pepper flakes
⅛ tsp. freshly ground black pepper

1. Thoroughly mix the salsa, chipotle pepper, cider vinegar, cumin, black pepper and red pepper flakes in a small bowl. Rub this mixture into both sides of each steak piece. Allow to stand for 15 minutes at room temperature.
2. Air fry the steaks in the air fryer, two at a time, for about 6 to 9 minutes, or until they reach at least 145ºF (63ºC) on a meat thermometer.
3. Transfer the steaks to a clean plate and cover with aluminum foil to keep warm. Repeat with the remaining steaks.
4. Slice the steaks thinly against the grain and serve warm.

Beef Taco Wraps

Prep time: 10 minutes | Cook time: 2 minutes | Serves 6

olive oil
2 pounds (907 g) of lean ground beef
6 (12-inch) wheat tortillas
6 wheat tostadas
12 ounces (340 g) low-sodium nacho cheese

3 Roma tomatoes
2 cups shredded lettuce
2 cups sour cream
2 cups Mexican blend cheese
2 packets low-sodium taco seasoning

1. Ensure your air fryer is preheated to 400ºF (205ºC).
2. Make beef according to taco seasoning packets.
3. Add ⅔ cup prepared beef, 1 tostada, 4 tbsps. nacho cheese, ⅓ cup sour cream, ⅓ cup lettuce, ⅙ of tomatoes and ⅓ cup Mexican blend cheese on each tortilla.
4. Gently fold up tortillas edges and repeat with remaining ingredients.
5. Lay the folded sides of tortillas down into the air fryer and lightly spray with olive oil.
6. Air fry for about 2 minutes at 400ºF (205ºC).
7. Enjoy!

Spicy Beef and Brown Rice Stuffed Bell Peppers

Prep time: 10 minutes | Cook time: 15 minutes | Serves 4

2 tsps. olive oil
4 medium bell peppers, any colors, rinsed, tops removed
1 cup chopped cooked low-sodium roast beef
1 cup cooked brown rice

2 medium beefsteak tomatoes, chopped
½ cup grated carrot
1 medium onion, chopped
1 tsp. dried marjoram

1. Remove the stems from the bell pepper tops and dice the tops.
2. Combine the chopped bell pepper tops, onion, carrot and olive oil in a 6-by-2-inch pan. Cook for 2 to 4 minutes, or until the vegetables are crisp-tender.
3. Take the vegetables to a medium bowl. Add the tomatoes, roast beef, brown rice and marjoram. Stir to mix well.
4. Stuff the vegetable mixture into the bell peppers. Put the bell peppers in the air fryer basket. Air fry for 11 to 16 minutes, or until the peppers are soft and the filling is hot. Serve hot.

Peruvian Stir-Fried Beef and Tomato with Fries

Prep time: 10 minutes | Cook time: 32 minutes | Serves 4

1 tbsp. vegetable oil plus more for spraying
1 pound (454 g) beef sirloin
2 russet potatoes
2 tomatoes, cut into wedges
½ red onion, sliced
2 cloves garlic, minced

Juice of 1 lime
2 tbsps. soy sauce plus more for serving
2 tsps. aji amarillo (Peruvian yellow chile powder or paste)
Kosher salt and pepper, to taste

1. Peel the potatoes and cut them into ¼-inch slices. Cut each slice into 4 or 5 thick fries. (Halve any especially long pieces. You're looking for fries the size of your finger.) Put the cut potatoes into a bowl of cold water and allow them to soak for at least 30 minutes to get rid of excess starch.
2. While the potatoes are soaking, marinate the beef. Slice the beef sirloin into strips approximately ½ to 1 inch wide and 4 to 5 inches long. Whisk together the garlic, lime juice, soy sauce and aji amarillo in a medium bowl. Add the beef and toss to combine well. Marinate at room temperature for about 15 minutes.
3. While the beef is marinating, cook the onion and tomatoes. Preheat the air fryer to 375ºF (190ºC). Spray the air fryer basket lightly with oil. Place the vegetables in a single layer in the basket and spray with oil. Season with salt and pepper to taste. Air fry for 9 to 10 minutes until the vegetables begin to char and soften. Remove the vegetables to a large bowl.
4. Take the beef from the marinade and, working in batches as necessary, put the beef in a single layer in the air fryer basket. Air fry for about 3 to 4 minutes at 375ºF (190ºC) until the meat is browned on the outside but pink inside. Place the beef in the bowl with the vegetables.
5. Drain the potatoes and dry them well. Toss the potatoes with 1 tbsp. of oil and salt. Spread the potatoes in a single layer in the air fryer basket. (Depending on the size of your machine, you may have to work in 2 batches. Do not overcrowd the basket.) Air fry for 10 minutes. Open the air fryer and shake the basket to redistribute the potatoes. Cook for another 10 to 12 minutes until all the potatoes are browned and crisp. Repeat with the remaining potatoes if necessary.
6. Quickly reheat the meat and vegetables in a large skillet over medium heat. If desired, add the fries to the skillet and stir to combine well. (You can also serve the fries on the side if you prefer. Both ways are common in Peru.) Taste and adjust the seasoning, adding more soy sauce, salt and pepper if needed. Serve hot with rice.

Beef and Bell Pepper Risotto

Prep time: 10 minutes | Cook time: 20 minutes | Serves 4

2 tsps. olive oil
¾ cup short-grain rice
½ cup chopped cooked roast beef
½ cup chopped red bell pepper

1 onion, finely chopped
1¼ cups low-sodium beef broth
3 garlic cloves, minced
3 tbsps. grated Parmesan cheese

1. Combine the olive oil, onion, garlic, and red bell pepper in a 6-by-2-inch pan. Place the pan in the air fryer for 2 minutes, or until the vegetables are crisp-tender. Remove from the air fryer.
2. Add the rice, roast beef and beef broth. Take the pan back to the air fryer and air fry for 18 to 22 minutes, stirring once during cooking, until the rice is tender and the beef reaches at least 145ºF (63ºC) on a meat thermometer. Take the pan from the air fryer.
3. Toss in the Parmesan cheese and serve hot.

Sherry Beef Steak and Broccoli

Prep time: 10 minutes | Cook time: 12 minutes | Serves 4

1 tbsp. olive oil
2 tsps. sesame oil
1 pounds broccoli
¾ pound (340 g) round steak
⅓ cup sherry
⅓ cup oyster sauce

1 minced garlic clove
1 sliced ginger root
1 tsp. almond flour
1 tsp. sweetener of choice
1 tsp. low-sodium soy sauce

1. Remove stems from broccoli and cut into florets. Slice steak into thin strips.
2. Mix sweetener, sherry, almond flour, soy sauce, sesame oil and oyster sauce together, stirring till the sweetener dissolves.
3. Place steak strips into the mixture and allow to marinate for 45 minutes to 2 hours.
4. Put broccoli and marinated steak to air fryer. Add ginger, garlic and olive oil on top.
5. Air fry for 12 minutes at 400ºF (205ºC). Serve hot with cauliflower rice!

Classic Onion Beef Brisket

Prep time: 10 minutes | Cook time: 1¼ hours | Serves 4

2 tbsps. olive oil
1½ pounds (680 g) beef brisket
1 tsp. onion powder
1 tsp. garlic powder
1 tsp. dried parsley flakes
1 tsp. dried thyme
Sea salt and ground black pepper, to taste

1. Toss the beef with the remaining ingredients. Put the beef in the air fryer basket.
2. Air fry for 15 minutes at 390ºF (200ºC), turn the beef over and turn the temperature to 360ºF (180ºC).
3. Continue to cook the beef for another 55 minutes. Bon appétit!

Quick Ribeye Steak

Prep time: 5 minutes | Cook time: 13 minutes | Serves 4

1 tbsp. olive oil
2 pounds (907 g) of ribeye steak
salad for serving
Pepper and salt, to taste

1. Sprinkle meat on both sides with pepper and salt.
2. Rub all sides of meat with olive oil.
3. Preheat air fryer to 356ºF (180ºC) and spray lightly with olive oil.
4. Select the Steak function, adjust time to 7 minutes, then press Start/Pause. Flip and cook for an additional 6 minutes.
5. Let meat stand for 2 to 5 minutes to rest. Slice and serve warm with salad.

Herbed Roast Beef

Prep time: 10 minutes | Cook time: 20 minutes | Serves 10 to 12

2 tsps. olive oil
4 pounds (1.8 kg) top round roast beef
1 tsp. dried thyme
½ tsp. fresh rosemary
1 tsp. salt
¼ tsp. pepper

1. Ensure your air fryer is preheated to 360ºF (180ºC).
2. Rub olive oil all over beef.
3. Mix rosemary, thyme, salt and pepper together and proceed to rub all sides of beef with spice mixture.
4. Put the seasoned beef into air fryer. Select the Steak function, adjust time to 20 minutes, then press Start/Pause.
5. Let roast rest for 10 minutes before slicing to serve.

Garlic Skirt Steak

Prep time: 5 minutes | Cook time: 12 minutes | Serves 4

2 tbsps. olive oil
1½ pounds (680 g) skirt steak
2 garlic cloves, minced
1 tsp. cayenne pepper
¼ tsp. cumin powder
Kosher salt and freshly cracked black pepper, to taste

1. Toss the steak with the other ingredients, then put the steak in the air fryer basket.
2. Select the Steak function, adjust time to 12 minutes, then press Start/Pause, turning it over halfway through the cooking time.
3. Serve warm!

Garlic Ribeye Steak

Prep time: 5 minutes | Cook time: 15 minutes | Serves 4

2 tbsps. butter, room temperature
1 pound (454 g) ribeye steak, bone-in
2 garlic cloves, minced
2 rosemary sprigs, leaves picked, chopped
Sea salt and ground black pepper, to taste

1. Toss the ribeye steak with the butter, garlic, rosemary, salt and black pepper. Put the steak in the air fryer basket.
2. Select the Steak function, adjust time to 15 minutes, then press Start/Pause, turning it over halfway through the cooking time.
3. Bon appétit!

Simple Beef Empanadas

Prep time: 5 minutes | Cook time: 32 minutes | Serves 8

olive oil
8 Goya empanada discs (thawed)
1 cup picadillo
1 egg white
1 tsp. water

1. Ensure your air fryer is preheated to 320ºF (160ºC).
2. Spray the air fryer basket lightly with olive oil.
3. Put 2 tbsps. of picadillo into the center of each disc. Gently fold the disc in half and use a fork to seal the edges. Repeat with all the ingredients.
4. Whisk egg white with water, then brush the tops of empanadas with egg wash.
5. Place 2 to 3 empanadas to air fryer. Air fry for 8 minutes at 320ºF (160ºC). Repeat till you cook all the filled empanadas. Serve warm.

French Filet Mignon

Prep time: 5 minutes | Cook time: 14 minutes | Serves 4

3 tbsps. olive oil
1 pound (454 g) beef filet mignon
4 tbsps. dry French wine

1 tbsp. Dijon mustard
1 tsp. cayenne pepper
Sea salt and ground black pepper, to taste

1. Toss the filet mignon with the remaining ingredients, then put the filet mignon in the air fryer basket.
2. Select the Steak function, adjust time to 14 minutes, then press Start/Pause, turning it over halfway through the cooking time.
3. Enjoy!

Skirt Steak Sliders with Mustard

Prep time: 10 minutes | Cook time: 15 minutes | Serves 4

2 tbsps. olive oil
1½ pounds (680 g) skirt steak
8 Hawaiian buns
2 tbsps. Dijon mustard

1 tsp. steak dry rub
½ tsp. cayenne pepper
Sea salt and ground black pepper, to taste

1. Toss the beef with the spices and olive oil. Put the beef in the air fryer basket.
2. Select the Steak function, adjust time to 15 minutes, then press Start/Pause, turning it over halfway through the cooking time.
3. Cut the beef into slices and serve warm with mustard and Hawaiian buns. Bon appétit!

Old-Fashioned Shallot Meatloaf

Prep time: 10 minutes | Cook time: 25 minutes | Serves 4

2 tbsps. olive oil
1½ pounds (680 g) ground chuck
1 egg, beaten
½ cup shallots, minced
2 garlic cloves, minced
4 tbsps. crackers,

crushed
1 tbsp. fresh rosemary, chopped
1 tbsp. fresh thyme, chopped
Sea salt and ground black pepper, to taste

1. Thoroughly mix all the ingredients until everything is well combined.
2. Scrape the beef mixture into a lightly oiled baking pan and take it to the air fryer basket.
3. Air fry for 25 minutes at 390ºF (200ºC). Bon appétit!

Herbed New York Strip Steak

Prep time: 5 minutes | Cook time: 15 minutes | Serves 4

2 tbsps. butter, melted
1½ pounds (680 g) New York strip steak
1 tsp. dried thyme

1 tsp. dried rosemary
1 tsp. paprika
Sea salt and ground black pepper, to taste

1. Toss the beef with the remaining ingredients, then place the beef in the air fryer basket.
2. Select the Steak function, adjust time to 15 minutes, then press Start/Pause, turning it over halfway through the cooking time.
3. Serve warm!

Parsley Roast Beef

Prep time: 10 minutes | Cook time: 50 minutes | Serves 4

2 tbsps. olive oil
1½ pounds (680 g) bottom round roast
2 garlic cloves, minced
1 tsp. parsley

1 tsp. rosemary
1 tsp. oregano
Sea salt and freshly ground black pepper, to taste

1. Toss the beef with the garlic, spices and olive oil. Put the beef in the air fryer basket.
2. Select the Steak function, adjust time to 50 minutes, then press Start/Pause, turning it over halfway through the cooking time.
3. Cut the beef into slices and serve warm with dinner rolls. Bon appétit!

Authentic Mexican Carnitas

Prep time: 5 minutes | Cook time: 1¼ hours | Serves 4

2 tbsps. olive oil
1½ pounds (680 g) beef brisket
4 medium-sized flour

tortillas
1 tsp. chili powder
Sea salt and ground black pepper, to taste

1. Toss the beef brisket with the olive oil, chili powder, salt and black pepper; now, put the beef brisket in the air fryer basket.
2. Air fry for 15 minutes at 390ºF (200ºC), turn the beef over and reduce the temperature to 360ºF (180ºC).
3. Continue to cook the beef brisket for about 55 minutes or until cooked through.
4. Use two forks to shred the beef and serve warm with tortillas and toppings of choice. Bon appétit!

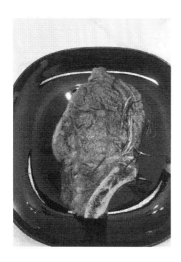

Traditional Montreal Ribeye Steak, page 85

Tenderloin Steaks with Mushrooms, page 89

Thai Curry Lime Beef Meatballs, page 86

French Filet Mignon, page 83

Traditional Montreal Ribeye Steak

Prep time: 5 minutes | Cook time: 15 minutes | Serves 4

2 tbsps. butter
1½ pounds (680 g) ribeye steak, bone-in
1 Montreal seasoning mix
Sea salt and ground black pepper, to taste

1. Toss the ribeye steak with the rest of ingredients, then put the ribeye steak in a lightly oiled air fryer basket.
2. Air fry for 15 minutes at 400ºF (205ºC), turning it over halfway through the cooking time.
3. Serve warm!

Italian Rump Roast with Onion

Prep time: 10 minutes | Cook time: 55 minutes | Serves 4

2 tbsps. olive oil
1½ pounds (680 g) rump roast
1 onion, sliced
¼ cup red wine
2 cloves garlic, peeled
1 tsp. Italian seasoning mix
Sea salt and ground black pepper, to taste

1. Toss the rump roast with the remaining ingredients, then put the rump roast in a lightly oiled air fryer basket.
2. Air fry for 55 minutes at 390ºF (200ºC), turning it over halfway through the cooking time.
3. Bon appétit!

Ketchup Pulled Beef

Prep time: 10 minutes | Cook time: 1¼ hours | Serves 4

2 tbsps. olive oil
1½ pounds (680 g) beef brisket
3 garlic cloves, pressed
2 tbsps. tomato ketchup
2 tbsps. Dijon mustard
1 tsp. red pepper flakes, crushed
Sea salt and ground black pepper, to taste

1. Toss the beef brisket with the olive oil, garlic, red pepper, salt and black pepper. Then put the beef brisket in the air fryer basket.
2. Air fry for 15 minutes at 390ºF (200ºC), turn the beef over and reduce the temperature to 360ºF (180ºC).
3. Continue to cook the beef brisket for about 55 minutes or until cooked through.
4. Use two forks to shred the beef, add the ketchup and mustard and stir to combine well. Bon appétit!

Mustard Filet Mignon

Prep time: 5 minutes | Cook time: 14 minutes | Serves 4

2 tbsps. butter, melted
1½ pounds (680 g) filet mignon
2 tbsps. soy sauce
1 tsp. mustard powder
1 tsp. garlic powder
Sea salt and ground black pepper, to taste

1. Toss the filet mignon with the rest of ingredients, then put the filet mignon in the air fryer basket.
2. Select the Steak function, adjust time to 14 minutes, then press Start/Pause, turning it over halfway through the cooking time.
3. Serve warm!

Classic BBQ Cheeseburgers

Prep time: 5 minutes | Cook time: 15 minutes | Serves 3

¾ pound (340 g) ground chuck
3 hamburger buns
3 slices cheese
2 tbsps. BBQ sauce
1 tsp. garlic, minced
Sea salt and ground black pepper, to taste

1. Mix the ground chuck, BBQ sauce, garlic, salt and black pepper until everything is well combined. Shape the mixture into three patties.
2. Air fry for about 15 minutes at 380ºF (195ºC), or until cooked through, making sure to turn them over halfway through the cooking time.
3. Place a slice of cheese on top of each burger. Serve your burgers on the hamburger buns and enjoy!

Parsley Top Round Roast

Prep time: 10 minutes | Cook time: 55 minutes | Serves 5

2 tbsps. extra-virgin olive oil
2 pounds (907 g) top round roast
2 cloves garlic, pressed
1 tbsp. fresh parsley, chopped
1 tbsp. fresh rosemary, chopped
1 tsp. red chili powder
Kosher salt and freshly ground black pepper, to taste

1. Toss the beef with the remaining ingredients, then put the beef in the air fryer basket.
2. Select the Steak function, adjust time to 55 minutes, then press Start/Pause, turning it over halfway through the cooking time.
3. Serve warm!

Quick Paprika Flank Steak

Prep time: 5 minutes | Cook time: 12 minutes | Serves 5

2 tbsps. olive oil	1 tsp. paprika
2 pounds (907 g) flank steak	Sea salt and ground black pepper, to taste

1. Toss the steak with the rest of ingredients and put the steak in the air fryer basket.
2. Select the Steak function, adjust time to 12 minutes, then press Start/Pause, turning over halfway through the cooking time.
3. Serve warm!

Classic Corned Beef Brisket

Prep time: 10 minutes | Cook time: 1¼ hours | Serves 4

2 tbsps. olive oil	1 tbsp. English mustard powder
1½ pounds (680 g) beef brisket	1 tsp. ground cumin
2 garlic cloves, pressed	1 tsp. chili pepper flakes
1 tbsp. smoked paprika	

1. Toss the beef with the rest ingredients; then put the beef in the air fryer basket.
2. Air fry for 15 minutes at 390ºF (200ºC), turn the beef over and reduce the temperature to 360ºF (180ºC).
3. Continue to cook the beef for another 55 minutes. Bon appétit!

Thai Curry Lime Beef Meatballs

Prep time: 5 minutes | Cook time: 15 minutes | Serves 4

Cooking spray	lemongrass
1 tbsp. sesame oil	1 tsp. red Thai curry paste
1 pound (454 g) ground beef	1 tsp. Thai seasoning blend
Juice and zest of ½ lime	
2 tsps. chopped	

1. Spray the air fryer basket with cooking spray.
2. Combine all the ingredients until well blended in a medium bowl.
3. Form the meat mixture into 24 meatballs and put them in the air fryer basket, working in 2 batches if necessary to avoid overcrowding. Select the Steak function, adjust time to 15 minutes, then press Start/Pause. Flip halfway through to ensure even cooking.
4. Take the meatballs to plates. Allow to cool for 5 minutes before serving.

Tasty Barbecue Beef Brisket

Prep time: 5 minutes | Cook time: 1¼ hours | Serves 4

¼ cup barbecue sauce	brisket
1½ pounds (680 g) beef	2 tbsps. soy sauce

1. Toss the beef with the rest of ingredients, then put the beef in the air fryer basket.
2. Air fry for 15 minutes at 390ºF (200ºC), turn the beef over and turn the temperature to 360ºF (180ºC).
3. Continue to cook the beef for another 55 minutes. Bon appétit!

Beef Sausage and Bell Peppers

Prep time: 10 minutes | Cook time: 15 minutes | Serves 4

2 tbsps. olive oil	1 tsp. thyme
1 pound (454 g) smoked beef sausage	1 tsp. sage
2 bell peppers, sliced	Sea salt and red pepper, to season
2 garlic cloves, pressed	

1. Place all the ingredients in a lightly oiled air fryer basket.
2. Select the Steak function, adjust time to 15 minutes, then press Start/Pause, tossing the basket halfway through the cooking time.
3. Serve hot and enjoy!

Parsley London Broil

Prep time: 10 minutes | Cook time: 28 minutes | Serves 4

3 tbsps. butter, cold	1 tbsp. Dijon mustard
1½ pounds (680 g) London broil	1 tsp. garlic, pressed
1 tbsp. fresh parsley, chopped	¼ tsp. ground bay leaf
	Kosher salt and ground black pepper, to taste

1. Toss the beef with salt and black pepper, then put the beef in a lightly oiled air fryer basket.
2. Select the Steak function, adjust time to 28 minutes, then press Start/Pause, turning over halfway through the cooking time.
3. At the same time, mix the butter with the remaining ingredients and put it in the refrigerator until well-chilled.
4. Serve hot beef with chilled garlic butter on the side. Bon appétit!

Parsley Coulotte Roast

Prep time: 5 minutes | Cook time: 55 minutes | Serves 5

2 tbsps. olive oil
2 pounds (907 g) Coulotte roast
2 garlic cloves, minced
1 tbsp. fresh parsley, finely chopped
1 tbsp. fresh cilantro, finely chopped
Kosher salt and ground black pepper, to taste

1. Toss the roast beef with the rest of ingredients, then put the roast beef in the air fryer basket.
2. Select the Steak function, adjust time to 55 minutes, then press Start/Pause, turning over halfway through the cooking time.
3. Serve warm!

Traditional Mexican-Style Meatloaf

Prep time: 10 minutes | Cook time: 25 minutes | Serves 4

2 tbsps. olive oil
1½ pounds (680 g) ground chuck
¼ cup tortilla chips, crushed
1 egg, whisked
½ onion, chopped
1 tsp. habanero pepper, minced
1 tsp. garlic, minced
Sea salt and ground black pepper, to taste

1. Thoroughly mix all the ingredients until everything is well combined.
2. Scrape the beef mixture into a lightly oiled baking pan and take it to the air fryer basket.
3. Air fry for 25 minutes at 390ºF (200ºC). Serve warm!

Tasty Beef Burgers

Prep time: 10 minutes | Cook time: 15 minutes | Serves 3

¾ pound (340 g) ground beef
3 hamburger buns
2 tbsps. onion, minced
1 tsp. garlic, minced
1 tsp. cayenne pepper
1 tsp. red chili powder
Sea salt and ground black pepper, to taste

1. Mix the beef, onion, garlic, cayenne pepper, red chili powder, salt and black pepper, until everything is well combined. Shape the mixture into three patties.
2. Select the Steak function, adjust time to 15 minutes, then press Start/Pause, turning them over halfway through the cooking time.
3. Serve your beef burgers on the prepared buns and enjoy!

Simple Beef Sliders

Prep time: 5 minutes | Cook time: 15 minutes | Serves 4

1 pound (454 g) ground beef
8 dinner rolls
1 tsp. paprika
½ tsp. garlic powder
½ tsp. onion powder
Sea salt and ground black pepper, to taste

1. Combine all the ingredients, except for the dinner rolls. Form the mixture into four patties.
2. Air fry for 15 minutes at 380ºF (195ºC), or until cooked through, making sure to turn them over halfway through the cooking time.
3. Serve your burgers on the prepared rolls and enjoy!

Brandy Paprika Rump Roast

Prep time: 5 minutes | Cook time: 50 minutes | Serves 4

2 tbsps. olive oil
1½ pounds (680 g) rump roast
¼ cup brandy
2 tbsps. cold butter
1 tsp. paprika
Ground black pepper and kosher salt, to taste

1. Toss the rump roast with the olive oil, black pepper, salt, paprika and brandy, then put the rump roast in a lightly oiled air fryer basket.
2. Select the Steak function, adjust time to 50 minutes, then press Start/Pause, turning it over halfway through the cooking time.
3. Serve rump roast with the cold butter and enjoy!

Lemon Marinated London Broil

Prep time: 10 minutes | Cook time: 28 minutes | Serves 4

2 tbsps. olive oil
1 pound (454 g) London broil
1 small lemon, freshly squeezed
3 cloves garlic, minced
1 tbsp. fresh parsley, chopped
1 tbsp. fresh coriander, chopped
Kosher salt and ground black pepper, to taste

1. Toss the beef with the remaining ingredients and allow it to marinate for an hour.
2. Put the beef in a lightly oiled air fryer basket and discard the marinade.
3. Select the Steak function, adjust time to 28 minutes, then press Start/Pause, turning it over halfway through the cooking time.
4. Serve warm!

Beef Patties with Mushroom

Prep time: 10 minutes | Cook time: 15 minutes | Serves 4

1 pound (454 g) ground chuck	1 small onion, chopped
4 brioche rolls	2 garlic cloves, minced
1 cup mushrooms, chopped	1 tsp. cayenne pepper
	Sea salt and ground black pepper, to taste

1. Mix the ground chuck, mushrooms, garlic, onion, cayenne pepper, salt and black pepper until everything is well combined. Shape the mixture into four patties.
2. Air fry for 15 minutes at 380ºF (195ºC), or until cooked through, making sure to turn them over halfway through the cooking time.
3. Serve your beef patties on the brioche rolls and enjoy!

Sicilian Beef and Tomato Stuffed Peppers

Prep time: 15 minutes | Cook time: 31 minutes | Serves 4

Vegetable oil for spraying	1 cup grated Mozzarella cheese
2 tbsps. extra-virgin olive oil	1 yellow onion, diced
¾ pound (340 g) ground beef	¼ cup pine nuts
2 medium tomatoes or 1 large tomato	¼ cup raisins
4 red bell peppers	3 cloves garlic, minced
1 cup cooked rice	3 tbsps. red wine vinegar
	2 tsps. kosher salt
	Pinch red pepper flakes

1. In a large, deep skillet over medium heat, heat the olive oil. When the oil is shimmering, add the onion and sauté until softened, for about 5 minutes. Place the garlic and sauté for an additional minute. Add the ground beef, salt and red pepper flakes and cook until the meat is no longer pink, about 6 minutes. If the meat has given off a lot of grease, gently remove it from the pan with a spoon.
2. Slice off the stem end of the tomatoes and grate them using the coarse side of a box grater. Discard the skin. Add the tomato pulp, raisins, pine nuts and vinegar to the meat mixture and sauté for a few additional minutes to thicken. Add the cooked rice and stir to combine well. Remove from the heat and set aside.
3. Cut off the top third of the peppers and remove the seeds and inner membranes. Distribute the meat

mixture evenly among the 4 peppers. Place the tops back on the peppers and put them carefully in the air fryer basket. Lightly spray or brush the outsides and tops of the peppers with oil. Air fry for 15 minutes at 375ºF (190ºC), cooking the peppers halfway through. Remove the tops and place ¼ cup grated Mozzarella to each pepper. Cook for 4 minutes until the cheese is melted and browned. Serve warm.

Beef Shoulder and Onion

Prep time: 10 minutes | Cook time: 55 minutes | Serves 4

2 tbsps. olive oil	1 tsp. cayenne pepper
1½ pounds (680 g) beef shoulder	1 tsp. Dijon mustard
1 onion, cut into slices	½ tsp. ground cumin
2 cloves garlic, minced	Sea salt and ground black pepper, to taste

1. Toss the beef with the spices, mustard, garlic and olive oil; then put the beef in a lightly oiled air fryer basket.
2. Select the Steak function, adjust time to 45 minutes, then press Start/Pause, turning it over halfway through the cooking time.
3. Place the onion slices and continue to cook for another 10 minutes.
4. Serve warm!

Garlicky Chuck Roast

Prep time: 10 minutes | Cook time: 55 minutes | Serves 5

2 pounds (907 g) chuck roast	minced
½ cup red wine	1 tsp. red pepper flakes, crushed
1 tbsp. corn flour	Sea salt and ground black pepper, to taste
1 tbsp. Dijon mustard	
1 tbsp. fresh garlic,	

1. Place the wine, red pepper, mustard, garlic, salt, black pepper and chuck roast in a ceramic bowl. Cover the bowl and allow the meat to marinate for 3 hours in your refrigerator.
2. Toss the roast beef with the corn flour and put the roast beef in the air fryer basket.
3. Select the Steak function, adjust time to 55 minutes, then press Start/Pause, turning them over halfway through the cooking time.
4. Serve warm!

T-Bone Steak and Tomato Salad

Prep time: 10 minutes | Cook time: 12 minutes | Serves 5

¼ cup extra-virgin olive oil
2 pounds (907 g) T-bone steak
1 tomato, diced
1 bell pepper, seeded and sliced
1 red onion, sliced
2 tbsps. lime juice
1 tsp. garlic powder
Sea salt and ground black pepper, to taste

1. Toss the steak with the garlic powder, salt and black pepper; then put the steak in the air fryer basket.
2. Air fry for 12 minutes at 400ºF (205ºC), turning it over halfway through the cooking time.
3. Cut the steak into slices and add the rest of ingredients. Serve at room temperature or well-chilled.
4. Bon appétit!

Sirloin Roast with Carrots and Herbs

Prep time: 10 minutes | Cook time: 55 minutes | Serves 5

2 tbsps. olive oil
2 pounds (907 g) top sirloin roast
2 carrots, sliced
1 tbsp. fresh coriander
1 tbsp. fresh thyme
1 tbsp. fresh rosemary
Sea salt and ground black pepper, to taste

1. Toss the beef with the olive oil, salt and ground black pepper, then put the beef in the air fryer basket.
2. Air fry for 45 minutes at 390ºF (200ºC), turning it over halfway through the cooking time.
3. Place the carrots and herbs on top of the beef. Continue to cook for an additional 10 minutes.
4. Serve warm!

Tenderloin Steaks with Mushrooms

Prep time: 10 minutes | Cook time: 15 minutes | Serves 4

2 tbsps. butter, melted
1½ pounds (680 g) tenderloin steaks
½ pound (227 g) cremini mushrooms, sliced
1 tsp. garlic powder
1 tsp. cayenne pepper
½ tsp. mustard powder
Sea salt and ground black pepper, to taste

1. Toss the beef with 1 tbsp. of the butter and spices, then put the beef in the air fryer basket.
2. Select the Steak function, adjust time to 10 minutes, then press Start/Pause, turning it over halfway through the cooking time.
3. Place the mushrooms along with the remaining 1 tbsp. of the butter. Continue to cook for another 5 minutes. Serve hot.
4. Bon appétit!

Spicy Beef Burgers

Prep time: 10 minutes | Cook time: 10 minutes | Serves 4

1 pound (454 g) lean ground beef
1 tsp. dried parsley
1 tsp. Worcestershire sauce
½ tsp. dried oregano
½ tsp. onion powder
½ tsp. garlic powder
Few drops of liquid smoke
½ tsp. salt
½ tsp. pepper

1. Ensure your air fryer is preheated to 350ºF (180ºC).
2. Mix all the seasonings together until combined well.
3. In a bowl, place beef and seasonings. Mix well, but do not overmix.
4. Make 4 patties from the mixture and make an indent in the center of each patty by using your thumb.
5. Place patties to air fryer basket and air fry for about 10 minutes. No need to turn!

Chuck Eye Roast with Jalapeno Pepper

Prep time: 5 minutes | Cook time: 55 minutes | Serves 4

2 tbsps. olive oil, melted
1½ pounds (680 g) chuck eye roast
1 jalapeno pepper, chopped
1 large-sized tomato, sliced
1 tsp. red pepper flakes, crushed
Sea salt and ground black pepper, to taste

1. Toss the roast beef with red pepper flakes, salt, black pepper and olive oil; put the roast beef in a lightly oiled air fryer basket.
2. Select the Steak function, adjust time to 45 minutes, then press Start/Pause, turning it over halfway through the cooking time.
3. Place the tomato and jalapeno pepper on top of roast beef. Continue to cook for 10 minutes more. Enjoy!

Herbed Filet Mignon

Prep time: 10 minutes | Cook time: 14 minutes | Serves 4

2 tbsps. olive oil
1½ pounds (680 g) filet mignon
2 cloves garlic, minced
1 tsp. dried rosemary
1 tsp. dried thyme
1 tsp. dried basil
Sea salt and ground black pepper, to taste

1. Toss the beef with the rest of ingredients, then put the beef in the air fryer basket.
2. Select the Steak function, adjust time to 14 minutes, then press Start/Pause, turning it over halfway through the cooking time.
3. Serve warm!

Juicy Tomahawk Steaks with Bell Pepper

Prep time: 10 minutes | Cook time: 14 minutes | Serves 4

2 tbsps. butter, melted
1½ pounds (680 g) Tomahawk steaks
2 bell peppers, sliced
2 tbsps. fish sauce
2 tsps. Montreal steak seasoning
Sea salt and ground black pepper, to taste

1. Place all the ingredients in the air fryer basket.
2. Air fry for 14 minutes at 400ºF (205ºC), turning it over halfway through the cooking time.
3. Serve warm!

Chinese-Style Spiced Beef Tenderloin

Prep time: 10 minutes | Cook time: 20 minutes | Serves 4

2 tbsps. sesame oil
1½ pounds (680 g) beef tenderloin, sliced
2 garlic cloves, minced
2 tbsps. soy sauce
1 tsp. Five-spice powder
1 tsp. fresh ginger, peeled and grated

1. Toss the beef tenderloin with the rest ingredients, then put the beef tenderloin in the air fryer basket.
2. Select the Steak function, adjust time to 20 minutes, then press Start/Pause, turning it over halfway through the cooking time.
3. Serve warm!

Garlic Pulled Beef

Prep time: 10 minutes | Cook time: 1¼ hours | Serves 4

2 tbsps. olive oil
1½ pounds (680 g) beef brisket
1 tsp. dried oregano
2 cloves garlic, minced
2 tbsps. chives, chopped
2 tbsps. cilantro, chopped
1 tsp. mustard powder
½ tsp. ground cumin
Sea salt and freshly ground black pepper, to season

1. Toss the beef brisket with the remaining ingredients; now, put the beef brisket in the air fryer basket.
2. Air fry for 15 minutes at 390ºF (200ºC), turn the beef over and reduce the temperature to 360ºF (180ºC).
3. Continue to cook the beef brisket for about 55 minutes or until cooked through.
4. Use two forks to shred the beef and serve warm with toppings of choice. Bon appétit!

Ribeye Steak with Blue Cheese

Prep time: 10 minutes | Cook time: 15 minutes | Serves 4

2 tbsps. olive oil
1 pound (454 g) ribeye steak, bone-in
1 cup blue cheese, crumbled
1 tsp. garlic powder
½ tsp. onion powder
Sea salt and ground black pepper, to taste

1. Toss the ribeye steak with the olive oil, salt, black pepper, onion powder, and garlic powder; then put the ribeye steak in the air fryer basket.
2. Select the Steak function, adjust time to 15 minutes, then press Start/Pause, turning it over halfway through the cooking time.
3. Place the cheese on top of ribeye steak and serve warm. Bon appétit!

Chapter 7 Fish and Seafood

Fish Fillet with Crumb Coating

Prep time: 10 minutes | Cook time: 6 minutes | Serves 4

1 pound (454 g) fish fillets
1 tbsp. coarse brown mustard
1 tsp. Worcestershire sauce
½ tsp. hot sauce
Salt, to taste

FOR THE CRUMB COATING:
Oil for misting or cooking spray
¾ cup panko breadcrumbs
¼ cup stone-ground cornmeal
¼ tsp. salt

1. Slice fish fillets crosswise into slices 1-inch wide.
2. Mix the hot sauce, Worcestershire sauce and mustard together to make a paste and rub on all sides of the fish. Season with salt to taste.
3. Mix all the crumb coating ingredients together and spread on a sheet of wax paper.
4. Roll the fish fillets in the crumb mixture.
5. Spray all sides with olive oil or cooking spray and put in air fryer basket in a single layer.
6. Air fry for about 6 to 9 minutes at 390ºF (200ºC), until the fish flakes easily. Serve warm.

Pesto White Fish and Spinach Pie

Prep time: 10 minutes | Cook time: 15 minutes | Serves 4

Vegetable oil spray
1 pound (454 g) firm white fish, cut into 2-inch chunks
1 (10-ounce / 283-g) package frozen chopped spinach, thawed and squeezed dry
½ sheet frozen puff pastry, thawed

½ cup cherry tomatoes, quartered
¼ cup half-and-half
¼ cup grated Parmesan cheese
2 tbsps. prepared pesto
All-purpose flour
1 tsp. kosher salt
1 tsp. black pepper

1. Combine the pesto, half-and-half, Parmesan, salt and pepper in a small bowl. Stir until well combined and keep aside.
2. Spray a 7 × 3-inch round heatproof pan lightly with vegetable oil spray. Spread the spinach evenly across the bottom of the pan. Top with the fish and tomatoes. Add the pesto mixture evenly over everything.
3. On a lightly floured surface, gently roll the puff pastry sheet into a circle. Put the pastry on top of the pan and tuck it in around the edges of the pan. (Or, do what I do and stretch it with your hands and then pat it into place.)
4. Place the pan in the air fryer basket. Air fry for about 15 minutes at 400ºF (205ºC), or until the pastry is well browned. Allow to stand for 5 minutes before serving.

Coconut Shrimp and Tomato Po' Boys

Prep time: 10 minutes | Cook time: 12 minutes | Serves 4

Oil for misting or cooking spray
1 pound (454 g) shrimp, peeled and deveined
1 large tomato, thinly sliced
2 large hoagie rolls
1½ cups shredded lettuce
¾ cup shredded coconut

½ cup panko breadcrumbs
2 eggs
½ cup cornstarch
2 tbsps. milk
Old Bay seasoning, to taste
Honey mustard or light mayonnaise

1. Add cornstarch in a shallow dish or plate.
2. Beat together eggs and milk in another shallow dish.
3. Mix the coconut and panko crumbs in a third dish.
4. Sprinkle the shrimp with Old Bay seasoning.
5. Dip shrimp in cornstarch to coat lightly, dip in egg mixture, shake off excess, and roll in coconut mixture to coat well.
6. Spray both sides of coated shrimp lightly with oil or cooking spray.
7. Air fry for 5 minutes at 390ºF (200ºC).
8. Repeat to cook the remaining shrimp.
9. Split each hoagie lengthwise, leaving one long edge intact.
10. Put in air fryer basket and cook at 390ºF (200ºC), and set time to 1 to 2 minutes or until heated through.
11. Take the buns, break apart, and put on 4 plates, cut side up.
12. Evenly spread with honey mustard or mayonnaise.
13. Add shredded lettuce, tomato slices and coconut shrimp on top. Serve warm.

Spicy Bang Bang Shrimp

Prep time: 10 minutes | Cook time: 14 minutes | Serves 4

FOR THE SAUCE:
¼ cup sweet chili sauce
½ cup mayonnaise
2 to 4 tbsps. sriracha
1 tsp. minced fresh ginger
FOR THE SHRIMP:

Vegetable oil spray
1 pound (454 g) jumbo raw shrimp, peeled and deveined
2 tbsps. cornstarch or rice flour
½ tsp. kosher salt

MAKE THE SAUCE:
1. Combine the mayonnaise, chili sauce, sriracha and ginger in a large bowl. Stir until well combined. Remove half of the sauce to serve as a dipping sauce.

MAKE THE SHRIMP:
2. Put the shrimp in a medium bowl. Scatter the cornstarch and salt over the shrimp and toss until well coated.
3. Arrange the shrimp in the air fryer basket in a single layer. (If they won't fit in a single layer, set a rack or trivet on top of the bottom layer of shrimp and place the rest of the shrimp on the rack.) Spray generously with vegetable oil spray. Air fry for 10 minutes at 350ºF (180ºC), turning and spraying with additional oil spray halfway through the cooking time.
4. Remove the shrimp and toss in the bowl with half of the sauce. Put the shrimp back in the air fryerbasket. Air fry for another 4 to 5 minutes at 350ºF (180ºC), or until the sauce has formed a glaze.
5. Serve the shrimp with the reserved sauce for dipping.

Fried Shrimp with Peanut Mix

Prep time: 10 minutes | Cook time: 10 minutes | Serves 4

FOR THE PEANUT MIX:
2 tsps. vegetable oil
1 cup roasted and salted red-skinned Spanish peanuts
3 dried red arbol chiles, broken into pieces
8 cloves garlic, smashed

and peeled
1 tbsp. cumin seeds
FOR THE SHRIMP:
2 tbsps. vegetable oil
1 pound (454 g) jumbo raw shrimp, peeled and deveined
Lime wedges, for serving

MAKE THE PEANUT MIX:
1. In a 6 × 3-inch round heatproof pan, combine all the ingredients and toss well. Put the pan in the air fryer basket. Air fry for 5 minutes at 400ºF (205ºC), or until all the spices are toasted. Remove the pan from the air fryer and allow the mixture to cool.

2. When completely cool, take the mixture to a mortar and pestle or clean coffee or spice grinder, then crush or pulse to a very coarse texture that won't fall through the grate of the air fryer basket.

MAKE THE SHRIMP:
3. Combine the shrimp and oil in a large bowl. Toss until well combined. Add the peanut mix and toss again. Put the shrimp and peanut mix in the air fryer basket. Air fry for 5 minutes at 350ºF (180ºC).
4. Take to a serving dish. Cover and let the shrimp finish cooking in the residual heat, about 5 minutes. Serve warm with lime wedges.

Authentic Cajun Fried Shrimp with Remoulade

Prep time: 20 minutes | Cook time: 8 minutes | Serves 4

FOR THE REMOULADE:
½ cup mayonnaise
1 clove garlic, minced
1 green onion, finely chopped
2 tbsps. Creole mustard
1 tbsp. sweet pickle relish
2 tsps. fresh lemon juice
½ tsp. Worcestershire sauce
½ tsp. hot pepper sauce
¼ tsp. smoked paprika

¼ tsp. kosher salt
FOR THE SHRIMP:
Vegetable oil spray
1 pound (454 g) jumbo raw shrimp, peeled and deveined
2 cups finely ground cornmeal
1½ cups buttermilk
1 large egg
3 tsps. salt-free Cajun seasoning, divided
Kosher salt and black pepper

MAKE THE REMOULADE:
1. Stir together all the ingredients until well combined in a small bowl. Cover the sauce and chill until serving time.

MAKE THE SHRIMP:
2. Whisk together the buttermilk, egg, and 1 tsp. of the Cajun seasoning in a large bowl. Add the shrimp and toss to combine well. Refrigerate for at least 15 minutes, or up to 1 hour.
3. Meanwhile, whisk together the remaining 2 tsps. Cajun seasoning, cornmeal, and salt and pepper to taste in a shallow dish.
4. Spray the air fryer basket lightly with vegetable oil spray. Dredge the shrimp in the cornmeal mixture until well coated. Shake off any excess and put the shrimp in the air fryer basket. Spray with oil spray.
5. Air fry for 8 minutes at 350ºF (180ºC), carefully turning and spraying the shrimp with the oil spray halfway through the cooking time.
6. Serve the hot shrimp with the remoulade.

Honey Mustard Breaded Salmon Fillet

Prep time: 10 minutes | Cook time: 10 minutes | Serves 4

2 tbsps. olive oil
4 (6-ounce / 170-g) skinless salmon fillets
⅓ cup crushed potato chips

¼ cup panko bread crumbs
3 tbsps. honey mustard
½ tsp. dried thyme
½ tsp. dried basil

1. Place the salmon on a plate. Combine the mustard, thyme and basil in a small bowl, and spread evenly over the salmon.
2. Combine the bread crumbs and potato chips in another small bowl, and mix well. Drizzle in the olive oil and mix until combined.
3. Put the salmon in the air fryer basket and gently but tightly press the bread crumb mixture onto the top of each fillet.
4. Air fry for about 9 to 12 minutes or until the salmon reaches at least 145ºF (63ºC) on a meat thermometer and the topping is browned and crisp.

Marinaded Shrimp and Grits

Prep time: 15 minutes | Cook time: 20 minutes | Serves 4

1 pound (454 g) raw shelled shrimp, deveined
FOR THE MARINADE:
1 tbsp. olive oil
2 tbsps. Worcestershire sauce
2 tbsps. lemon juice
1 tsp. Old Bay seasoning
½ tsp. hot sauce
FOR THE GRITS:
¾ cup quick cooking grits (not instant)

3 cups water
½ tsp. salt
½ cup chopped green bell pepper
½ cup chopped celery
½ cup chopped onion
2 ounces (57 g) sharp Cheddar cheese, grated
1 tbsp. butter
½ tsp. oregano
¼ tsp. Old Bay seasoning

1. Stir together all the marinade ingredients. Add marinade over shrimp and keep aside.
2. For grits, heat water and salt to boil in saucepan on stovetop. Stir in grits, reduce heat to medium-low, and cook for about 5 minutes or until thick and done.
3. Put butter, bell pepper, celery, and onion in air fryer basket. Air fry for 2 minutes at 390ºF (200ºC) and stir. Cook for 6 or 7 minutes longer, until crisp and soft.
4. Place oregano and 1 tsp. Old Bay to cooked vegetables. Stir in grits and cheese and air fry for

1 minute at 390ºF (200ºC). Stir and cook for 1 to 2 minutes longer to melt the cheese.
5. Remove baking pan from air fryer. Cover with plate to keep warm while shrimp cooks.
6. Drain marinade from shrimp. Arrange shrimp in air fryer basket. Select the Shrimp function, adjust time to 3 minutes, then press Start/Pause. Stir or shake the basket. Air-fry for 2 to 4 more minutes, until done.
7. Scoop grits onto plates and top with shrimp. Serve warm.

Lush Stuffed Tail-on Shrimp

Prep time: 15 minutes | Cook time: 24 minutes | Serves 4

Oil for misting or cooking spray
16 tail-on shrimp, peeled and deveined (last tail section intact)
¾ cup crushed panko breadcrumbs
FOR THE STUFFING:
1 egg, beaten
2 (6-ounce / 170-g) cans lump crabmeat
½ cup crushed saltine crackers
2 tbsps. chopped shallots

2 tbsps. chopped green onions
2 tbsps. chopped celery
2 tbsps. chopped green bell pepper
2 tsps. dried parsley flakes
2 tsps. fresh lemon juice
2 tsps. Worcestershire sauce
1 tsp. Old Bay seasoning
1 tsp. garlic powder
¼ tsp. ground thyme

1. Rinse shrimp. Remove the tail section (shell) from 4 shrimp, discard, and chop the meat finely.
2. To prepare the remaining 12 shrimp, cut a deep slit down the back side so that the meat lies open flat. Do not cut all the way through.
3. Preheat air fryer to 360ºF (180ºC).
4. Put the chopped shrimp in a large bowl with all the stuffing ingredients and stir to combine well.
5. Distribute stuffing into 12 portions, about 2 tbsps. each.
6. Add one stuffing portion onto the back of each shrimp and form into a ball or oblong shape. Press tightly so that stuffing sticks together and adheres to shrimp.
7. Carefully roll each stuffed shrimp in panko crumbs and mist with oil or cooking spray.
8. Put 6 shrimp in air fryer basket and air fry for 10 minutes at 360ºF (180ºC). Mist with oil or spray and cook for 2 minutes longer or until stuffing cooks through inside and is crispy outside.
9. Repeat step 8 to cook the remaining shrimp. Serve warm.

Louisiana Shrimp Po Boy with Remoulade

Prep time: 15 minutes | Cook time: 10 minutes | Serves 4

olive oil	**SAUCE:**
1 pound (454 g) deveined shrimp	½ cup vegan mayo
	1 chopped green onion
½ cup Louisiana Fish Fry	Juice of ½ a lemon
¼ cup buttermilk	1 tsp. hot sauce
8 slices of tomato	1 tsp. Dijon mustard
Lettuce leaves	1 tsp. Worcestershire
1 tsp. creole seasoning	sauce
FOR THE REMOULADE	½ tsp. creole seasoning

1. Mix all the sauce ingredients until well incorporated. Chill while you cook shrimp.
2. Liberally season the shrimp with the seasoning.
3. Place buttermilk to a bowl. Dip each shrimp into milk and put in a Ziploc bag. Chill half an hour to marinate.
4. Add fish fry to a bowl. Transfer shrimp from marinating bag and dip into fish fry, then add to air fryer.
5. Ensure your air fryer is preheated to 400ºF (205ºC).
6. Spray shrimp lightly with olive oil. Air fry for 5 minutes at 400ºF (205ºC), flip and then cook another 5 minutes.
7. Assemble "Keto" Po Boy by pouring sauce to lettuce leaves, along with shrimp and tomato.

Crispy Marinaded Shrimp

Prep time: 10 minutes | Cook time: 16 minutes | Serves 4

1 pound (454 g) shrimp, peeled, deveined, and butterflied (last tail section of shell intact)	1 tbsp. baking powder
	FOR THE COATING:
	Oil for misting or cooking spray
FOR THE MARINADE:	1 cup crushed panko breadcrumbs
2 eggs, beaten	½ tsp. Old Bay seasoning
1 (5-ounce / 142-g) can evaporated milk	½ tsp. paprika
2 tbsps. white vinegar	¼ tsp. garlic powder

1. Toss together all the marinade ingredients until well mixed. Place shrimp and stir to coat well. Refrigerate for 1 hour.
2. When ready to cook, preheat the air fryer to 390ºF (200ºC).
3. In a shallow dish, combine the coating ingredients.
4. Remove shrimp from marinade, roll in crumb mixture, and lightly spray with olive oil or cooking spray.
5. Cooking in two batches, put shrimp in air fryer basket in single layer, close but not overlapping. Air fry for about 6 to 8 minutes at 390ºF (200ºC), until light golden brown and crispy.
6. Repeat step 5 to cook the remaining shrimp. Serve warm.

One-Pot Shrimp and Egg Fried Rice

Prep time: 15 minutes | Cook time: 25 minutes | Serves 4

FOR THE SHRIMP:	carrots, thawed
1 pound (454 g) jumbo raw shrimp, peeled and deveined	¼ cup chopped green onions (white and green parts)
1 tsp. cornstarch	1 tbsp. soy sauce
½ tsp. kosher salt	½ tsp. kosher salt
¼ tsp. black pepper	1 tsp. black pepper
FOR THE RICE:	**FOR THE EGGS:**
3 tbsps. toasted sesame oil	2 large eggs, beaten
	¼ tsp. kosher salt
2 cups cold cooked rice	¼ tsp. black pepper
1 cup frozen peas and	

MAKE THE SHRIMP:
1. Whisk together the cornstarch, salt, and pepper until well combined in a small bowl. In a large bowl, add the shrimp and sprinkle the seasoned cornstarch over. Toss until well coated and keep aside.

MAKE THE RICE:
2. Combine the rice, peas and carrots, green onions, sesame oil, soy sauce, salt and pepper in a 6 × 3-inch round heatproof pan. Toss and stir until well combined.
3. Put the pan in the air fryer basket. Air fry for 15 minutes at 350ºF (180ºC), stirring and tossing the rice halfway through the cooking time.
4. Put the shrimp on top of the rice. Air fry for 5 minutes at 350ºF (180ºC).

MAKE THE EGGS:
5. Beat the eggs with salt and pepper in a medium bowl.
6. Open the air fryer and pour the eggs over the shrimp and rice mixture. Air fry for 5 minutes at 350ºF (180ºC).
7. Take the pan from the air fryer. Stir to break up the rice and mix in the eggs and shrimp. Serve warm.

Lime Mackerel Fillets

Prep time: 5 minutes | Cook time: 14 minutes | Serves 4

1 tbsp. olive oil, or more to taste
1½ pounds (680 g) mackerel fillets
2 garlic cloves, minced
2 tbsps. fresh lime juice
2 tbsps. parsley
Sea salt and ground black pepper, taste

1. Toss the fish fillets with the rest of ingredients and arrange them in a lightly oiled air fryer basket.
2. Select the Seafood function, adjust time to 14 minutes, then press Start/Pause, turning them over halfway through the cooking time.
3. Serve warm!

Buttery Garlic Sea Scallops

Prep time: 5 minutes | Cook time: 7 minutes | Serves 4

2 tbsps. butter, room temperature
1 pound (454 g) sea scallops
2 garlic cloves, crushed
¼ cup dry white wine
2 tbsps. lemon juice
Salt and fresh ground black pepper to taste

1. Place all the ingredients in a lightly greased air fryer basket.
2. Select the Seafood function, adjust time to 7 minutes, then press Start/Pause, tossing the basket halfway through the cooking time.
3. Serve warm!

Chili Pollock

Prep time: 10 minutes | Cook time: 14 minutes | Serves 4

2 tbsps. olive oil
1 pound (454 g) pollock, chopped
4 ciabatta buns
4 tbsps. all-purpose flour
1 tsp. smoked paprika
1 tsp. chili sauce
Sea salt and ground black pepper, to taste

1. In a bowl, mix all the ingredients, except for the ciabatta buns. Form the mixture into four patties and arrange them in a lightly oiled air fryer basket.
2. Air fry for about 14 minutes at 400ºF (205ºC), turning them over halfway through the cooking time.
3. Serve warm on ciabatta buns and enjoy!

Mediterranean Cheesy Squid

Prep time: 10 minutes | Cook time: 5 minutes | Serves 4

2 tbsps. butter, melted
1½ pounds (680 g) small squid tubes
¼ cup dry white wine
1 chili pepper, chopped
2 garlic cloves, minced
2 tbsps. fresh lemon juice
2 tbsps. Parmigiano-Reggiano cheese, grated
1 tsp. Mediterranean herb mix
1 tsp. red pepper flakes
Sea salt and ground black pepper, to taste

1. Mix all the ingredients, except for the Parmigiano-Reggiano cheese, in a lightly greased air fryer basket.
2. Air fry for 5 minutes at 400ºF (205ºC), tossing the basket halfway through the cooking time.
3. Place the cheese on top of warm squid. Bon appétit!

Lemon Cilantro Swordfish Steak

Prep time: 10 minutes | Cook time: 10 minutes | Serves 4

4 tbsps. olive oil
1 pound (454 g) swordfish steaks
4 garlic cloves, peeled
2 tbsps. fresh lemon juice, more for later
1 tbsp. fresh cilantro, roughly chopped
1 tsp. Spanish paprika
Sea salt and ground black pepper, to taste

1. Toss the swordfish steaks with the rest of ingredients and put them in a lightly oiled air fryer basket.
2. Select the Seafood function, adjust time to 10 minutes, then press Start/Pause, turning them over halfway through the cooking time.
3. Serve warm!

Basil Mahi-Mahi Fillets

Prep time: 10 minutes | Cook time: 14 minutes | Serves 4

2 tbsps. butter, at room temperature
1 pound (454 g) mahi-mahi fillets
2 tbsps. fresh lemon juice
1 tsp. dried basil
1 tsp. dried oregano
1 tsp. garlic, minced
1 tsp. smoked paprika
Kosher salt and freshly ground black pepper, to taste

1. Toss the fish fillets with the remaining ingredients and place them in a lightly oiled air fryer basket.
2. Select the Seafood function, adjust time to 14 minutes, then press Start/Pause, turning them over halfway through the cooking time.
3. Serve warm!

Buttery Halibut Steaks

Prep time: 5 minutes | Cook time: 12 minutes | Serves 4

1 pound (454 g) halibut steaks
¼ cup butter
Sea salt, to taste
2 tbsps. fresh chives, chopped
1 tsp. garlic, minced
1 tsp. mixed peppercorns, ground

1. Toss the halibut steaks with the rest of the ingredients and put them in a lightly oiled air fryer basket.
2. Select the Seafood function, adjust time to 12 minutes, then press Start/Pause, turning them over halfway through the cooking time.
3. Serve warm!

Chili Squid with Capers

Prep time: 10 minutes | Cook time: 5 minutes | Serves 5

2 tbsps. olive oil
1½ pounds (680 g) squid, cut into pieces
1 chili pepper, chopped
1 small lemon, squeezed
2 garlic cloves, minced
2 tbsps. parsley, chopped
1 tbsp. capers, drained
1 tbsp. coriander, chopped
1 tsp. sweet paprika
Sea salt and ground black pepper, to taste

1. Place all the ingredients in a lightly greased air fryer basket.
2. Air fry for 5 minutes at 400ºF (205ºC), tossing the basket halfway through the cooking time.
3. Serve warm!

Garlic Calamari with Sherry Wine

Prep time: 10 minutes | Cook time: 5 minutes | Serves 4

2 tbsps. butter, melted
1 pound (454 g) calamari, sliced into rings
4 garlic cloves, smashed
2 tbsps. sherry wine
2 tbsps. fresh lemon juice
1 tsp. paprika
1 tsp. dried oregano
Coarse sea salt and ground black pepper, to taste

1. Place all the ingredients in a lightly greased air fryer basket.
2. Select the Seafood function, adjust time to 5 minutes, then press Start/Pause, tossing the basket halfway through the cooking time.
3. Serve warm!

Lemon Shrimp and Broccoli Floret

Prep time: 10 minutes | Cook time: 6 minutes | Serves 4

1 tbsp. olive oil
1 pound (454 g) raw shrimp, peeled and deveined
½ pound (227 g) broccoli florets
1 garlic clove, minced
2 tbsps. freshly squeezed lemon juice
1 tsp. paprika
Coarse sea salt and ground black pepper, to taste

1. Place all the ingredients in a lightly greased air fryer basket.
2. Air fry for 6 minutes at 400ºF (205ºC), tossing the basket halfway through the cooking time.
3. Serve warm!

Exotic Hot Paprika Fried Prawns

Prep time: 10 minutes | Cook time: 9 minutes | Serves 4

2 tbsps. coconut oil
1½ pounds (680 g) prawns, peeled and deveined
½ cup whole-wheat flour
2 tbsps. lemon juice
2 garlic cloves, minced
2 tbsps. fresh chives, chopped
1 tsp. hot paprika
½ tsp. sweet paprika
Salt and freshly ground black pepper, to taste

1. Place all the ingredients in a lightly greased air fryer basket.
2. Air fry for 9 minutes at 400ºF (205ºC), tossing the basket halfway through the cooking time.
3. Serve warm!

Mustard Coated Calamari

Prep time: 5 minutes | Cook time: 5 minutes | Serves 4

2 tbsps. olive oil
1 pound (454 g) calamari, sliced into rings
2 cups flour
1 tbsp. mustard
1 tsp. garlic, minced
Sea salt and ground black pepper, to taste

1. Thoroughly combine the flour, salt, black pepper, garlic, mustard and olive oil in a mixing bowl. Mix to combine well.
2. Now, dip your calamari into the flour mixture to coat well.
3. Air fry for 5 minutes at 400ºF (205ºC), turning them over halfway through the cooking time.
4. Serve warm!

Parsley Calamari

Prep time: 5 minutes | Cook time: 5 minutes | Serves 4

2 tbsps. butter
1 pound (454 g) calamari, sliced into rings
2 garlic cloves, minced
2 tbsps. parsley, chopped

1 tsp. cayenne pepper
Sea salt and freshly ground black pepper, to taste

1. Place all the ingredients in a lightly greased air fryer basket.
2. Air fry for 5 minutes at 400ºF (205ºC), tossing the basket halfway through the cooking time.
3. Enjoy!

Quick Fried Calamari Rings

Prep time: 10 minutes | Cook time: 5 minutes | Serves 4

2 tbsps. olive oil
1 pound (454 g) calamari, sliced into rings
1 cup all-purpose flour
½ cup tortilla chips, crushed

1 tbsp. dried parsley
1 tsp. mustard powder
1 tsp. cayenne pepper
Sea salt and freshly ground black pepper, to taste

1. Thoroughly combine the flour, tortilla chips, spices and olive oil in a mixing bowl. Mix to combine well.
2. Now, dip your calamari into the flour mixture to coat well.
3. Air fry for 5 minutes at 400ºF (205ºC), turning them over halfway through the cooking time.
4. Serve warm!

Classic Mediterranean Calamari

Prep time: 10 minutes | Cook time: 5 minutes | Serves 4

2 tbsps. olive oil
1 pound (454 g) calamari, sliced into rings
2 garlic cloves, minced
2 tbsps. fresh lemon juice
2 tbsps. dry white wine
1 tsp. basil, chopped

1 tsp. dill, chopped
1 tsp. parsley, chopped
1 tsp. red pepper flakes
Coarse sea salt and freshly cracked black pepper, to taste

1. Place all the ingredients in a lightly greased air fryer basket.
2. Select the Seafood function, adjust time to 5 minutes, then press Start/Pause, tossing the basket halfway through the cooking time.
3. Enjoy!

Pepper Air-Fried Shrimp

Prep time: 5 minutes | Cook time: 6 minutes | Serves 4

1 tbsp. olive oil
1½ pounds (680 g) raw shrimp, peeled and deveined

1 tsp. cayenne pepper
1 tsp. garlic, minced
½ tsp. lemon pepper
Sea salt, to taste

1. Place all the ingredients in a lightly greased air fryer basket.
2. Select the Shrimp function, adjust time to 6 minutes, then press Start/Pause, tossing the basket halfway through the cooking time.
3. Serve warm!

Herb Salmon Fillets

Prep time: 10 minutes | Cook time: 12 minutes | Serves 4

2 tbsps. olive oil
1½ pounds (680 g) salmon fillets
1 small lemon, juiced
2 sprigs fresh rosemary
2 cloves garlic, chopped
1 tbsp. fresh basil

1 tbsp. fresh thyme
1 tbsp. fresh dill
1 tsp. stone-ground mustard
Sea salt and ground black pepper, to taste

1. Toss the salmon with the remaining ingredients, then arrange them in a lightly oiled air fryer basket.
2. Air fry for about 12 minutes at 380ºF (195ºC), turning them over halfway through the cooking time.
3. Serve hot and enjoy!

Cheesy Tilapia Fish Fillets Burgers

Prep time: 10 minutes | Cook time: 14 minutes | Serves 4

1 tbsp. olive oil
1 pound (454 g) tilapia fish fillets, chopped
8 dinner rolls
8 slices Provolone

cheese
½ cup breadcrumbs
2 garlic cloves, minced
4 tbsps. shallots, chopped

1. In a bowl, mix all the ingredients, except for the dinner rolls and cheese. Form the mixture into four patties and arrange them in a lightly oiled air fryer basket.
2. Air fry for about 14 minutes at 400ºF (205ºC), turning them over halfway through the cooking time.
3. Serve warm with the cheese and dinner rolls. Enjoy!

Lemon Cilantro Swordfish Steak, page 96

Buttery Halibut Steaks, page 97

Quick Fried Calamari Rings, page 98

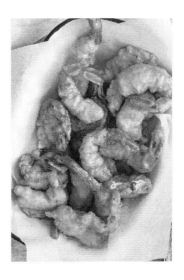

Exotic Hot Paprika Fried Prawns, page 97

Garlic Orange Roughy Fillets

Prep time: 5 minutes | Cook time: 10 minutes | Serves 4

2 tbsps. butter
1 pound (454 g) orange roughy fillets

2 cloves garlic, minced
Sea salt and red pepper flakes, to taste

1. Toss the fish fillets with the rest of ingredients and arrange them in a lightly oiled air fryer basket.
2. Select the Seafood function, adjust time to 10 minutes, then press Start/Pause, turning them over halfway through the cooking time.
3. Serve warm!

Chili Calamari with Red Chili

Prep time: 10 minutes | Cook time: 5 minutes | Serves 4

½ cup milk
1 cup all-purpose flour
2 tbsps. olive oil
1 tsp. turmeric powder
Sea salt and ground

black pepper, to taste
1 tsp. paprika
1 red chili, minced
1 pound (454 g) calamari, cut into rings

1. Thoroughly combine the milk, flour, olive oil, turmeric powder, salt, black pepper, paprika and red chili in a mixing bowl. Mix to combine well.
2. Now, dip your calamari into the flour mixture to coat well.
3. Air fry for 5 minutes at 400ºF (205ºC), turning them over halfway through the cooking time.
4. Serve warm!

Mayonnaise King Prawn Salad

Prep time: 10 minutes | Cook time: 6 minutes | Serves 4

1½ pounds (680 g) king prawns, peeled and deveined
1 cup mayonnaise
1 tbsp. fresh lemon juice
1 shallot, chopped
1 tbsp. fresh parsley,

roughly chopped
1 tsp. Dijon mustard
1 tsp. fresh dill, minced
Coarse sea salt and ground black pepper, to taste

1. Season the prawns with salt and black pepper in a lightly greased air fryer basket.
2. Air fry for 6 minutes at 400ºF (205ºC), tossing the basket halfway through the cooking time.
3. Place the prawns to a salad bowl, add the rest of ingredients and stir to combine well.
4. Serve warm!

Sea Scallops with Rosemary

Prep time: 5 minutes | Cook time: 7 minutes | Serves 4

4 tbsps. butter, melted
1½ pounds (680 g) sea scallops
2 rosemary sprigs, leaves picked and chopped

4 tbsps. dry white wine
1 tbsp. garlic, minced
Sea salt and ground black pepper, to season

1. Place all the ingredients in a lightly greased air fryer basket.
2. Air fry for 7 minutes at 400ºF (205ºC), tossing the basket halfway through the cooking time.
3. Serve warm!

Buttermilk Coconut Shrimp

Prep time: 10 minutes | Cook time: 9 minutes | Serves 4

2 tbsps. olive oil
1½ pounds (680 g) shrimp, peeled and deveined
1 cup coconut, shredded
½ cup whole wheat flour

¼ cup buttermilk
2 garlic cloves, crushed
1 tbsp. fresh lemon juice
Sea salt and red pepper flakes, to taste

1. In a mixing bowl, mix the flour, coconut, buttermilk, olive oil, garlic, lemon juice, salt and red pepper.
2. Dip the shrimp in the batter and arrange them in a well-greased air fryer basket.
3. Air fry for 9 minutes at 400ºF (205ºC), tossing the basket halfway through the cooking time.
4. Serve warm!

Sea Scallop and Tomato Salad

Prep time: 10 minutes | Cook time: 7 minutes | Serves 4

2 tbsps. olive oil
1½ pounds (680 g) sea scallops
1 small tomato, diced
1 cup mixed baby greens
2 garlic cloves, minced

1 tbsp. balsamic vinegar
2 tsps. fresh tarragon, minced
1 tsp. Dijon mustard
Sea salt and ground black pepper, to taste

1. Toss the scallops, salt and black pepper in a lightly greased air fryer basket.
2. Air fry for 7 minutes at 400ºF (205ºC), tossing the basket halfway through the cooking time.
3. Mix the scallops with the remaining ingredients and serve at room temperature or well-chilled.
4. Bon appétit!

Simple Tilapia Fillet and Chips

Prep time: 5 minutes | Cook time: 15 minutes | Serves 3

2 (4- to 6-ounce / 113- to 170-g) tilapia fillets	breadcrumbs
1 egg	Frozen crinkle cut fries
½ cup panko	Old Bay seasoning
	2 tbsps. almond flour

1. Add almond flour to one bowl, beat egg in another bowl and place panko breadcrumbs to the third bowl, mixed with Old Bay seasoning.
2. Dredge tilapia in flour, then in egg, and then in breadcrumbs.
3. Put the coated fish in air fryer along with fries.
4. Air fry for 15 minutes at 390ºF (200ºC). Serve warm.

Jumbo Shrimp with Chives

Prep time: 5 minutes | Cook time: 8 minutes | Serves 4

2 tbsps. butter, at room temperature	2 tbsps. fresh cilantro, chopped
1 pound (454 g) jumbo shrimp	2 garlic cloves, crushed
2 tbsps. fresh chives, chopped	Coarse sea salt and lemon pepper, to taste

1. Add all the ingredients in a lightly greased air fryer basket.
2. Select the Shrimp function, adjust time to 8 minutes, then press Start/Pause, tossing the basket halfway through the cooking time.
3. Serve warm!

Pink Salmon Patties

Prep time: 10 minutes | Cook time: 7 minutes | Serves 4

1 can wild Alaskan pink salmon	1 cup almond flour
1 egg	¼ tsp. salt
	⅛ tsp. pepper

1. Drain can of salmon into a bowl and keep liquid. Discard skin and bones.
2. Add ½ egg, salt, and pepper to salmon, mixing well with hands to incorporate, then make patties.
3. Dredge in flour and the remaining egg. If it seems dry, scoop reserved salmon liquid from the can onto patties.
4. Place patties to air fryer. Air fry for 7 minutes at 378ºF (192ºC), making sure to flip once during the cooking process. Serve warm.

Breaded Sea Scallops

Prep time: 5 minutes | Cook time: 16 minutes | Serves 4

Oil for misting or cooking spray	2 eggs
1½ pounds (680 g) sea scallops	½ cup plain breadcrumbs
	½ cup flour
	Salt and pepper, to taste

1. Rinse scallops and remove the tough side muscle. Sprinkle with salt and pepper to taste.
2. In a shallow dish, beat eggs together. Place flour in a second shallow dish and breadcrumbs in a third.
3. Preheat air fryer to 390ºF (200ºC).
4. Dip scallops in flour, then eggs, and then roll in breadcrumbs. Mist with oil or cooking spray.
5. Put scallops in air fryer basket in a single layer, leaving some space between. You may cook about a dozen at a time.
6. Air fry for 6 to 8 minutes at 390ºF (200ºC), watching carefully so as not to overcook. Scallops are cooked when they turn opaque all the way through. They will feel slightly firm when pressed with the tines of a fork.
7. Repeat step 6 to cook the remaining scallops. Serve warm.

Tandoori Shrimp with Cilantro

Prep time: 10 minutes | Cook time: 6 minutes | Serves 4

2 tbsps. olive oil (for Paleo) or melted ghee	1 tbsp. minced fresh ginger
1 pound (454 g) jumbo raw shrimp, peeled and deveined	2 tsps. fresh lemon juice
3 cloves garlic, minced	1 tsp. ground turmeric
¼ cup chopped fresh cilantro or parsley, plus more for garnish	1 tsp. garam masala
	1 tsp. smoked paprika
	1 tsp. kosher salt
	½ to 1 tsp. cayenne pepper

1. Combine the shrimp, ginger, garlic, cilantro, turmeric, garam masala, paprika, salt and cayenne in a large bowl. Toss to coat well. Add the oil or ghee and toss again. Marinate at room temperature for about 15 minutes, or cover and refrigerate for up to 8 hours.
2. Put the shrimp in a single layer in the air fryer basket. Air fry for 6 minutes at 325ºF (160ºC). Take the shrimp to a serving platter. Cover and allow the shrimp to finish cooking in the residual heat, for about 5 minutes.
3. Spritz the shrimp with the lemon juice and toss to coat well. Sprinkle with additional cilantro and serve warm.

Panko Breaded Shrimp

Prep time: 5 minutes | Cook time: 10 minutes | Serves 3

12 raw large shrimp
1 cup panko breadcrumbs
1 cup almond flour

1 cup unsweetened, dried coconut
1 egg white
1 tbsp. coconut flour

1. Place shrimp on paper towels to drain.
2. Mix the coconut and panko breadcrumbs together. Then in a different bowl, mix in coconut flour and almond flour. Set aside.
3. Dip shrimp into flour mixture, then into egg white, and then into coconut mixture.
4. Put into air fryer basket. Repeat with the remaining shrimp.
5. Air fry for 10 minutes at 350ºF (180ºC). Turn halfway through the cooking process. Serve warm.

Herbed Tilapia Fillet Nuggets

Prep time: 10 minutes | Cook time: 10 minutes | Serves 4

2 tbsps. olive oil
1½ pounds (680 g) tilapia fillets, cut into 1½-inch pieces
1½ cups all-purpose flour
1 tbsp. dried oregano

1 tbsp. dried thyme
1 tbsp. Dijon mustard
½ tsp. baking powder
Sea salt and ground black pepper, to taste

1. Use kitchen towels to pat the fish dry.
2. Thoroughly combine all remaining ingredients until well mixed in a mixing bowl. Now, dip the fish pieces into the batter to coat well.
3. Air fry for 10 minutes at 400ºF (205ºC), shaking the basket halfway through the cooking time.
4. Serve warm!

Breaded Cod Fish Fingers

Prep time: 10 minutes | Cook time: 10 minutes | Serves 4

1½ tbsps. olive oil
1 pound (454 g) cod fish fillets, sliced into pieces
¼ cup plain breadcrumbs
2 eggs

½ cup all-purpose flour
½ tsp. onion powder
¼ tsp. garlic powder
Sea salt and ground black pepper, to taste

1. Thoroughly combine the eggs, flour and spices in a mixing bowl. In a separate bowl, thoroughly combine

the breadcrumbs and olive oil.
2. Mix to combine well.
3. Now, dip the fish pieces into the flour mixture to coat well; roll the fish pieces over the breadcrumb mixture until they are well coated on all sides.
4. Air fry for 10 minutes at 400ºF (205ºC), turning them over halfway through the cooking time.
5. Serve warm!

Codfish Fillet Tacos with Avocado-Mayonnaise

Prep time: 10 minutes | Cook time: 14 minutes | Serves 4

1 tbsp. olive oil
1 pound (454 g) codfish fillets
8 small corn tortillas
1 habanero pepper, chopped

1 avocado, pitted, peeled and mashed
4 tbsps. mayonnaise
1 shallot, chopped
1 tsp. mustard

1. Toss the fish fillets with the olive oil, then put them in a lightly oiled air fryer basket.
2. Select the Seafood function, adjust time to 14 minutes, then press Start/Pause, turning them over halfway through the cooking time.
3. Assemble your tacos with the chopped fish and the rest of ingredients and serve hot. Bon appétit!

Cheesy English Muffin Tuna

Prep time: 10 minutes | Cook time: 14 minutes | Serves 4

1 tbsp. olive oil
1 pound (454 g) tuna, boneless and chopped
4 English muffins
4 Mozzarella cheese slices
2 eggs, whisked

½ cup all-purpose flour
½ cup breadcrumbs
2 tbsps. buttermilk
½ tsp. cayenne pepper
Kosher salt and ground black pepper, to taste

1. In a bowl, mix all the ingredients, except for the cheese and English muffins. Form the mixture into four patties and put them in a lightly oiled air fryer basket.
2. Select the Seafood function, adjust time to 14 minutes, then press Start/Pause, turning them over halfway through the cooking time.
3. Add the cheese slices on the warm patties and serve on hamburger buns and enjoy!

Italian-Style Sea Bass with White Wine

Prep time: 5 minutes | Cook time: 10 minutes | Serves 4

2 tbsps. olive oil
1 pound (454 g) sea bass
¼ cup dry white wine
2 garlic cloves, minced

1 tbsp. Italian seasoning mix
Sea salt and ground black pepper, to taste

1. Toss the fish with the rest of ingredients; then put them in a lightly oiled air fryer basket.
2. Select the Seafood function, adjust time to 10 minutes, then press Start/Pause, turning them over halfway through the cooking time.
3. Serve warm!

Garlic Halibut Burgers

Prep time: 10 minutes | Cook time: 14 minutes | Serves 4

1 tbsp. olive oil
1 pound (454 g) halibut, chopped
4 hamburger buns
2 garlic cloves, crushed
4 tbsps. scallions,

chopped
1 tsp. smoked paprika
A pinch of grated nutmeg
Sea salt and ground black pepper, to taste

1. In a bowl, mix all the ingredients, except for the hamburger buns. Form the mixture into four patties and arrange them in a lightly oiled air fryer basket.
2. Select the Seafood function, adjust time to 14 minutes, then press Start/Pause, turning them over halfway through the cooking time.
3. Serve warm on hamburger buns and enjoy!

Swordfish Steaks with Red Wine

Prep time: 10 minutes | Cook time: 10 minutes | Serves 4

2 tbsps. olive oil
1 pound (454 g) swordfish steaks
¼ cup dry red wine
2 sprigs rosemary

1 sprig thyme
1 tbsp. grated lemon rind
2 tsps. tamari sauce
Salt and freshly ground pepper, to taste

1. In a ceramic dish, toss the swordfish steaks with the rest of ingredients; cover and allow it to marinate in your refrigerator for about 2 hours.
2. Then, discard the marinade and arrange the fish in a

lightly oiled air fryer basket.
3. Select the Seafood function, adjust time to 10 minutes, then press Start/Pause, turning them over halfway through the cooking time.
4. Serve warm!

Old-Fashioned Fish and Olive Salad

Prep time: 10 minutes | Cook time: 12 minutes | Serves 4

2 tbsps. olive oil
1 pound (454 g) salmon fillets
½ cup Kalamata olives, pitted and sliced
1 bell pepper, sliced
½ lemon, juiced

2 garlic cloves, minced
1 shallot, chopped
1 tsp. Aleppo pepper, minced
Sea salt and ground black pepper, to taste

1. Toss the salmon fillets with the olive oil, salt and black pepper, then arrange them in a lightly oiled air fryer basket.
2. Air fry for about 12 minutes at 380ºF (195ºC), turning them over halfway through the cooking time.
3. Use two forks to chop the salmon fillets and place them to a salad bowl, add the remaining ingredients and toss to combine well.
4. Serve warm!

Light Asian Tuna Steak

Prep time: 10 minutes | Cook time: 9 minutes | Serves 4

2 tsps. sesame oil
4 small tuna steaks
1 stalk lemongrass, bent in half
3 tbsps. lemon juice
2 tbsps. low-sodium soy

sauce
1 tbsp. water
2 tsps. rice wine vinegar
1 tsp. grated fresh ginger
⅛ tsp. pepper

1. Place the tuna steaks on a plate.
2. Combine the soy sauce, sesame oil, rice wine vinegar and ginger in a small bowl, and mix well. Add this mixture over the tuna and marinate for about 10 minutes. Rub the soy sauce mixture gently into both sides of the tuna. Sprinkle with pepper to taste.
3. Put the lemongrass on the air fryer basket and top with the steaks. Pour the lemon juice and 1 tbsp. water in the pan below the basket.
4. Air fry for 8 to 10 minutes or until the tuna registers at least 145ºF (63ºC). Discard the lemongrass and serve the tuna right away.

Old Bay Tiger Prawns with Sherry Wine

Prep time: 10 minutes | Cook time: 9 minutes | Serves 4

1 tbsp. coconut oil
1½ pounds (680 g) tiger prawns, peeled and deveined
¼ cup sherry wine
1 tsp. garlic, crushed

1 tsp. Old Bay seasoning
1 tsp. Dijon mustard
Coarse sea salt and ground black pepper, to taste

1. Mix all the ingredients in a lightly greased air fryer basket.
2. Air fry for 9 minutes at 400ºF (205ºC), tossing the basket halfway through the cooking time.
3. Serve warm!

Easy Old Bay Calamari

Prep time: 10 minutes | Cook time: 15 minutes | Serves 6 to 8

5-6 tbsps. olive oil
1½ pounds (680 g) baby squid
½ cup semolina flour
½ cup almond flour

⅓ cup plain cornmeal
½ tsp. Old Bay seasoning
1-2 pinches of salt and pepper

1. Rinse squid in cold water and slice tentacles, keeping just ¼-inch of the hood in one piece.
2. Mix 1-2 pinches of pepper, salt, cornmeal, Old Bay seasoning and both flours together. Dredge squid pieces into flour mixture and put into air fryer. Spray liberally with olive oil.
3. Air fry for 15 minutes at 345ºF (174ºC), till coating turns a golden brown. Serve warm.

Buttery Lobster Tail

Prep time: 5 minutes | Cook time: 8 minutes | Serves 4

4 tbsps. butter, room temperature
1 pound (454 g) lobster tails
2 garlic cloves, minced

4 tbsps. spring onions
1 tbsp. fresh lime juice
Coarse sea salt and freshly cracked black pepper, to taste

1. Butterfly the lobster tails by cutting through the shell and arrange them in a lightly oiled air fryer basket.
2. Thoroughly combine the remaining ingredients in a mixing bowl.

3. Now, evenly spread ½ of the butter mixture over the top of the lobster meat. Air fry for 4 minutes at 380ºF (195ºC).
4. After that, spread another ½ of the butter mixture on top and continue to cook for another 4 minutes.
5. Serve warm!

Tuna and Spinach Salad with a Twist

Prep time: 10 minutes | Cook time: 10 minutes | Serves 4

1 pound (454 g) fresh tuna steak
2 cups baby spinach
1 carrot, julienned
1 small onion, thinly sliced

2 tbsps. parsley, roughly chopped
2 tbsps. fresh lemon juice
Sea salt and ground black pepper, to taste

1. Toss the fish with salt and black pepper, then put your tuna in a lightly oiled air fryer basket.
2. Air fry for about 10 minutes at 400ºF (205ºC), turning it over halfway through the cooking time.
3. Use two forks to chop your tuna and place the remaining ingredients. Stir to combine well and serve well-chilled.
4. Serve warm!

Coated Tilapia Fillet

Prep time: 10 minutes | Cook time: 10 minutes | Serves 4

1 pound (454 g) tilapia fillets, cut into strips
1 large egg
½ cup all-purpose flour
½ cup crackers, crushed

2 tbsps. buttermilk
1 tsp. garlic powder
½ tsp. cayenne pepper
Sea salt and ground black pepper, to taste

1. In a shallow bowl, add the flour. In a second bowl, whisk the egg and buttermilk, and mix the crushed crackers and spices in a third bowl.
2. Dip the fish strips in the flour mixture, then in the whisked eggs; finally, roll the fish strips over the cracker mixture until they are well coated on all sides.
3. Place the fish sticks in the air fryer basket.
4. Air fry for 10 minutes at 400ºF (205ºC), shaking the basket halfway through the cooking time.
5. Serve warm!

Greek Monkfish Fillet Pita with Avocado

Prep time: 10 minutes | Cook time: 14 minutes | Serves 4

1 tbsp. olive oil	4 tbsps. coleslaw
1 pound (454 g) monkfish fillets	1 tbsp. fresh parsley, chopped
4 (6-½ inch) Greek pitas, warmed	1 tsp. cayenne pepper
1 avocado, pitted, peeled and diced	Sea salt and ground black pepper, to taste

1. Toss the fish fillets with the olive oil, then arrange them in a lightly oiled air fryer basket.
2. Select the Seafood function, adjust time to 14 minutes, then press Start/Pause, turning them over halfway through the cooking time.
3. Assemble your pitas with the chopped fish and the rest of ingredients and serve hot. Bon appétit!

Shrimp and Cucumber Salad Sandwich

Prep time: 15 minutes | Cook time: 6 minutes | Serves 4

1 tsp. olive oil	chopped
1 pound (454 g) shrimp, peeled and chilled	1 tbsp. fresh parsley, roughly chopped
4 hoagie rolls	1 tbsp. apple cider vinegar
1 English cucumber, sliced	1½ tsps. Dijon mustard
1 stalk celery, sliced	1 tsp. Creole seasoning mix
½ cup mayonnaise	
1 shallot, sliced	Coarse sea salt and lemon pepper, to taste
1 tbsp. fresh lime juice	
1 tbsp. fresh dill, roughly	

1. Toss the shrimp and olive oil in the air fryer basket.
2. Select the Shrimp function, adjust time to 6 minutes, then press Start/Pause, tossing the basket halfway through the cooking time.
3. Put the shrimp in a mixing bowl along with the rest of ingredients, except for hoagie rolls. Toss to combine well and serve warm on the hoagie rolls.
4. Bon appétit!

Italian Cheesy Monkfish Fingers

Prep time: 10 minutes | Cook time: 10 minutes | Serves 4

1 pound (454 g) monkfish, sliced into strips	1 tbsp. Italian parsley, chopped
1 egg, whisked	1 tsp. cayenne pepper
½ cup Pecorino Romano cheese, grated	1 tsp. garlic powder
	½ tsp. onion powder
½ cup all-purpose flour	Sea salt and ground black pepper, to taste

1. Mix the flour, spices, egg and cheese in a shallow bowl. Dip the fish strips in the batter until they are well coated on all sides.
2. Place the fish strips in the air fryer basket.
3. Air fry for 10 minutes at 400ºF (205ºC), shaking the basket halfway through the cooking time.
4. Serve warm!

Panko-Crusted Shrimp with Bang Bang Sauce

Prep time: 10 minutes | Cook time: 8 minutes | Serves 4

1 pound (454 g) raw shrimp (peeled and deveined)	Montreal chicken seasoning
¾ cup panko bread crumbs	**FOR THE BANG BANG SAUCE:**
½ cup almond flour	⅓ cup plain Greek yogurt
1 egg white	¼ cup sweet chili sauce
1 tsp. paprika	2 tbsps. sriracha sauce

1. Ensure your air fryer is preheated to 400ºF (205ºC).
2. Season all the shrimp with paprika and seasoning.
3. Place flour to one bowl, egg white to another, and breadcrumbs to a third.
4. Dip seasoned shrimp in flour, then egg whites, and then breadcrumbs.
5. Spray coated shrimp lightly with olive oil and put to air fryer basket.
6. Air fry for about 4 minutes at 400ºF (205ºC), flip and cook for another 4 minutes.
7. Make the sauce by mixing together all the sauce ingredients until smooth.

Chapter 8 Bread, Sandwiches and Pizza

Cheddar and Mango Chutney Puff Pie

Prep time: 5 minutes | Cook time: 20 minutes | Serves 1 to 2

1 sheet puff pastry
¼ cup chunky mango chutney
3 ounces (85 g) extra-sharp Cheddar cheese, cut into thin slices
Egg wash
Crackers and crudités, for serving
Kosher salt and freshly ground black pepper, to taste

1. Roll the puff pastry sheet into a 14-inch square with a rolling pin. Cut out two 7-inch rounds and discard the scraps (or save for another use). Place the Cheddar in the middle of one round, then top with the chutney and season with salt and pepper to taste. Lightly brush the edge of the round with egg wash and top with the second pastry round. Press and crimp the edges together with a fork.
2. Take the pastry round to the air fryer and cook for about 20 minutes at 325ºF (160ºC), or until the pastry is puffed and golden brown and the cheese is melted inside.
3. Remove the puff pie to a cutting board and allow to cool for 5 minutes. Cut the pie into 4 wedges and serve hot with crackers and crudités.

Spicy Chimichurri Beef Empanadas

Prep time: 10 minutes | Cook time: 24 minutes | Serves 2

1 tbsp. olive oil
12 ounces (340 g) pizza dough
½ pound (227 g) trimmed beef sirloin, cut into ½-inch pieces, at room temperature
2 garlic cloves, minced
1 tbsp. chopped fresh flat-leaf parsley leaves
1 tbsp. chopped fresh cilantro leaves
1 tbsp. chopped fresh mint leaves
2 tsps. red wine vinegar
¼ tsp. ground cumin
½ tsp. kosher salt
Freshly ground black pepper, to taste

1. Toss together the beef, parsley, cilantro, mint, olive oil, vinegar, salt, cumin, garlic and pepper in a bowl.
2. Divide the dough in half and gently flatten each portion into a 10-inch round. Divide the beef mixture evenly between the 2 dough rounds, then fold them in half to create 2 half-moons. With a fork or your fingers, crimp and twist the edges of the dough on itself to seal the empanadas completely.
3. Put one empanada in the air fryer basket, cut a hole in the top with a paring knife to vent, and cook for about 12 minutes at 350ºF (180ºC), or until the dough is golden brown and the beef is cooked through. Take the empanada to a plate and allow to cool for 2 minutes before serving. Repeat for the second empanada.

Fluffy Mini Pita Breads

Prep time: 10 minutes | Cook time: 6 minutes | Makes 8 mini pitas

1 tbsp. olive oil, plus more for brushing
3¼ cups all-purpose flour
1¼ to 1½ cups warm water, 100ºF (38ºC)
2 tsps. active dry yeast
1 tbsp. sugar
2 tsps. salt
Kosher salt (optional)

1. Dissolve the yeast, sugar and water in the bowl of a stand mixer. Allow the mixture to sit for 5 minutes to make sure the yeast is active – it should foam a little. (If there's no foaming, discard and start again with new yeast.) Mix the flour and salt in a bowl, and add it to the water, along with the olive oil. Mix with the dough hook until combined. Place a little more flour if needed to get the dough to pull away from the sides of the mixing bowl, or pour a little more water if the dough seems too dry.
2. Knead the dough until it is smooth and elastic (about 8 minutes in the mixer or 15 minutes by hand). Take the dough to a lightly oiled bowl, cover and allow it to rise in a warm place until doubled in bulk.
3. Evenly divide the dough into 8 portions and roll each portion into a circle about 4-inches in diameter. Don't roll the balls too thin, or you won't get the pocket inside the pita.
4. Preheat the air fryer to 400ºF (205ºC).
5. Brush both sides of the dough lightly with olive oil, and season with kosher salt if desired. Work in 2 batches if necessary to avoid overcrowding. Select the Bread function, adjust time to 6 minutes, then press Start/Pause, flipping it over when there are two minutes left in the cooking time.

Healthy Banana Bread

Prep time: 10 minutes | Cook time: 20 minutes | Makes 1 loaf

Cooking spray
2 tbsps. coconut oil
1 egg
1 cup white wheat flour
½ cup mashed ripe banana

¼ cup plain yogurt
¼ cup pure maple syrup
½ tsp. pure vanilla extract
½ tsp. baking powder
¼ tsp. baking soda
¼ tsp. salt

1. Preheat air fryer to 330ºF (165ºC).
2. Spray 6 x 6-inch baking dish lightly with cooking spray.
3. Mix together the flour, baking powder, salt and soda in a medium bowl.
4. Beat the egg and add the mashed banana, yogurt, syrup, oil and vanilla in a separate bowl. Mix until well combined.
5. Add liquid mixture into dry ingredients and stir gently to blend. Do not beat. Batter may be slightly lumpy.
6. Pour batter into baking dish and select the Bread function, adjust time to 20 minutes, then press Start/Pause, until the toothpick inserted in the center of the loaf comes out clean.

Cheesy Pull-Apart Bread with Anchovies

Prep time: 10 minutes | Cook time: 20 minutes | Serves 2 to 4

2 tbsps. olive oil
1 small sourdough boule
⅔ cup grated smoked Mozzarella cheese
2 garlic cloves, minced
2 tbsps. grated pecorino cheese
1 tbsp. sherry vinegar

2 tsps. Worcestershire sauce
1 tsp. minced anchovies or anchovy paste (optional)
Kosher salt and freshly ground black pepper, to taste

1. Put the sourdough boule on a cutting board and, if necessary, trim its edges so it fits snugly within your air fryer basket. Cut through the top of the bread in a crisscross pattern, spacing the cuts every ½ inch and making sure to not cut all the way through so the bread stays together.
2. Whisk together the olive oil, vinegar, Worcestershire, anchovies (if using), and garlic in a bowl. Season liberally with salt and pepper and whisk again to combine well. Working on a cutting board, drizzle the dressing evenly into all the grooves of the bread.

Evenly sprinkle the bread with the Mozzarella and then the pecorino.

3. Put the bread in the air fryer, tent with a round of foil, and select the Bread function, adjust time to 12 minutes, then press Start/Pause. Uncover the bread and cook until the bread is toasted at the edges and the cheese is golden brown, about 8 minutes more. Transfer the bread to a plate and serve warm.

Honey Rosemary Knots

Prep time: 15 minutes | Cook time: 14 minutes | Makes 8 garlic knots

2 tbsps. olive oil
2 tbsps. unsalted butter, at room temperature, plus more for greasing and brushing
¼ cup milk, heated to 115ºF (46ºC) in the microwave
⅔ cup all-purpose flour, plus more for dusting
2 garlic cloves, minced

1 tbsp. finely chopped fresh rosemary
1 tbsp. honey or agave syrup
1 tsp. garlic powder
½ tsp. active dry yeast
½ tsp. kosher salt
¼ tsp. freshly ground black pepper
Flaky sea salt

1. Whisk together the milk, yeast and honey in a large bowl, and let stand until foamy, about 10 minutes. Stir in the flour and kosher salt until just combined. Toss in the butter until completely absorbed. Scrape the dough onto a lightly floured work surface and knead until smooth, for about 6 minutes. Take the dough to a bowl lightly greased with more butter, cover loosely with a sheet of plastic wrap or a kitchen towel, and let sit until nearly doubled in size, about 1 hour.
2. Uncover the dough, lightly press it down to expel the bubbles, then portion it into 8 equal pieces. Roll each piece into a 6-inch rope, then tie it into a simple knot, tucking the loose ends into each side of the "hoop" made by the knot. Take the knots back to the bowl they proofed in, then add the olive oil, rosemary, fresh garlic, garlic powder and pepper. Toss the knots until coated in the oil and spices, then nestle them side by side in the air fryer basket. Cover the knots loosely with plastic wrap and allow to sit until lightly risen and puffed, about 20 to 30 minutes.
3. Uncover the knots and air fry for 14 minutes at 280ºF (138ºC), or until the knots are golden brown outside and tender and fluffy inside. Remove the garlic knots from the air fryer and brush with a little more butter, if you like, and scatter with a pinch of flaky sea salt. Serve hot.

Garlic Bacon Cheese Pizza

Prep time: 10 minutes | Cook time: 20 minutes | Serves 4

Flour, for dusting
Nonstick baking spray with flour
4 frozen large whole-wheat dinner rolls, thawed
8 slices precooked bacon, cut into 1-inch pieces
1¼ cups shredded Cheddar cheese
¾ cup pizza sauce
5 cloves garlic, minced
½ tsp. dried oregano
½ tsp. garlic salt

1. Press out each dinner roll to a 5-by-3-inch oval on a lightly floured surface.
2. Spray four 6-by-4-inch pieces of heavy duty foil lightly with nonstick spray and put one crust on each piece.
3. Air fry, two at a time, for about 2 minutes or until the crusts are set, but not browned.
4. Meanwhile, combine the garlic, pizza sauce, oregano and garlic salt in a small bowl. When the pizza crusts are set, evenly spread each with some of the sauce. Top with the bacon pieces and Cheddar cheese.
5. Cook, two at a time, for 8 minutes more or until the crust is browned and the cheese is melted and starting to brown. Serve warm.

Healthy Corn Bread

Prep time: 15 minutes | Cook time: 25 minutes | Serves 6

Cooking oil spray (sunflower, safflower, or refined coconut)
½ cup cornmeal
½ cup whole-wheat pastry flour
½ cup plus 1 tbsp. nondairy milk (unsweetened)
⅓ cup coconut sugar
¼ cup neutral-flavored oil (such as sunflower, safflower, or melted refined coconut)
3 tbsps. water
2 tbsps. ground flaxseed
½ tbsp. baking powder
¼ tsp. sea salt
¼ tsp. baking soda
½ tbsp. apple cider vinegar
vegan margarine (optional)

1. Combine the flaxseed and water in a small bowl. Keep aside for 5 minutes, or until thick and gooey.
2. Add the cornmeal, flour, sugar, baking powder, salt and baking soda in a medium bowl. Combine thoroughly, stirring with a whisk. Keep aside.
3. Add the milk, vinegar and oil to the flaxseed mixture and stir well.
4. Place the wet mixture to the dry mixture and stir gently, just until thoroughly combined.
5. Spray (or coat) a 6-inch round, 2-inch deep baking pan lightly with oil. Add the batter into it and select the Bread function, adjust time to 25 minutes, then press Start/Pause, until golden-browned and a knife inserted in the center comes out clean. Cut into wedges, top with a little vegan margarine if desired.

Garlicky Parmesan Bread Ring

Prep time: 10 minutes | Cook time: 30 minutes | Serves 6 to 8

Olive oil
1 pound (454 g) frozen bread dough, defrosted
1 egg, beaten
¾ cup grated Parmesan cheese
½ cup unsalted butter, melted
3 to 4 cloves garlic, minced
1 tbsp. chopped fresh parsley
¼ tsp. salt (omit if using salted butter)

1. In a small bowl, combine the melted butter, salt, Parmesan cheese, garlic and chopped parsley.
2. Roll the dough out into a rectangle that measures 8 inches by 17 inches. Evenly spread the butter mixture over the dough, leaving a half-inch border un-buttered along one of the long edges. Roll the dough from one long edge to the other, ending with the un-buttered border. Pinch the seam shut tightly. Form the log into a circle sealing the ends together by pushing one end into the other and stretching the dough around it.
3. Cut out a circle of aluminum foil that is the same size as the air fryer basket. Lightly brush the foil circle with oil and put an oven safe ramekin or glass in the center. Transfer the dough ring to the aluminum foil circle, around the ramekin. This will help you make sure the dough will fit in the basket and maintain its ring shape. With kitchen shears, cut 8 slits around the outer edge of the dough ring halfway to the center. Brush the dough ring with egg wash.
4. Preheat the air fryer to 400ºF (205ºC), and set time to 4 minutes. When it has preheated, brush the sides of the basket with oil and take the dough ring, foil circle and ramekin into the basket. Slide the drawer back into the air fryer, but do not turn the air fryer on. Allow the dough to rise inside the warm air fryer for 30 minutes.
5. After the bread has proofed in the air fryer for 30 minutes, air fry for 15 minutes at 340ºF (170ºC). Flip the bread over by inverting it onto a plate or cutting board and sliding it back into the air fryer basket. Cook for 15 minutes more.

Cheesy Salami and Kale Pizza

Prep time: 10 minutes | Cook time: 8 minutes | Makes 1 pizza

2 tsps. olive oil
4 ounces (113 g) pizza dough
5 (1½- to 2-inch-diameter) slices salami
¼ cup packed torn kale leaves
3 tbsps. grated Asiago

cheese
2 tbsps. shredded low-moisture Mozzarella cheese
Kosher salt and freshly ground black pepper, to taste

1. Roll and stretch the pizza dough into a 6-inch round.
2. Lay the dough round in the air fryer, then lightly brush with 1 tsp. of olive oil. Place the kale leaves over the dough, followed by the salami slices. Sprinkle with the Asiago and Mozzarella. Season with salt and pepper to taste, drizzle with the remaining 1 tsp. olive oil, and air fry for about 8 minutes at 350ºF (180ºC), or until the dough is cooked through and the cheese is melted and golden brown.
3. Take the pizza to a plate and serve warm.

Coconut Banana Chia Bread

Prep time: 15 minutes | Cook time: 27 minutes | Serves 6

Cooking oil spray (sunflower, safflower, or refined coconut)
2 tbsps. neutral-flavored oil (sunflower or safflower)
2 large bananas, very ripe, peeled
1 cup whole-wheat pastry flour

¼ cup coconut sugar
2 tbsps. maple syrup
½ tbsp. chia seeds
½ tsp. vanilla
½ tbsp. ground flaxseed
½ tsp. cinnamon
¼ tsp. nutmeg
¼ tsp. baking powder
¼ tsp. baking soda
¼ tsp. salt

1. In a medium bowl, use a fork to mash the peeled bananas until very mushy. Add the oil, chia, maple syrup, vanilla and flaxseeds and stir well.
2. Add the flour, sugar, cinnamon, salt, nutmeg, baking soda and baking powder, and stir just until thoroughly combined.
3. Preheat a 6-inch round, 2-inch deep baking pan in the air fryer for 2 minutes.
4. Open the air fryer to spray the basket with oil, and add the batter into it. Use a rubber spatula to smooth out the top and select the Bread function, adjust time to 25 minutes, then press Start/Pause, until a knife inserted in the center comes out clean.

5. Remove and allow to cool for a minute or two, then cut into wedges and serve warm.

Samosa Potato Pot Pie

Prep time: 15 minutes | Cook time: 51 minutes | Serves 2

3 tbsps. vegetable oil
All-purpose flour, for rolling/dusting
2 sheets puff pastry, thawed if frozen
1 pound (454 g) russet potatoes, peeled, boiled, and cut into 1-inch chunks
½ cup thawed frozen peas
1 medium yellow onion, roughly chopped
½ to 1 serrano chile,

seeded and minced
3 garlic cloves, minced
2 tsps. fresh lemon juice
1 tsp. brown mustard seeds
1 tsp. garam masala
1 tsp. ground coriander
½ tsp. ground cumin
½ tsp. ground turmeric
½ tsp. sweet paprika
Kosher salt and freshly ground black pepper, to taste

1. Heat the oil over medium-high heat in a medium saucepan. Place the mustard seeds and cook until they begin popping, 1 to 1½ minutes. Add the onion and chile and cook, stirring, until soft and caramelized at the edges, for about 10 minutes.
2. Place the garam masala, coriander, turmeric, paprika, cumin and garlic and cook for about 1 minute, until fragrant. Stir in the potatoes, peas, and lemon juice, breaking the potatoes up slightly and stirring until everything is coated in the yellow stain of the turmeric. Remove the pan from the heat, season the filling with salt and pepper to taste, and allow to cool completely. The filling can be made and stored in a bowl in the refrigerator for up to 3 days before you plan to cook the pie.
3. Working on a lightly floured surface, roll 1 pastry sheet into a 10-inch square, then cut out a 10-inch round, discarding the scraps. Mound the cooled potato filling in the center of the dough round, then tightly press and mold it with your hands into a 7-inch disk. Cut a 7-inch round out of the second pastry sheet (no need to roll) and put it over the filling disk. Brush the edge of the bottom dough round with water just to moisten, then lift it up to meet the top dough round. Pinch and fold the edges together all around the filling to form and enclose the pie.
4. Take the pie to the air fryer, and cut a slit in the top of the pie with a paring knife to vent. Cover the top of the pie loosely with a round of foil, and air fry for 20 minutes at 310ºF (154ºC). Remove the foil and cook at 330ºF (165ºC) until the pastry is golden brown and the filling is piping hot, about 20 minutes more.

Fluffy Mini Pita Breads, page 107

Chili BLT Sandwich, page 115

Zucchini Chocolate Bread, page 112

Honey Rosemary Knots, page 108

Strawberry Bread

Prep time: 10 minutes | Cook time: 28 minutes | Makes 1 loaf

Cooking spray
⅓ cup oil
1 egg, beaten
1 cup flour
½ cup frozen strawberries in juice,
completely thawed (do not drain)
½ cup sugar
1 tsp. cinnamon
½ tsp. baking soda
⅛ tsp. salt

1. Chop any large berries into smaller pieces no larger than ½ inch.
2. Preheat air fryer to 330ºF (165ºC).
3. Stir together the flour, sugar, cinnamon, soda and salt in a large bowl.
4. Mix together the egg, oil and strawberries in a small bowl. Add to dry ingredients and stir together gently.
5. Spray 6 x 6-inch baking pan lightly with cooking spray.
6. Add batter into prepared pan and select the Bread function, adjust time to 28 minutes, then press Start/Pause.
7. When the bread is done, allow to cool for 10 minutes before removing from the pan.

Healthy Crushed Tomato Pizza

Prep time: 10 minutes | Cook time: 8 minutes | Makes 1 pizza

2 tsps. olive oil
2 canned whole peeled tomatoes, crushed by hand and drained
4 ounces (113 g) pizza dough
1 tbsp. walnut halves
1 tbsp. thinly sliced fresh flat-leaf parsley
1½ tsps. nutritional yeast
½ tsp. garlic powder
Kosher salt and freshly ground black pepper, to taste

1. Set a Microplane grater over a small bowl and grate the walnuts into the bowl. Toss in the nutritional yeast and garlic powder. Roll and stretch the pizza dough into a 6-inch round.
2. Lay the dough round in the air fryer, then lightly brush with 1 tsp. of olive oil. Place the crushed tomatoes over the dough and sprinkle with the walnut "Parmesan" mixture. Season with salt and pepper to taste, drizzle with the remaining 1 tsp. olive oil, and air fry for about 8 minutes at 350ºF (180ºC), or until the dough is cooked through, the tomatoes are dried out and the "Parmesan" is browned.
3. Take the pizza to a plate, garnish with the parsley and serve warm.

Paprika Lamb, Green Olive and Cheese Pizza

Prep time: 10 minutes | Cook time: 8 minutes | Makes 1 pizza

2 tsps. olive oil
4 ounces (113 g) pizza dough
1½ ounces ground lamb, crumbled into small bits
6 pitted green olives, roughly chopped
1 ounce (28 g) Feta cheese, crumbled
¼ tsp. smoked paprika
¼ tsp. ground cumin
Kosher salt and freshly ground black pepper, to taste

1. Roll and stretch the pizza dough into a 6-inch round.
2. Lay the dough round in the air fryer, then lightly brush with 1 tsp. of olive oil. Place the lamb crumbles over the dough and sprinkle with the cumin and paprika, followed by the olives and Feta. Season with salt and pepper to taste, drizzle with the remaining 1 tsp. olive oil, and air fry for 8 minutes at 350ºF (180ºC), or until the dough is cooked through and the meat is browned and crisp on top.
3. Take the pizza to a plate and serve warm.

Zucchini Chocolate Bread

Prep time: 15 minutes | Cook time: 15 minutes | Serves 12

½ cup sunflower oil
1 cup zucchini, shredded and squeezed
1 cup flour
½ cup unsweetened cocoa powder
½ cup maple syrup
½ cup milk
⅓ cup chocolate chips
1 tbsp. flax egg (1 tbsp. flax meal + 3 tbsps. water)
1 tsp. vanilla extract
1 tsp. apple cider vinegar
1 tsp. baking soda
¼ tsp. salt

1. Preheat your Air Fryer to 350ºF (180ºC).
2. Place a baking dish small enough to fit inside the fryer and line it with parchment paper.
3. In a bowl, mix together the flax meal, zucchini, sunflower oil, maple, vanilla, apple cider vinegar and milk.
4. Incorporate the flour, salt, cocoa powder and baking soda, stirring all the time to combine everything well.
5. Finally, throw in the chocolate chips.
6. Take the batter to the baking dish and select the Bread function, adjust time to 15 minutes, then press Start/Pause. Make sure to test with a toothpick before serving by sticking it in the center. The bread is ready when the toothpick comes out clean.

Smoked Mozzarella and Oyster Mushroom Pizza

Prep time: 10 minutes | Cook time: 8 minutes | Makes 1 pizza

2 tsps. olive oil
4 ounces (113 g) pizza dough
½ cup oyster mushrooms, torn into small pieces
¼ cup shredded smoked

Mozzarella cheese
1 tsp. fresh thyme leaves
⅛ tsp. crushed red chile flakes
Kosher salt and freshly ground black pepper, to taste

1. Roll and stretch the pizza dough into a 6-inch round.
2. Lay the dough round in the air fryer, then lightly brush with 1 tsp. of olive oil. Place the mushrooms over the dough, followed by the thyme leaves. Scatter with the smoked Mozzarella and chile flakes. Season with salt and black pepper to taste, drizzle with the remaining 1 tsp. olive oil, and air fry for about 8 minutes at 350ºF (180ºC), or until the dough is cooked through and the cheese is melted and golden brown.
3. Take the pizza to a plate and serve warm.

Cinnamon Pumpkin Loaf

Prep time: 15 minutes | Cook time: 22 minutes | Makes 1 loaf

Cooking spray
⅓ cup oil
1 large egg
⅔ cup flour plus 1 tbsp.
½ cup granulated sugar
½ cup canned pumpkin (not pie filling)

1 tsp. pumpkin pie spice
½ tsp. vanilla
½ tsp. baking powder
½ tsp. baking soda
¼ tsp. cinnamon
½ tsp. salt

1. Lightly spray 6 x 6-inch baking dish with cooking spray.
2. Put baking dish in air fryer basket and preheat air fryer to 330ºF (165ºC).
3. In a large bowl, beat eggs and sugar together by using a hand mixer.
4. Add oil, vanilla and pumpkin and mix well.
5. Sift together all the dry ingredients. Place to pumpkin mixture and beat well, for about 1 minute.
6. Pour batter in baking dish and select the Bread function, adjust time to 22 minutes, then press Start/Pause, until toothpick inserted in the center of the loaf comes out clean.

Peanut Butter Banana Bread

Prep time: 5 minutes | Cook time: 5 minutes | Serves 3

1 tbsp. oil
4 slices bread

1 banana, sliced
2 tbsps. peanut butter

1. Spread the peanut butter evenly on top of each slice of bread, then place the banana slices on top. Sandwich two slices together, then the other two.
2. Oil the inside of the Air Fryer and select the Bread function, adjust time to 5 minutes, then press Start/Pause.
3. Enjoy!

Cheesy Olives and Roasted Red Pepper Bread

Prep time: 10 minutes | Cook time: 14 minutes | Serves 8

Olive oil
7-inch round bread boule
1 cup grated Mozzarella or Fontina cheese
½ cup black olives, sliced
½ cup green olives, sliced
½ cup coarsely chopped roasted red peppers

½ cup mayonnaise
¼ cup grated Parmesan cheese
2 tbsps. butter, melted
2 tbsps. minced red onion
½ tsp. dried oregano
Freshly ground black pepper, to taste

1. Preheat the air fryer to 370ºF (188ºC).
2. Cut the bread boule in half horizontally. If your bread boule has a rounded top, trim the top of the boule so that the top half will lie flat with the cut side facing up. Brush both sides of the boule halves lightly with olive oil.
3. Put one half of the boule into the air fryer basket with the center cut side facing down. Select the Bread function, adjust time to 2 minutes, then press Start/Pause. Repeat with the other half of the bread boule.
4. In a small bowl, combine the mayonnaise, butter, Mozzarella cheese, Parmesan cheese and dried oregano. Gently fold in the black and green olives, roasted red peppers and red onion and season with freshly ground black pepper to taste. Evenly spread the cheese mixture over the untoasted side of the bread, covering the entire surface.
5. Air-fry for 5 minutes at 350ºF (180ºC), until the cheese is melted and browned. Repeat with the other half. Cut into slices and serve hot.

Chicken English Muffin Sandwiches

Prep time: 5 minutes | Cook time: 12 minutes | Serves 4

1 tbsp. olive oil
1 pound (454 g) chicken breasts
4 English muffins, lightly toasted

4 slices Cheddar cheese
4 tsps. yellow mustard
Sea salt and black pepper, to taste

1. Use kitchen towels to pat the chicken dry. Toss the chicken breasts with the olive oil, salt and pepper.
2. Air fry for 12 minutes at 380ºF (195ºC), turning them over halfway through the cooking time.
3. With two forks, shred the chicken and serve with cheese, mustard and English muffins. Bon appétit!

Traditional Tuscan Toast

Prep time: 5 minutes | Cook time: 5 minutes | Serves 4

¼ cup butter
4 slices Italian bread, 1-inch thick
½ clove garlic

½ tsp. lemon juice
½ tsp. dried parsley flakes

1. In a food processor, add butter, lemon juice, garlic and parsley. Process about 1 minute, or until the garlic is pulverized and ingredients are well blended.
2. Evenly spread garlic butter on both sides of bread slices.
3. Put bread slices upright in air fryer basket. (They can lie flat but cook better standing on end.)
4. Air fry for 5 minutes at 390ºF (200ºC), or until toasty brown.

Mayonnaise Egg Salad Sandwich

Prep time: 10 minutes | Cook time: 22 minutes | Serves 3

6 eggs
6 slices whole-grain bread
¼ cup mayonnaise
¼ cup sour cream
2 tbsps. scallions,

chopped
2 garlic cloves, minced
1 tsp. yellow mustard
Sea salt and ground black pepper, to taste

1. Put the eggs in the air fryer basket.
2. Air fry for 15 minutes at 270ºF (132ºC).
3. Peel and chop the eggs, then put them in a salad bowl and add the remaining ingredients, except for bread. Toss to combine well.

4. Next, for the bread slices, air fry for 4 minutes at 330ºF (165ºC). Turn them over and cook for another 3 to 4 minutes.
5. Lastly, assemble sandwiches with the egg salad and bread.
6. Enjoy!

Sweet Cornbread

Prep time: 10 minutes | Cook time: 17 minutes | Serves 6 to 8

Cooking spray
2 tbsps. oil
1 egg
½ cup white cornmeal
½ cup milk

½ cup flour
4 tsps. sugar
2 tsps. baking powder
½ tsp. salt

1. Preheat air fryer to 360ºF (180ºC).
2. Spray air fryer basket lightly with nonstick cooking spray.
3. Stir together the cornmeal, flour, baking powder, salt and sugar in a medium bowl.
4. Beat together the egg, oil and milk in a small bowl. Stir into dry ingredients until well combined.
5. Add batter into the prepared basket.
6. Air fry for 17 minutes at 360ºF (180ºC), or until the toothpick inserted in the center comes out clean or with crumbs clinging.

Cheesy Broccoli Cornbread

Prep time: 10 minutes | Cook time: 18 minutes | Makes 1 loaf

Cooking spray
1 cup frozen chopped broccoli, thawed and drained
½ cup flour
½ cup yellow cornmeal
¼ cup cottage cheese

¼ cup milk, plus 2 tbsps.
1 egg, beaten
2 tbsps. minced onion
2 tbsps. melted butter
1 tsp. baking powder
½ tsp. salt

1. Put thawed broccoli in colander and tightly press with a spoon to squeeze out excess moisture.
2. In a large bowl, stir together the remaining ingredients.
3. Spray 6 x 6-inch baking pan lightly with cooking spray.
4. Spread batter in pan and air fry for about 18 minutes at 330ºF (165ºC), or until cornbread is lightly browned and the loaf starts to pull away from the sides of pan.

Sweet Italian Sausage Sandwich

Prep time: 5 minutes | Cook time: 15 minutes | Serves 3

2 tsps. mustard
6 white bread slices

1 pound (454 g) sweet
Italian sausage

1. Put the sausage in a lightly greased air fryer basket.
2. Air fry for 15 minutes at 370ºF (188ºC), tossing the basket halfway through the cooking time.
3. Assemble the sandwiches with the bread, mustard and sausage, and serve right away.
4. Bon appétit!

Chili BLT Sandwich

Prep time: 10 minutes | Cook time: 10 minutes | Serves 3

6 (½-inch) slices white bread
6 ounces (170 g) bacon, thick-cut
1 head lettuce, torn into leaves
2 medium tomatoes,

sliced
2 tbsps. brown sugar
1 tbsp. Dijon mustard
2 tsps. chipotle chile powder
1 tsp. cayenne pepper

1. Toss the bacon with the sugar, cayenne pepper, chipotle chile powder and mustard.
2. Put the bacon in the air fryer basket. Then air fry for 10 minutes at 400ºF (205ºC), tossing the basket halfway through the cooking time.
3. Assemble your sandwiches with the lettuce, bacon, tomato and bread.
4. Serve warm!

Cheesy Beef Sandwich

Prep time: 5 minutes | Cook time: 10 minutes | Serves 2

2 tbsps. butter, room temperature
½ pound (227 g) corned

beef
4 slices sourdough bread
4 slices Cheddar cheese

1. Butter one side of each slice of bread.
2. Use the cheese and corned beef to assemble your sandwiches.
3. Air fry for 10 minutes at 380ºF (195ºC).
4. Serve warm!

Cheesy Mushroom and Tomato Pita Pizza

Prep time: 10 minutes | Cook time: 3 minutes | Serves 4

1 tbsp. olive oil
4 (3-inch) pitas
1 cup grated Mozzarella or provolone cheese
1 cup sliced grape tomatoes

1 (4-ounce /113-g) jar sliced mushrooms, drained
¾ cup pizza sauce
2 green onions, minced
½ tsp. dried basil

1. Brush each piece of pita lightly with oil and top with the pizza sauce.
2. Place the mushrooms and scatter with basil and green onions. Top with the grated cheese.
3. Air fry for 3 to 6 minutes or until the cheese is melted and starts to brown. Place the grape tomatoes on top and serve right away.

Chapter 9 Snacks and Appetizers

Cheesy Bacon Wrapped Jalapeño Peppers

Prep time: 10 minutes | Cook time: 12 minutes | Serves 12

olive oil
12 jalapeño peppers
12 slices bacon, cut in half
1 (8-ounce / 227-g) package cream cheese, at room temperature
1 cup shredded Cheddar cheese
1 tsp. onion powder
1 tsp. salt
½ tsp. freshly ground black pepper

1. Spray the air fryer basket lightly with olive oil.
2. Cut each pepper in half, then scrape out the veins and seeds with a spoon.
3. Mix together the cream cheese, Cheddar cheese, onion powder, salt and pepper in a small mixing bowl.
4. Use a small spoon to fill each pepper half with the cheese mixture.
5. Gently wrap each stuffed pepper half with a half slice of bacon.
6. Put the bacon-wrapped peppers into the greased air fryer basket in a single layer. (You will need to cook the peppers in more than one batch.)
7. Air fry for about 12 minutes at 320ºF (160ºC).
8. Remove the peppers from the air fryer with tongs, place them on a platter and serve.

Buffalo Cheesy Meatballs

Prep time: 5 minutes | Cook time: 22 minutes | Makes 16 meatballs

8 tbsps. buffalo wing sauce
1 pound (454 g) ground chicken
2 ounces (57 g) Gruyère cheese, cut into 16 cubes
1 tbsp. maple syrup

1. Mix 4 tbsps. buffalo wing sauce into all the ground chicken.
2. Shape the chicken mixture into a log and divide into 16 equal portions.
3. With slightly damp hands, mold each chicken portion around a cube of cheese and shape into a firm ball. When you have shaped 8 meatballs, put them in air

fryer basket.
4. Air fry for about 5 minutes at 390ºF (200ºC). Shake the basket, reduce temperature to 360ºF (180ºC), and cook for 5 to 6 minutes longer.
5. While the first batch is cooking, shape the rest of chicken and cheese into 8 more meatballs.
6. Repeat step 4 to cook second batch of meatballs.
7. Mix the remaining 4 tbsps. of buffalo wing sauce with the maple syrup in a medium bowl. Add all the cooked meatballs and toss to coat well.
8. Put meatballs back into air fryer basket and air fry at 390ºF (200ºC), and set time to 2 to 3 minutes to set the glaze. Skewer each with a toothpick and serve warm.

Cheesy Spinach Dip with Bread Knots

Prep time: 10 minutes | Cook time: 8 minutes | Serves 6

Nonstick cooking spray
½ (11 ounces, 312 g) can refrigerated breadstick dough
1 (8 ounces, 227 g) package cream cheese, cut into cubes
½ cup frozen chopped spinach, thawed and
drained
½ cup grated Swiss cheese
¼ cup sour cream
2 green onions, chopped
3 tbsps. grated Parmesan cheese
2 tbsps. melted butter

1. Spray a 6-by-6-by-2-inch pan lightly with nonstick cooking spray.
2. Combine the cream cheese, sour cream, spinach, Swiss cheese and green onions in a medium bowl, and mix well. Lay into the prepared pan and cook for about 8 minutes or until hot.
3. While the dip is cooking, unroll six of the breadsticks and slice them in half crosswise to make 12 pieces.
4. Carefully stretch each piece of dough and tie into a loose knot; tuck in the ends.
5. When the dip is hot, take from the air fryer and gently put each bread knot on top of the dip, covering the surface of the dip. Rub each knot with melted butter and scatter Parmesan cheese on top.
6. Air fry for about 8 to 13 minutes, or until the bread knots are golden brown and cooked through. Serve hot.

Shrimp Cucumber Pirogues

Prep time: 10 minutes | Cook time: 5 minutes | Serves 8

12 ounces (340 g) small, peeled and deveined raw shrimp
4 small hothouse cucumbers, each approximately 6 inches long
3 ounces (85 g)
cream cheese, room temperature
2 tbsps. plain yogurt
1 tsp. lemon juice
1 tsp. dried dill weed, crushed
Salt, to taste

1. Add 4 tbsps. water in the bottom of air fryer drawer.
2. Arrange shrimp in air fryer basket in single layer and air fry for about 4 to 5 minutes at 390ºF (200ºC), just until cooked. Watch carefully because shrimp cooks immediately, and overcooking makes it tough.
3. Cut shrimp into small pieces, no larger than ½ inch.
4. Use a fork to mash and whip the cream cheese until smooth.
5. Toss in the yogurt and beat until smooth. Stir in dill weed, lemon juice and chopped shrimp.
6. Taste for seasoning. If needed, season with ¼ to ½ tsp. salt to suit your taste.
7. Store in the refrigerator until serving time.
8. When ready to serve, wash and pat cucumbers dry and split them lengthwise. Spoon out the seeds and turn the cucumbers upside down on paper towels to drain for about 10 minutes.
9. Just before filling, wipe centers of cucumbers dry with paper towels. Scoop the shrimp mixture into the pirogues and cut in half crosswise. Serve right away.

Beef Steak Sliders with Horseradish Mayonnaise

Prep time: 10 minutes | Cook time: 16 minutes | Makes 8 sliders

1 tbsp. extra-light olive oil
1 pound (454 g) top sirloin steaks, about ¾-inch thick
8 slider buns
2 large onions, thinly sliced
Salt and pepper, to taste
FOR THE
HORSERADISH MAYONNAISE:
4 tsps. prepared horseradish
1 cup light mayonnaise
2 tsps. Worcestershire sauce
1 tsp. coarse brown mustard

1. Put steak in air fryer basket and air fry for 6 minutes at 390ºF (200ºC). Turn and cook for 5 to 6 minutes for medium rare. If you prefer your steak medium, continue cooking for another 2 to 3 minutes.
2. While the steak is cooking, make the Horseradish Mayonnaise by combining all the ingredients together.
3. When the steak is cooked, remove from the air fryer, season with salt and pepper to taste, and keep aside to rest.
4. Toss the onion slices with the oil and put in air fryer basket. Cook at 390ºF (200ºC), and set time to 5 to 7 minutes, until the onion rings are tender and browned.
5. Slice steak into very thin slices.
6. Evenly spread slider buns with the horseradish mayo and pile on the meat and onions. Serve warm with the remaining horseradish dressing for dipping.

Asian Rice Logs with Orange Marmalade

Prep time: 15 minutes | Cook time: 5 minutes | Makes 8 rice logs

1 tsp. sesame oil
1½ cups cooked jasmine or sushi rice
¾ cup panko breadcrumbs
⅓ cup plain breadcrumbs
1 egg, beaten
2 tbsps. sesame seeds
1 tbsp. tamari sauce
2 tsps. five-spice powder
2 tsps. diced shallots
2 tsps. water
¼ tsp. salt
FOR THE ORANGE MARMALADE DIPPING SAUCE:
1 tbsp. soy sauce
½ cup all-natural orange marmalade

1. Prepare the rice according to package instructions. While the rice is cooking, make the dipping sauce by mixing the marmalade and soy sauce and keep aside.
2. Stir together the cooked rice, salt, shallots, five-spice powder and tamari sauce.
3. Evenly divide rice into 8 equal pieces. With slightly damp hands, mold each piece into a log shape. Chill in freezer for about 10 to 15 minutes.
4. In a shallow bowl, mix the egg, sesame oil and water together.
5. Place the plain breadcrumbs on a sheet of wax paper.
6. Mix the panko breadcrumbs with the sesame seeds and place on another sheet of wax paper.
7. Roll the rice logs in plain breadcrumbs, then dip in egg wash, and then dip in the panko and sesame seeds.
8. Air fry for about 5 minutes at 390ºF (200ºC), until golden brown.
9. Cool slightly and serve with orange marmalade dipping sauce.

Quick Mozzarella Cheese Sticks

Prep time: 5 minutes | Cook time: 8 minutes | Serves 6

olive oil
1 (8-ounce / 227-g) package crescent roll dough
1 package Mozzarella sticks

¼ cup panko bread crumbs
3 tbsps. unsalted butter, melted
Marinara sauce, for dipping (optional)

1. Spray the air fryer basket lightly with olive oil.
2. Slice each cheese stick into thirds.
3. Unroll the crescent roll dough. Cut the dough into 36 even pieces with a pizza cutter or sharp knife.
4. Gently wrap each small cheese stick in a piece of dough. Make sure that the dough is wrapped firmly around the cheese. Pinch the dough together at both ends, and pinch along the seam to ensure that the dough is entirely sealed.
5. With tongs, dip the wrapped cheese sticks in the melted butter, then in the panko bread crumbs.
6. Arrange the cheese sticks in the greased air fryer basket in a single layer. (You will need to cook the cheese sticks in more than one batch.)
7. Air fry for about 5 minutes at 370ºF (188ºC). After 5 minutes, the top should be golden brown.
8. Flip the cheese sticks with tongs and cook for another 3 minutes, or until golden brown on all sides.
9. Repeat until you have used all the dough.
10. Transfer the cheese sticks to a plate, serve with the marinara sauce (if you like), and enjoy!

Pepper-Brined Fried Calamari

Prep time: 10 minutes | Cook time: 8 minutes | Serves 2

Cooking spray
½ pound calamari bodies and tentacles, bodies cut into ½-inch-wide rings
1 jar (8 ounces) sweet or hot pickled cherry peppers
3 large eggs, lightly beaten

2 cups all-purpose flour
½ cup mayonnaise
1 lemon
1 garlic clove, minced
1 tsp. finely chopped rosemary
Kosher salt and freshly ground black pepper, to taste

1. Pour the pickled pepper brine into a large bowl and gently tear the peppers into bite-size strips. Place the pepper strips and calamari to the brine and allow to stand in the refrigerator for about 20 minutes or up to 2 hours.
2. Grate the lemon zest into a large bowl, then whisk in the flour and season to taste with salt and pepper.

Dip the calamari and pepper strips in the egg, then in the flour mixture until evenly coated. Liberally spray the calamari and peppers with cooking spray, then take half to the air fryer. Air fry for about 8 minutes at 400ºF (205ºC), shaking the basket halfway into cooking, until the calamari is done through and golden brown. Take the calamari to a plate and repeat with the remaining pieces.
3. Whisk together the mayonnaise, rosemary, and garlic in a small bowl. Squeeze half the zested lemon, then stir the juice into the sauce. Season with salt and pepper to taste. Slice the remaining zested lemon half into 4 small wedges and serve alongside the peppers, calamari and sauce.

Crispy Potato with Spicy Tomato Ketchup

Prep time: 10 minutes | Cook time: 18 minutes | Serves 2

2 tbsps. vegetable oil
1 (12-ounce/ 340-g) large russet potato
½ cup canned crushed tomatoes
2 tbsps. apple cider vinegar
1 tbsp. dark brown sugar
1 tbsp. Worcestershire sauce

1 tbsp. hot smoked paprika
1 tsp. mild hot sauce, such as Cholula or Frank's
½ tsp. garlic powder
Kosher salt and freshly ground black pepper, to taste

1. Spiralize the potato with a spiralizer, then place in a large colander. (If you don't have a spiralizer, slice the potato into thin ⅛-inch-thick matchsticks.) Rinse the potatoes with cold running water until the water runs clear. Lay the potatoes out on a double-thick layer of paper towels and pat entirely dry.
2. Combine the potatoes, oil, paprika, and garlic powder in a large bowl. Season with salt and pepper to taste and toss to combine well. Take the potatoes to the air fryer and air fry for 15 minutes at 400ºF (205ºC) until the potatoes are browned and crisp, shaking the basket halfway through.
3. Meanwhile, puree the tomatoes, vinegar, brown sugar, Worcestershire, and hot sauce until smooth in a small blender. Add into a small saucepan or skillet and simmer over medium heat until reduced by half, about 3 to 5 minutes. Place the homemade ketchup into a bowl and allow to cool.
4. Take the spiralized potato nest from the air fryer and serve warm with the ketchup.

Honey Glazed Chicken Wings

Prep time: 10 minutes | Cook time: 24 minutes | Serves 4

8 chicken wings	onion
4 stalks celery, cut into pieces	2 cloves garlic, minced
¾ cup low sodium barbecue sauce	3 tbsps. honey
	1 tbsp. lemon juice
¼ cup thinly sliced green	1 tbsp. low sodium chicken stock

1. Pat the chicken wings dry with paper towels. Cut off the small end piece and discard or freeze it to prepare chicken stock later.
2. Place the wings into the air fryer basket. Air fry for about 20 minutes, shaking the basket twice while cooking.
3. Meanwhile, combine the honey, chicken stock, lemon juice and garlic, and whisk until combined well.
4. Take the wings from the air fryer and put into a 6" x 2" pan. Add the sauce over the wings and toss to coat well.
5. Take the pan back to the air fryer and air fry for 4 to 5 minutes more or until the wings are glazed and a food thermometer registers 165ºF (74ºC). Scatter with the green onion and serve warm with the barbecue sauce and celery.

Cinnamon Apple Wedges

Prep time: 10 minutes | Cook time: 8 minutes | Serves 4

Oil for misting or cooking spray	¼ cup pecans
	¼ cup cornstarch
1 medium apple	1½ tsps. cinnamon
1 egg white	1½ tsps. brown sugar
¼ cup panko breadcrumbs	2 tsps. water

1. Combine panko, pecans, cinnamon and brown sugar in a food processor. Process to make small crumbs.
2. Put cornstarch in a plastic bag or bowl with a lid. Beat together the egg white and water in a shallow dish, until slightly foamy.
3. Preheat air fryer to 390ºF (200ºC).
4. Cut apple into small wedges. The thickest edge should be no more than ⅜- to ½-inch thick. Discard the core, but do not peel.
5. Arrange apple wedges in cornstarch, reseal bag or bowl, and shake to coat well.
6. Dip wedges in egg wash, shake off excess, and roll in crumb mixture. Lightly spray with oil.
7. Put apples in air fryer basket in single layer and air

fry for about 5 minutes. Shake the basket and break apart any apples that have stuck together. Mist lightly with oil and cook for about 3 to 4 minutes, until crispy.

Masala Onion Rings with Lemon-Mayo Dip

Prep time: 15 minutes | Cook time: 10 minutes | Serves 2 to 4

Cooking spray	1 scallion, finely chopped
1 (14- to 16-ounce / 397- to 454-g) large red onion	2 tbsps. sweet paprika
	2 tbsps. curry powder
6 large eggs, lightly beaten	2 tbsps. finely chopped fresh mint
2 cups all-purpose flour	2 tsps. fresh lemon juice
2 cups panko breadcrumbs	2 tbsps. kosher salt, plus more as needed
½ cup mayonnaise	Salt to taste
¼ cup garam masala	Ketchup, for serving

1. Trim the ends of the onion and peel the papery outer skin away. Slice the onion crosswise into ¾- to 1-inch-thick slices, then gently separate the slices into rings, discarding the feathery skin between the rings.
2. Whisk together the garam masala, paprika, curry powder and salt in a small bowl. Put the flour, eggs, and breadcrumbs in three separate shallow bowls and season each with one-third (2 tbsps. plus 2½ tsps.) of the spice mixture. Dip 1 onion ring in the spiced egg, dredge in the flour, then repeat with the egg and flour once more. Dip the ring back into the egg again, then coat evenly in the spiced breadcrumbs. Repeat to coat all the onion rings and spread them on a wire rack set over a baking sheet. Put the onion rings in the freezer and chill until firm, at least 30 minutes or up to 1 week.
3. Meanwhile, in a bowl, whisk together the mayonnaise, mint, lemon juice, and scallion and season with salt. Refrigerate to marry the flavors in the sauce when the onion rings freeze.
4. When ready to fry, liberally spray 5 or 6 of the onion rings with cooking spray and spread them loosely in the air fryer basket, laying some flat and leaning some against the side of the basket. Air fry for 10 minutes at 375ºF (190ºC) until the onion rings are soft and the breading is golden brown and crisp. Season with more salt to taste once they come out of the fryer and continue frying as many onion rings as you like. Serve warm with the mint-mayo sauce and ketchup on the side.

Stuffed Onion with Garlic-Lemon Breadcrumb

Prep time: 10 minutes | Cook time: 15 minutes | Serves 2

1 tbsp. olive oil
1 large yellow onion
¼ cup grated Parmesan cheese
¼ cup plus 2 tbsps. panko breadcrumbs
1 garlic clove, minced
3 tbsps. mayonnaise
1 tbsp. fresh lemon juice
1 tbsp. chopped fresh flat-leaf parsley
2 tsps. whole-grain Dijon mustard
Kosher salt and freshly ground black pepper, to taste

1. Put the onion on a cutting board and trim the top off and peel off the outer skin. Turn the onion upside down and use a paring knife to cut vertical slits halfway through the onion at ½-inch intervals around the onion, keeping the root intact. The onion should open up like the petals of a flower when you turn it right side up. Spritz the cut sides of the onion with the olive oil and season with salt and pepper to taste. Put petal-side up in the air fryer and air fry for about 10 minutes at 350ºF (180ºC).
2. Meanwhile, stir together the panko, Parmesan, mayonnaise, lemon juice, parsley, mustard and garlic in a bowl, until incorporated into a smooth paste.
3. Take the onion from the fryer and stuff the paste all over and in between the onion "petals." Take the onion back to the air fryer and cook at 375ºF (190ºC) for about 5 minutes, until the onion is soft in the center and the breadcrumb mixture is golden brown. Transfer the onion to a plate and serve hot.

Cheesy Dill Pickles

Prep time: 5 minutes | Cook time: 8 minutes | Serves 4

olive oil
1 (16-ounce / 454-g) jar sliced dill pickles
2 large eggs
⅔ cup panko bread
crumbs
⅓ cup grated Parmesan cheese
¼ tsp. dried dill

1. Line a platter with a double thickness of paper towels. Lay the pickles out in a single layer on the paper towels. Allow the pickles to drain on the towels for about 20 minutes. After 20 minutes have passed, pat the pickles again with a clean paper towel to make them as dry as possible before breading.
2. Spray the air fryer basket lightly with olive oil.
3. Combine the panko bread crumbs, Parmesan cheese and dried dill in a small mixing bowl. Mix well.

4. Crack the eggs and beat until frothy in a separate small bowl.
5. Dip each pickle into the egg mixture, then into the bread crumb mixture. Make sure the pickle is thoroughly coated in breading.
6. Arrange the breaded pickle slices in the greased air fryer basket in a single layer. (You will need to fry your pickles in more than one batch.)
7. Spray the pickles gently with a generous amount of olive oil.
8. Air fry for about 4 minutes at 390ºF (200ºC).
9. Open the air fryer drawer and flip the pickles with tongs. Spray them again with olive oil. Reset the timer and air fry for 4 minutes more.
10. Remove the pickles from the drawer with tongs. Plate, serve warm and enjoy!

Sesame Seasoned Sausage Rolls

Prep time: 10 minutes | Cook time: 10 minutes | Serves 6

FOR THE SEASONING:
2 tbsps. sesame seeds
1½ tsps. dried minced onion
1½ tsps. poppy seeds
1 tsp. dried minced garlic
1 tsp. salt
1 (12-ounce / 340-g) package mini smoked sausages (cocktail franks)
1 (8-ounce / 227-g) package crescent roll dough
FOR THE SAUSAGES:

MAKE THE SEASONING:
1. Combine the sesame seeds, poppy seeds, onion, salt and garlic in a small bowl, and set aside.
MAKE THE SAUSAGES:
2. Spray the air fryer basket lightly with olive oil.
3. Take the crescent dough from the package and spread it out on a cutting board. Separate the dough at the perforations. Cut each triangle of dough into fourths with a pizza cutter or sharp knife.
4. Drain the sausages and use a paper towel to pat them dry.
5. Roll each sausage in a piece of dough.
6. Scatter seasoning on top of each roll.
7. Put the seasoned sausage rolls into the greased air fryer basket in a single layer. (You may need to cook these in at least 2 batches.)
8. Air fry for about 5 minutes at 330ºF (165ºC).
9. Remove the sausages from the air fryer and place them on a platter with tongs.
10. Repeat steps 6 through 8 with the second batch.

Crispy Carrot Chips

Prep time: 5 minutes | Cook time: 6 minutes | Serves 6

2 tbsps. olive oil
1 pound (454 g) carrots, peeled and sliced ⅛ inch thick
1 tsp. sea salt

1. Combine the carrots, olive oil and salt in a large mixing bowl. Toss them together until the carrot slices are well coated with oil.
2. Arrange the carrot chips in the air fryer basket in a single layer. (You will need to fry the carrot chips in more than one batch.)
3. Air fry for about 3 minutes at 360ºF (180ºC). Take the air fryer drawer and shake to redistribute the chips for even cooking. Reset the timer and cook for another 3 minutes.
4. Check the carrot chips for doneness. If you like them extra crispy, shake the basket again and cook them for 1 to 2 minutes more.
5. When the chips are cooked, take the air fryer basket from the drawer, pour the chips into a bowl and serve warm.

Crispy Avocado Fries

Prep time: 10 minutes | Cook time: 10 minutes | Serves 4

Oil for misting or cooking spray
1 large avocado
¾ cup panko breadcrumbs
¼ cup cornmeal
¼ cup almond or coconut milk
2 tbsps. flour
1 tbsp. lime juice
⅛ tsp. hot sauce
¼ tsp. salt

1. Whisk together the almond or coconut milk, lime juice and hot sauce in a small bowl.
2. Put flour on a sheet of wax paper.
3. Mix cornmeal, panko, and salt and place on another sheet of wax paper.
4. Split avocado in half and remove the pit. Peel or use a spoon to lift avocado halves out of the skin.
5. Slice avocado lengthwise into ½-inch slices. Dip each in flour, then milk mixture, then roll in panko mixture.
6. Mist with oil or cooking spray and air fry for about 10 minutes at 390ºF (200ºC), until the crust is brown and crispy. Serve warm.

Loaded Potato Skins with Bacon

Prep time: 10 minutes | Cook time: 12 minutes | Serves 4

Olive oil
4 medium russet potatoes, baked
2 cups shredded Cheddar cheese
4 slices cooked bacon, chopped
Sour cream, for topping
Finely chopped olives, for topping
Finely chopped scallions, for topping
Salt, to taste
Freshly ground black pepper, to taste

1. Spray the air fryer basket lightly with oil.
2. Cut each baked potato in half with a sharp knife.
3. Scoop out the center of each potato half with a large spoon, leaving about 1 inch of the potato flesh around the edges and the bottom.
4. Brush olive oil over the inside of each baked potato half and season with salt and pepper to taste, then put the potato skins in the greased air fryer basket.
5. Air fry for about 10 minutes at 400ºF (205ºC).
6. After 10 minutes, take the potato skins and place the shredded Cheddar cheese and bacon to fill them, then cook in the air fryer for 2 minutes more, just until the cheese is melted.
7. Garnish the potato skins with the scallions, olives and sour cream.

Crispy String Bean Fries

Prep time: 10 minutes | Cook time: 5 minutes | Serves 4

Oil for misting or cooking spray
½ pound (227 g) fresh string beans
½ cup white flour
½ cup breadcrumbs
2 eggs
4 tsps. water
¼ tsp. dry mustard (optional)
¼ tsp. salt
¼ tsp. ground black pepper

1. Preheat air fryer to 360ºF (180ºC).
2. Gently trim stem ends from string beans, wash and wipe dry.
3. Beat eggs and water together in a shallow dish, until well blended.
4. In a second shallow dish, add flour.
5. Stir together the breadcrumbs, salt, pepper and dry mustard (if using) in a third shallow dish.
6. Dip each string bean in egg mixture, flour, egg mixture again, then breadcrumbs.
7. When you finish coating all the string beans, open air fryer and arrange them in the basket.
8. Air fry for about 3 minutes.
9. Stop and gently mist string beans with oil or cooking spray.
10. Cook for another 2 to 3 minutes, or until the string beans are crispy and nicely browned. Serve warm.

Buffalo Cheesy Meatballs, page 117

Panko Breaded Eggplant Fries, page 124

Garlic Coated Chicken Wings, page 127

Simple Curried Chickpeas, page 124

Simple Curried Chickpeas

Prep time: 5 minutes | Cook time: 15 minutes | Makes 1 cup

1 tbsp. olive oil
1 (15-ounce / 425-g) can chickpeas, drained

2 tsps. curry powder
¼ tsp. salt

1. Drain chickpeas thoroughly and arrange in a single layer on paper towels. Use another paper towel to cover and press carefully to remove extra moisture. Don't press too hard or you'll crush the chickpeas.
2. Combine curry powder and salt together.
3. In a medium bowl, add chickpeas and season with seasonings. Stir to coat well.
4. Pour olive oil and stir again to distribute oil.
5. Air fry for about 15 minutes at 390ºF (200ºC), stopping to shake the basket about halfway through cooking time.
6. Cool entirely and store in airtight container.

Crispy Fried Peaches

Prep time: 10 minutes | Cook time: 6 minutes | Serves 4

Oil for misting or cooking spray
2 medium, very firm peaches, peeled and pitted
1 cup crisp rice cereal

2 egg whites
¼ cup cornstarch
¼ cup sliced almonds
2 tbsps. brown sugar
1 tbsp. water
½ tsp. almond extract

1. Preheat air fryer to 390ºF (200ºC).
2. In a shallow dish, beat together egg whites and water.
3. Combine the almonds, brown sugar and almond extract in a food processor. Process until the ingredients combine well and the nuts are finely chopped.
4. Place cereal and pulse just until cereal crushes. Add crumb mixture into a shallow dish or onto a plate.
5. Slice each peach into eighths and put in a plastic bag or container with a lid. Add cornstarch, seal, and shake to coat well.
6. Take peach slices from bag or container, tapping them hard to shake off the excess cornstarch. Dip in egg wash, then roll in crumbs. Lightly spray with oil.
7. Arrange in air fryer basket and air fry for 5 minutes. Shake the basket, separate any that have stuck together, and spray a little oil on any spots that aren't browning.
8. Cook for another 1 to 3 minutes, until golden brown and crispy. Serve warm.

Crispy Yellow Potato Chips

Prep time: 5 minutes | Cook time: 15 minutes | Serves 4

1 tbsp. olive oil
4 yellow potatoes

1 tbsp. salt (plus more for topping)

1. Slice the potatoes into ⅛-inch-thick slices with a mandoline or sharp knife.
2. Toss the potato slices with the olive oil and salt in a medium mixing bowl, until the potatoes are evenly coated with oil.
3. Arrange the potatoes in the air fryer basket in a single layer. (You will need to fry the potato chips in more than one batch.)
4. Air fry for 15 minutes at 375ºF (190ºC).
5. During cooking, shake the basket several times, so the chips crisp evenly and don't burn.
6. Check to see if they are fork-tender; if not, cook for 5 to 10 minutes more, checking frequently. They will crisp up when they are removed from the air fryer.
7. Season with a pinch of salt, if desired.

Panko Breaded Eggplant Fries

Prep time: 10 minutes | Cook time: 15 minutes | Serves 4

Oil for misting or cooking spray
1 medium eggplant
1 cup crushed panko breadcrumbs
1 large egg

2 tbsps. water
1 tsp. ground coriander
1 tsp. cumin
1 tsp. garlic powder
½ tsp. salt

1. Peel and slice the eggplant into fat fries, ⅜- to ½-inch thick.
2. Preheat air fryer to 390ºF (200ºC).
3. Mix together the coriander, cumin, garlic and salt in a small cup.
4. In a shallow dish, combine 1 tsp. of the seasoning mix and panko crumbs.
5. Put eggplant fries in a large bowl, season with remaining seasoning, and stir to combine well.
6. Beat eggs and water together and add over eggplant fries. Stir to coat well.
7. Remove eggplant from egg wash, shaking off excess, and roll in panko crumbs.
8. Lightly spray with oil.
9. Put half of the fries in air fryer rotisserie basket.
10. Air fry for about 5 minutes. Shake basket, mist lightly with oil, and cook for another 2 to 3 minutes, or until browned and crispy.
11. Repeat step 10 to cook the remaining eggplant.

Lemony Pita Chips

Prep time: 5 minutes | Cook time: 6 minutes | Serves 4

3 tbsps. olive oil
2 pieces whole wheat
pita bread
1 tsp. freshly squeezed
lemon juice

1 tsp. dried basil
1 tsp. garlic powder
1 tsp. Salt
your choice of dip
(optional)

1. Spray the air fryer basket lightly with olive oil.
2. Cut the pita bread into small wedges with a pair of kitchen shears or a pizza cutter.
3. In a small mixing bowl, place the wedges, olive oil, salt, lemon juice, dried basil and garlic powder.
4. Mix well, coating each wedge well.
5. Arrange the seasoned pita wedges in the greased air fryer basket in a single layer, being careful not to overcrowd them. (You will need to fry the pita chips in more than one batch.)
6. Air fry for about 6 minutes at 350ºF (180ºC). Every 2 minutes or so, take the drawer and shake the pita chips so they can redistribute in the basket for even cooking.
7. Enjoy with your choice of dip or alone as a tasty snack.

Hot Fried Dill Pickles

Prep time: 5 minutes | Cook time: 11 minutes | Makes 2 cups

Oil for misting or cooking
spray
2 cups sliced dill pickles,
well drained

¾ cup breadcrumbs
1 egg
1 tbsp. milk
¼ tsp. hot sauce

1. Preheat air fryer to 390ºF (200ºC).
2. Beat together milk, egg and hot sauce in a bowl large enough to hold all the pickles.
3. Put pickles to the egg wash and stir to coat well.
4. Add breadcrumbs in a large plastic bag or container with a lid.
5. Drain egg wash from pickles and put them in the bag with breadcrumbs. Shake to coat well.
6. Place pickles into air fryer basket and lightly spray with oil.
7. Air fry for about 5 minutes. Shake the basket and lightly spray with oil.
8. Cook for another 5 minutes. Shake and spray again. Separate any pickles that have stuck together and mist any spots you've missed.
9. Cook for 1 to 5 minutes more, or until dark golden brown and crispy. Serve warm.

Sweet-Spicy Chicken Wings

Prep time: 10 minutes | Cook time: 25 minutes | Makes 16 wings

1 tbsp. olive oil
8 chicken wings
⅓ cup brown sugar
⅓ cup apple cider
vinegar

2 cloves garlic, minced
2 tbsps. honey
½ tsp. dried red pepper
flakes
¼ tsp. salt

1. Gently cut each chicken wing into three pieces. You'll have one large piece, one medium piece, and one small end. Discard the small end or freeze it for stock.
2. Toss the wings with the oil in a medium bowl. Take to the air fryer basket and air fry for about 20 minutes, shaking the basket twice while cooking.
3. Meanwhile, combine the sugar, honey, vinegar, red pepper flakes and salt in a small bowl, and whisk until combined.
4. Take the wings from the air fryer basket and place into a 6-by-6-by-2-inch pan. Add the sauce over the wings and toss well.
5. Return to the air fryer and cook for another 5 minutes or until the wings are glazed. Serve hot.

Cheddar Cheese Bites

Prep time: 5 minutes | Cook time: 5 minutes | Makes 4 dozen

Oil for misting or cooking
spray
½ cup crisp rice cereal
½ cup flour

¼ cup butter
4 ounces (113 g) sharp
Cheddar cheese, grated
¼ tsp. salt

1. Cream the butter and grated cheese together. Use a stand mixer is faster and easier than by hands.
2. Sift flour and salt together. Place it to the cheese mixture and combine until well blended.
3. Gently stir in cereal.
4. Put dough on wax paper and shape into a long roll about 1 inch in diameter. Wrap well with wax paper and chill for at least 4 hours.
5. Once ready to cook, preheat the air fryer to 360ºF (180ºC).
6. Slice cheese roll into ¼-inch slices.
7. Spritz air fryer basket lightly with oil or cooking spray and put slices in a single layer, close but not touching.
8. Air fry for about 5 to 6 minutes, or until golden brown. When done, arrange them on paper towels to cool.
9. Repeat the previous step to cook the remaining cheese bites.

Ranch Chickpeas

Prep time: 5 minutes | Cook time: 10 minutes | Serves 4

1 tbsp. olive oil
1 (15-ounce / 425-g) can chickpeas, drained and rinsed
3 tbsps. ranch seasoning mix
2 tbsps. freshly squeezed lemon juice
1 tsp. salt

1. Spray the air fryer basket lightly with olive oil.
2. Pat the chickpeas dry with paper towels.
3. Mix together the chickpeas, oil, seasoning mix, salt and lemon juice in a medium mixing bowl.
4. Arrange the chickpeas in the air fryer basket and spread them out in a single layer. (You may need to cook the chickpeas in more than one batch.)
5. Air fry for about 4 minutes at 350ºF (180ºC). Take the drawer and shake vigorously to redistribute the chickpeas so they can cook evenly. Reset the timer and cook for another 6 minutes.
6. When the time is up, remove the air fryer basket from the drawer and transfer the chickpeas to a bowl. Season with a pinch of salt, if desired. Enjoy!

Potatoes Wedges

Prep time: 5 minutes | Cook time: 20 minutes | Serves 4

1 to 3 tbsps. olive oil, divided
4 russet potatoes
1 tsp. paprika
2 tsps. salt, divided
1 tsp. freshly ground black pepper

1. Gently cut the potatoes into ½-inch-thick wedges. Try to make the wedges uniform in size, so they can cook at an even rate.
2. Combine the potato wedges with 1 tsp. of salt, pepper, paprika and 1 tbsp. of olive oil in a medium mixing bowl. Toss until all the potatoes are thoroughly coated with oil. Pour additional oil, if needed.
3. Arrange the potato wedges in the rotisserie basket. (You will have to cook them in batches.)
4. Air fry for about 5 minutes at 400ºF (205ºC).
5. After 5 minutes, shake the potatoes to keep them from sticking. Reset the timer and cook for 5 minutes more, then shake again. Repeat this process until the potatoes have cooked for a total of 20 minutes.
6. Check and see if the potatoes are done. If they are not fork-tender, air fry for another 5 minutes.
7. Transfer the potato wedges to a bowl with tongs. Toss with the remaining salt and serve.

Greek Street Feta and Hummus Tacos

Prep time: 5 minutes | Cook time: 3 minutes | Makes 8 small tacos

Olive oil for misting
8 (4-inch diameter) small flour tortillas
8 tbsps. crumbled Feta cheese
8 tbsps. hummus
8 tbsps. chopped kalamata or other olives (optional)

1. Put 1 tbsp. of hummus in the center of each tortilla. Place 1 tsp. of Feta crumbles and 1 tsp. of chopped olives (if using) on top.
2. Use your finger or a small spoon to moisten the edges of the tortilla all around with water.
3. Gently fold tortilla over to make a half-moon shape. Press center gently. Then press the edges tightly to seal in the filling.
4. Mist both sides with olive oil.
5. Put in air fryer basket, working in 2 batches if necessary to avoid overcrowding.
6. Air fry for about 3 minutes at 390ºF (200ºC), just until lightly browned and crispy.

Turkey, Pineapple and Bell Pepper Burger Sliders

Prep time: 10 minutes | Cook time: 5 minutes | Makes 8 sliders

1 pound (454 g) ground turkey
8 slider buns
½ cup slivered green or red bell pepper
½ cup fresh chopped pineapple (or pineapple tidbits from kids' fruit cups, drained)
½ cup slivered red onions
Light cream cheese, softened
1 tsp. hoisin sauce
¼ tsp. curry powder
½ tsp. salt

1. Mix turkey, Hoisin sauce, curry powder, and salt and combine together well.
2. Form turkey mixture into 8 small patties.
3. Arrange patties in air fryer basket, working in 2 batches if necessary to avoid overcrowding. Air fry for about 5 to 7 minutes at 360ºF (180ºC), until patties are well cooked and juices run clear.
4. Put each patty on the bottom half of a slider bun and top with peppers, onions, and pineapple. Brush the remaining bun halves with cream cheese to taste, place on top and serve warm.

Authentic Tomatillo Salsa Verde

Prep time: 5 minutes | Cook time: 15 minutes | Serves 4

1 tbsp. vegetable oil
12 tomatillos
1 cup chopped fresh
cilantro leaves

2 fresh serrano chiles
1 tbsp. minced garlic
1 tsp. kosher salt

1. Remove and discard the papery husks of the tomatillos and rinse them with warm running water to remove the sticky coating.
2. Arrange the tomatillos and peppers in a 7-inch round baking pan with 4-inch sides. Put the pan in the air-fryer basket. Air fry for about 15 minutes at 350ºF (180ºC).
3. Take the tomatillos and peppers to a blender, add the cilantro, garlic, vegetable oil and salt, and blend until almost smooth. (If not used right away, omit the salt and add it just before serving.)

Garlic Coated Chicken Wings

Prep time: 15 minutes | Cook time: 13 minutes | Serves 4

Cooking spray
2 pounds (907 g) chicken
wings
FOR THE MARINADE:
1 cup buttermilk
2 cloves garlic, mashed
flat
1 bay leaf

1 tsp. Worcestershire
sauce
FOR THE COATING:
¾ cup breadcrumbs
1½ cups grated
Parmesan cheese
1½ tbsps. garlic powder
½ tsp. salt

1. Combine all the marinade ingredients together.
2. Remove the wing tips (the third joint) and discard or freeze for later use. Cut the remaining wings at the joint, then toss them into the marinade, stirring to coat well. Refrigerate for at least an hour but no more than 8 hours.
3. When ready to cook, mix all coating ingredients in a shallow dish.
4. Take wings from marinade, shaking off excess, and roll into coating mixture. Press coating into wings so that it adheres well. Lightly spray wings with oil.
5. Spray the air fryer basket with cooking spray. Put the wings in the basket in single layer, close but not touching.
6. Air fry for about 13 to 15 minutes at 360ºF (180ºC), or until the chicken is cooked and juices run clear.
7. Repeat the previous step to cook the remaining wings.

Asian-Style Chicken Wings

Prep time: 5 minutes | Cook time: 13 minutes | Serves 4

½ cup Asian-style salad
dressing
2 pounds (907 g) chicken

wings
2 tbsps. Chinese five-
spice powder

1. Cut off wing tips and discard or freeze for stock. Cut the remaining wing pieces in two at the joint.
2. Arrange wing pieces in a large sealable plastic bag. Add the Asian dressing, seal bag, and massage the marinade into the wings until coated well. Refrigerate for at least an hour.
3. Take wings from bag, drain off excess marinade, and put wings in air fryer basket.
4. Select the Poultry function, adjust time to 13 minutes, then press Start/Pause. About halfway through cooking time, shake the basket or stir wings for more even cooking.
5. Take cooked wings to plate in a single layer. Scatter half of the Chinese five-spice powder on the wings, turn, and scatter the other side with the remaining seasoning.

Chicken Tender with Blue Cheese

Prep time: 10 minutes | Cook time: 7 minutes | Serves 4

2 tbsps. olive oil
1 pound (454 g) chicken
tenders, cut into thirds
crosswise
1 cup panko bread
crumbs
⅔ cup sour cream
¼ cup crumbled blue

cheese
¼ cup creamy blue
cheese salad dressing
1 celery stalk, finely
chopped
3 tbsps. Buffalo chicken
wing sauce

1. Combine the sour cream, salad dressing, blue cheese, and celery in a small bowl, and set aside.
2. Combine the chicken pieces and Buffalo wing sauce in a medium bowl, and stir to coat well. Allow to sit while you get the bread crumbs ready.
3. On a plate, combine the bread crumbs and olive oil and mix well.
4. Coat the chicken pieces in the bread crumb mixture, patting each piece to make the crumbs adhere.
5. Air fry for about 7 to 9 minutes, shaking the basket once, until the chicken is cooked to 165ºF (74ºC) and is golden brown. Serve warm with the blue cheese sauce on the side.

Spicy Red Beets Chips

Prep time: 5 minutes | Cook time: 30 minutes | Serves 4

1 tbsp. olive oil
1 pound (454 g) red
beets, peeled and cut
into ⅛-inch slices

1 tsp. cayenne pepper
Sea salt and ground
black pepper, to taste

1. Preheat your Air Fryer to 330ºF (165ºC).
2. Toss the beets with the rest of ingredients and arrange them in the air fryer basket.
3. Air fry for about 30 minutes, shaking the basket occasionally. Work in batches.
4. Serve hot!

Parmesan Zucchini Fries

Prep time: 110 minutes | Cook time: 20 minutes | Serves 4

2 tbsps. olive oil
1 pound (454 g) zucchini,
cut into sticks
1 egg, whisked
½ cup almond flour

½ cup Parmesan cheese
1 tsp. hot paprika
Sea salt and ground
black pepper, to taste

1. Preheat your Air Fryer to 390ºF (200ºC).
2. Toss the zucchini sticks with the rest of ingredients and spread them in a single layer in the rotisserie basket.
3. Air fry for 10 minutes at 390ºF (200ºC), shaking the basket halfway through the cooking time. Work in batches.
4. Enjoy!

Bread Crumbs Stuffed Button Mushrooms

Prep time: 5 minutes | Cook time: 10 minutes | Serves 4

5 to 6 tbsps. olive oil
12 medium button
mushrooms
½ cup bread crumbs

1 tsp. salt
½ tsp. freshly ground
black pepper

1. Spray the air fryer basket lightly with olive oil.
2. Separate the cap from the stem of each mushroom, then discard the stems.
3. Combine the bread crumbs, salt, pepper and olive oil in a small mixing bowl, until you have a wet mixture.
4. Brush the mushrooms with olive oil on all sides.
5. Use a spoon to fill each mushroom with the bread crumb stuffing.
6. Arrange the mushrooms in the greased air fryer basket in a single layer.
7. Air fry for about 10 minutes at 360ºF (180ºC).
8. Remove the mushrooms from the air fryer with tongs, place them on a platter, and serve.

Sweet Cinnamon Bagel Chips

Prep time: 5 minutes | Cook time: 3 minutes | Makes 2½ cups

Butter-flavored cooking
spray
1 large plain bagel

2 tsps. sugar
1 tsp. ground cinnamon

1. Preheat air fryer to 390ºF (200ºC).
2. Cut bagel into ¼-inch slices or thinner.
3. Mix the seasonings together in a bowl.
4. Spread out the slices, spray with oil or cooking spray, and scatter with half of the seasonings.
5. Turn over and repeat to coat the other side with oil or cooking spray and seasonings.
6. Put in air fryer basket and air fry for 2 minutes at 390ºF (200ºC). Shake the basket or stir a little and continue cooking for about 1 to 2 minutes or until toasty brown and crispy.

Crispy Potato Chips

Prep time: 5 minutes | Cook time: 15 minutes | Serves 2 to 3

Oil for misting or cooking
spray
2 tsps. extra-light olive oil

2 medium potatoes
Salt and pepper, to taste

1. Peel the potatoes.
2. Shave potatoes into thin slices with a mandoline or paring knife, dropping them into a bowl of water as you cut them.
3. Use paper towels or a clean dish towel to dry potatoes as thoroughly as possible. Toss potato slices with the oil to coat completely.
4. Lightly spray air fryer basket with cooking spray and place potato slices.
5. Stir and separate by using a fork.
6. Air fry for 5 minutes at 390ºF (200ºC). Stir and separate potato slices. Cook for 5 minutes more. Stir and separate potatoes again. Cook for an additional 5 minutes.
7. Season to taste.

Mozzarella Eggplant Chips

Prep time: 10 minutes | Cook time: 15 minutes | Serves 4

2 tbsps. butter, melted
1 pound (454 g) eggplant, cut into slices
1 cup Mozzarella cheese, shredded

1 tsp. Italian seasoning
½ tsp. smoked paprika
Sea salt and ground black pepper, to taste

1. Toss the eggplant with the butter, cheese and spices. Spread the eggplant slices in the air fryer basket.
2. Air fry for 15 minutes at 400ºF (205ºC), shaking the basket halfway through the cooking time.
3. Enjoy!

Chapter 10 Desserts

Tasty Caramelized Peach Shortcakes

Prep time: 15 minutes | Cook time: 23 minutes | Serves 4

FOR THE SHORTCAKES:
Vegetable oil for spraying
1 cup self-rising flour
½ cup plus 1 tbsp. heavy cream

FOR THE CARAMELIZED PEACHES:
1 tbsp. unsalted butter, melted

2 peaches, preferably freestone
2 tsps. brown sugar
1 tsp. cinnamon

FOR THE WHIPPED CREAM:
1 cup cold heavy cream
1 tbsp. granulated sugar
Zest of 1 lime
½ tsp. vanilla extract (optional)

MAKE THE SHORTCAKES:

1. In a medium bowl, add the flour and whisk to remove any lumps. Create a well in the center of the flour. While stirring with a fork, gently pour in ½ cup plus 1 tbsp. of the heavy cream. Continue to stir until the dough has mostly come together. Gather the dough, incorporating any dry flour, and shape into a ball with your hands.

2. Put the dough on a lightly floured board and pat into a rectangle that is ½ to ¾ inch thick. Gently fold in half. Turn and repeat. Pat the dough into a ¾-inch-thick square. Slice the dough into 4 equally sized square biscuits.

3. Preheat the air fryer to 325ºF (160ºC). Spray the air fryer basket lightly with oil to prevent sticking. Arrange the biscuits in the air fryer basket. Air fry for about 15 to 18 minutes until the tops are browned and the insides completely cooked. (May be done ahead.)

MAKE THE PEACHES:

4. Cut the peaches in half and remove the pit. Brush the peach halves with the melted butter and sprinkle ½ tsp. of the brown sugar and ¼ tsp. of the cinnamon on each peach half. Arrange the peaches in a single layer in the air fryer basket. Air fry at 375ºF (190°C) for 8 to 10 minutes until the peaches are soft and the tops caramelized.

5. While the peaches are cooking, whip the cream. Add the cold heavy cream, vanilla (if using) and sugar into the bowl of a stand mixer or a metal mixing bowl. Use the whisk attachment for your stand mixer or a handheld electric mixer to beat on high speed until stiff peaks form, about 1 minute. (If you don't use the cream right away, cover with plastic wrap and refrigerate until needed.)

6. To assemble the shortcakes, slice each biscuit in half horizontally. Add a peach on the bottom half of each biscuit and put the top half on top of the peach. Place the whipped cream and a sprinkle of lime zest on top of each shortcake. Serve hot.

Strawberry Scone Shortcake with Powdered Sugar

Prep time: 10 minutes | Cook time: 20 minutes | Serves 4 to 6

1⅓ cups all-purpose flour
1⅓ cups heavy cream, chilled
1 cup quartered fresh strawberries
8 tbsps. unsalted butter, cubed and chilled
3 tbsps. granulated sugar

2 tbsps. powdered sugar, plus more for dusting
1½ tsps. baking powder
½ tsp. vanilla extract
1 tsp. kosher salt
Turbinado sugar, such as Sugar In The Raw, for sprinkling

1. Whisk together the flour, granulated sugar, baking powder and salt in a large bowl. Add the butter and break apart the butter pieces with your fingers while working them into the flour mixture, until pea-size pieces form. Add ⅔ cup of the cream over the flour mixture and mix the ingredients together with a rubber spatula, until just combined.

2. Take the dough to a work surface and shape into a 7-inch-wide disk. Brush the top with water, then scatter with some turbinado sugar. Transfer the dough to the air fryer with a large metal spatula. Select the Desserts function, adjust time to 20 minutes, then press Start/Pause, until golden brown and fluffy. Allow to cool in the air fryer basket for 5 minutes, then turn out onto a wire rack, right-side up, to cool completely.

3. Meanwhile, beat the remaining ⅔ cup cream, the powdered sugar and vanilla in a bowl, until stiff peaks form. Split the scone like a hamburger bun and lay the strawberries over the bottom. Add the whipped cream and cover with the top of the scone. Dust with powdered sugar and cut into wedges before serving.

Coconut Almond Chocolate Cake

Prep time: 15 minutes | Cook time: 20 minutes | Serves 6

nonstick cooking spray
1 stick butter, melted
2 eggs, at room temperature
½ cup almond flour
½ cup brown sugar
¼ cup cocoa powder
¼ cup all-purpose flour
5 ounces (142 g)

chocolate chips
2 ounces (57 g) almonds, slivered
4 tbsps. coconut milk
½ tsp. pure almond extract
½ tsp. pure vanilla extract
½ tsp. baking powder

1. Preheat your Air Fryer to 340ºF (170ºC). Then, lightly spray the sides and bottom of a baking pan with a nonstick cooking spray.
2. Beat the butter and sugar until fluffy in a mixing bowl. Next, gently fold in the eggs and beat again until combined well.
3. After that, place the remaining ingredients. Mix until everything is well combined.
4. Select the Desserts function, adjust time to 20 minutes, then press Start/Pause. Enjoy!

Spoon Chocolate Brownies

Prep time: 10 minutes | Cook time: 30 minutes | Serves 4 to 6

1 cup granulated sugar
2 large eggs, lightly beaten
½ cup roughly chopped bittersweet chocolate
⅓ cup Dutch-process cocoa powder
¼ cup all-purpose flour

8 tbsps. unsalted butter, melted
1 tsp. vanilla extract
½ tsp. kosher salt
Vanilla ice cream and flaky sea salt (optional), for serving

1. Whisk together the sugar, cocoa powder and salt in a bowl. Then place the vanilla, melted butter, and eggs and whisk until smooth. Stir in the flour and chocolate and drop the batter into a 7-inch round cake or pizza pan insert, or metal cake pan. Put the pan in the air fryer and cook for about 30 minutes at 310ºF (154ºC), until the brownie "pudding" is set at the edges but still jiggly in the middle (it may form a "skin" in the middle, but it doesn't affect the taste).
2. Allow the brownie pan to cool in the air fryer for 5 minutes, enough time to grab some bowls and let the ice cream soften to the perfect scooping consistency. Divide the gooey brownies evenly between serving bowls and top with a scoop of ice cream and a

decent pinch of flaky sea salt, if you like.

Persian Doughnuts with Saffron Syrup

Prep time: 10 minutes | Cook time: 27 minutes | Makes 18 to 20 doughnuts

FOR THE DOUGHNUTS:
Vegetable oil for spraying
2 eggs
1 cup all-purpose flour
1 cup water
3 tbsps. unsalted butter
1 tbsp. granulated sugar

FOR THE SYRUP:
1 cup granulated sugar
¾ cup water
Pinch saffron threads dissolved in ¼ cup boiling water
1 tsp. rose water

1. In a medium saucepan, combine the butter, sugar and water and melt the butter over low heat. Place the flour and stir to form a cohesive dough. Cook over medium-low heat for about 2 minutes to get rid of the raw flour taste. Turn off the heat and let cool to room temperature. Beat the eggs in one at a time, making sure the first egg is entirely incorporated before the adding the second. The dough will look curdled at first, but keep beating vigorously until the dough turns smooth. Once the eggs are completely incorporated, allow the dough to rest for 30 minutes.
2. While the dough is resting, make the rose water syrup. In a small saucepan, combine the sugar and water and bring to a boil, stirring to dissolve the sugar. Reduce the heat and simmer for about 5 minutes until thickened. Turn off the heat and pour the rose water and 1 tbsp. of the saffron water, reserving the remaining saffron water for another use, such as rice pilaf. Keep warm.
3. Once the dough has rested, put the dough in a piping bag outfitted with a large, star-shaped tip. Lightly spray the air fryer basket with oil. Pipe the dough directly onto the air fryer basket, forming doughnuts about 3 inches long and 1 inch wide. Cut the dough with a knife or scissors when you have achieved the desired length. Work in batches so as not to overcrowd the basket. Spritz lightly with oil. Air fry for about 10 to 12 minutes at 360ºF (180ºC), shaking the basket once or twice, until the outside of the doughnuts is golden brown and the inside is completely cooked and airy.
4. In a shallow bowl, pour the warm syrup and place the first batch of doughnuts in the syrup. Let them soak for about 5 minutes, then take to a plate or platter. Repeat the process with the remaining dough and syrup. Enjoy!

Lemony Apple Cake

Prep time: 15 minutes | Cook time: 30 minutes | Serves 6

Vegetable oil
2 cups diced peeled Gala apples
1¼ cups unbleached all-purpose flour
2 large eggs
⅓ cup granulated sugar
¼ cup unsalted butter, softened
¼ cup whole milk

1 tbsp. fresh lemon juice
1 tbsp. apple pie spice
1½ tsps. baking powder
½ tsp. ground ginger
¼ tsp. ground cardamom
¼ tsp. ground nutmeg
½ tsp. kosher salt
Confectioners' sugar, for dusting

1. Grease a 3-cup Bundt pan with oil and keep aside.
2. Toss the apples with the lemon juice until well coated in a medium bowl, keep aside.
3. Combine the butter and sugar in a large bowl. Use an electric hand mixer to beat on a medium speed until the sugar has fully dissolved. Place the eggs and beat until fluffy. Put the flour, baking powder, apple pie spice, ginger, nutmeg, cardamom, salt and milk. Mix until the batter is thick but pourable.
4. Add the batter into the prepared pan. Top batter evenly with the apple mixture. Put the pan in the air fryer basket. Air fry for about 30 minutes at 350ºF (180ºC), or until a toothpick inserted in the center of the cake comes out clean. Turn off the air fryer and allow the cake to rest for 10 minutes. Turn the cake out onto a wire rack and let cool completely.
5. Dust the cake with confectioners' sugar before serving.

Frosted Chocolate Cookie with Peanut Butter

Prep time: 10 minutes | Cook time: 8 minutes | Serves 4

3 tbsps. butter, at room temperature
1 egg yolk
⅔ cup flour
½ cup semisweet chocolate chips

⅓ cup plus 1 tbsp. brown sugar
5 tbsps. peanut butter, divided
1 tsp. vanilla
¼ tsp. baking soda

1. Beat the butter and brown sugar together until fluffy in a medium bowl. Stir in the egg yolk.
2. Place the flour, 3 tbsps. of peanut butter, vanilla and baking soda, and mix well.
3. Line a 6-by-6-by-2-inch baking pan with parchment paper.

4. Lay the batter into the prepared pan, leaving a ½-inch border on all sides.
5. Air fry for about 7 to 10 minutes, or until the cookie is light brown and just barely set.
6. Take the pan from the air fryer and allow to cool for about 10 minutes. Remove the cookie from the pan, remove the parchment paper, and allow to cool on a wire rack.
7. Combine the chocolate chips with the remaining 2 tbsps. of peanut butter in a small heatproof cup. Cook for another 1 to 2 minutes or until the chips are melted. Stir to combine well and spread on the cookie. Enjoy!

Raisin Apple Turnovers

Prep time: 10 minutes | Cook time: 45 minutes | Serves 4

1 pound (454 g) frozen puff pastry, defrosted according to package instructions
1 egg beaten with 1 tbsp. water
3½ ounces (99 g) dried apples

¼ cup golden raisins
1 tbsp. freshly squeezed lemon juice
1 tbsp. granulated sugar
Turbinado or demerara sugar for sprinkling
½ tsp. cinnamon

1. In a medium saucepan, add the dried apples and cover with 2 cups water. Bring the mixture to a boil over medium-high heat, then turn the heat to low, cover, and simmer for about 20 minutes, until the apples have absorbed most of the liquid. Take the apples from the heat and let cool. Add the raisins, lemon juice, sugar and cinnamon to the rehydrated apples and keep aside.
2. Gently roll the puff pastry out to a 12-inch square on a well-floured board. Slice the square into 4 equal quarters. Divide the filling evenly among the 4 squares, mounding it in the middle of each square. Use water to brush the edges of each square and fold the pastry diagonally over the apple mixture, making a triangle. Seal the edges by using the tines of a fork to press them. Take the turnovers to a sheet pan lined with parchment paper.
3. Use egg wash to brush the top of 2 turnovers and sprinkle with turbinado sugar. Create 2 small slits in the top of the turnovers for venting and air fry for about 25 to 30 minutes at 325ºF (160ºC), until the top is browned and puffed and the pastry is cooked through. Transfer the cooked turnovers to a cooling rack and cook the remaining 2 turnovers in the same manner. Enjoy!

Lavender Lemon Doughnuts

Prep time: 10 minutes | Cook time: 10 minutes | Makes 6 to 8 doughnuts

Vegetable oil for spraying divided
1 egg
2 cups all-purpose flour
1½ cups powdered sugar, sifted
½ cup milk, warmed to between 100°F and 110°F (38°C to 43°C)
¼ cup granulated sugar,
Zest and juice of 1 lemon
4 tbsps. unsalted butter, melted
1 tsp. yeast
½ tsp. kosher salt
Dried lavender for culinary use (optional)

1. In a small bowl, combine the warm milk, yeast and a pinch of the sugar and whisk to combine well. Let sit for about 5 to 10 minutes until the yeast blooms and looks bubbly. Meanwhile, whisk together the remaining sugar, salt and flour. Place the zest of the lemon to the dry ingredients.
2. When the yeast has bloomed, pour the milk mixture to the dry ingredients and stir to combine well. Place the melted butter and the egg and stir to form a thick dough. Turn the dough onto a well-floured board and knead for 1 to 2 minutes until smooth. Put the dough in an oiled bowl, cover, and let rise in the refrigerator overnight.
3. The following day, take the dough from the refrigerator and let it come to room temperature. Turn the risen dough out onto a well-floured board. Roll the dough out until it is about ¼ inch thick. Cut out as many doughnuts as possible with a 3- or 4-inch circular cookie cutter. Then cut out holes in the center of each doughnut with a 1-inch round cookie cutter. With the dough scraps, you can either cut out extra doughnut holes by using a 1-inch cutter or, if desired, gather the scraps and roll them out again to cut out more doughnuts. (The doughnuts from the rerolled scraps will not rise as well as the other doughnuts.)
4. Take the doughnuts and doughnut holes to a lined baking sheet. Use a clean kitchen towel to cover and let proof in a warm place for about 30 minutes to 1 hour, until puffy and, when pressed with a finger, the dough slowly springs back.
5. While the dough is proofing, make the glaze. Whisk together the sifted powdered sugar and the juice from the lemon in a medium bowl. Keep aside.
6. When the doughnuts have proofed, spray the air fryer basket lightly with oil. Take no more than 3 or 4 of the doughnuts and 2 or 3 of the holes to the air fryer basket. Lightly spray the doughnuts with oil. Air fry for about 5 to 6 minutes at 360ºF (180ºC), gently flipping once halfway through, until browned and cooked through. Take the cooked doughnuts and holes to a cooling rack and repeat with the remaining doughnuts and holes.
7. When the doughnuts are cool enough to handle, dip the tops into the glaze. Take the dipped doughnuts back to the rack to let the excess glaze drip off. Once the glaze has hardened, dip each doughnut again to create a nice opaque finish. When the second glaze is still wet, scatter a few buds of lavender on top of each doughnut, if desired.

Simple Brownies with a Twist

Prep time: 10 minutes | Cook time: 20 minutes | Serves 6

1 stick butter, melted
2 eggs
1 cup brown sugar
¾ cup all-purpose flour
¼ cup cocoa powder
2 tbsps. coconut oil
1 tsp. coconut extract
½ tsp. baking powder
A pinch of sea salt

1. Preheat your Air Fryer to 340ºF (170ºC). Now, lightly spray the sides and bottom of a baking pan with a nonstick cooking spray.
2. Beat the melted butter and sugar until fluffy in a mixing bowl. Next, gently fold in the eggs and beat again until combined well.
3. After that, place the remaining ingredients. Mix until everything is entirely incorporated.
4. Air fry for about 20 minutes at 340ºF (170ºC). Enjoy!

Lemony Apple Pie

Prep time: 10 minutes | Cook time: 35 minutes | Serves 4

3 cups apples, peeled and thinly sliced
12 ounces (340 g) refrigerated 2 pie crusts
¼ cup brown sugar
1 tbsp. lemon juice
½ tsp. cinnamon
1 tsp. pure vanilla extract
A pinch of ground cardamom
A pinch of kosher salt

1. Put the first pie crust in a lightly greased pie plate.
2. Make the filling by thoroughly combining the remaining ingredients in a mixing bowl. Scoop the filling into the prepared pie crust.
3. Unroll the second pie crust and put it on top of the filling.
4. Select the Desserts function, adjust time to 35 minutes, then press Start/Pause, until the top is golden brown. Bon appétit!

Cinnamon Coconut Pancake Cups

Prep time: 10 minutes | Cook time: 5 minutes | Serves 4

1 tbsp. coconut oil, melted
2 eggs
½ cup flour
⅓ cup coconut milk
1 tsp. vanilla paste
¼ tsp. ground cinnamon
A pinch of ground cardamom
your favorite toppings

1. Mix all the ingredients until combined well.
2. Allow the batter to stand for 20 minutes. Scoop the batter into a greased muffin tin.
3. Air fry for about 4 to 5 minutes at 330ºF (165ºC), or until golden brown. Serve with your favorite toppings.
4. Bon appétit!

Pumpkin Bread Pudding

Prep time: 15 minutes | Cook time: 50 minutes | Serves 6

FOR THE BREAD PUDDING:
4 tbsps. unsalted butter, melted
4 cups 1-inch cubed day-old baguette or crusty country bread
1 large egg plus 1 yolk
¾ cup heavy whipping cream
½ cup canned pumpkin
⅓ cup whole milk
⅓ cup sugar
½ tsp. pumpkin pie spice
⅛ tsp. kosher salt
FOR THE SAUCE:
½ cup heavy whipping cream
⅓ cup pure maple syrup
1 tbsp. unsalted butter
½ tsp. pure vanilla extract

MAKE THE BREAD PUDDING:
1. Combine the cream, pumpkin, milk, sugar, egg and yolk, pumpkin pie spice and salt in a medium bowl. Whisk until well combined.
2. Toss the bread cubes with the melted butter in a large bowl. Place the pumpkin mixture and gently toss until the ingredients are fully combined.
3. Take the mixture to an ungreased 6 × 3-inch heatproof pan. Put the pan in the air fryer basket. Air fry for about 35 minutes at 350ºF (180ºC), or until custard is set in the middle.
MAKE THE SAUCE:
4. Combine the syrup and butter in a small saucepan. Heat over medium heat, stirring, until the butter melts. Stir in the cream and simmer, stirring often, until the sauce has thickened, for about 15 minutes. Stir in the vanilla. Take the pudding from the air fryer.
5. Allow the pudding to stand for 10 minutes before serving with the warm sauce.

Coconut Chia Chocolate Cake

Prep time: 10 minutes | Cook time: 20 minutes | Serves 6

nonstick cooking spray
½ cup coconut oil, room temperature
2 chia eggs (2 tbsps. ground chia seeds + 4 tbsps. water)
1 cup brown sugar
½ cup cocoa powder
½ cup dark chocolate chips
¼ cup all-purpose flour
¼ cup coconut flour
2 tbsps. coconut milk
A pinch of grated nutmeg
A pinch of sea salt

1. Preheat your Air Fryer to 340ºF (170ºC). Now, lightly spray the sides and bottom of a baking pan with a nonstick cooking spray.
2. Beat the coconut oil and brown sugar until fluffy in a mixing bowl. Next, gently fold in the chia eggs and beat again until combined well.
3. After that, place the remaining ingredients. Mix until everything is entirely incorporated.
4. Select the Desserts function, adjust time to 20 minutes, then press Start/Pause. Enjoy!

Honey Basil Strawberry Tart

Prep time: 5 minutes | Cook time: 25 minutes | Serves 2

1 pound (454 g) strawberries, hulled and thinly sliced
1 sheet frozen puff pastry, thawed according to package instructions
1 egg beaten with 1 tbsp. water
1 sprig basil
1 tbsp. honey
1 tbsp. balsamic vinegar

1. Put the strawberries in a 7-inch round pizza pan insert for the air fryer and slightly mound them in the center. Whisk together the balsamic vinegar and honey in a small bowl. Pour the mixture over the strawberries. Slice the leaves of basil into ribbons and scatter them over the strawberries.
2. Cut out an 8-inch square from the sheet of puff pastry. Carefully drape the pastry over the strawberries in the pan. Use the tines of a fork to poke holes in the puff pastry. With the egg wash, brush the top of the pastry. Put the pan in the air fryer basket.
3. Select the Desserts function, adjust time to 27 minutes, then press Start/Pause, until the top of the pastry is golden brown and glossy and the underside of the pastry is cooked. Take the pan from the air fryer basket. Slice the pastry in half and distribute the dessert among 2 plates. Serve warm.

Coconut Almond Chocolate Cake, page 132

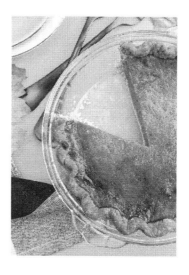

Autumn Walnut Pumpkin Pie, page 139

Chocolate Cupcakes with Raisin, page 139

Spoon Chocolate Brownies, page 132

Vanilla Apple Wedges

Prep time: 5 minutes | Cook time: 17 minutes | Serves 2

2 tsps. coconut oil
2 apples, peeled, cored, and cut into wedges
¼ cup water
2 tbsps. brown sugar
1 tsp. pure vanilla extract
1 tsp. ground cinnamon

1. Toss the apples with the coconut oil, vanilla, sugar and cinnamon.
2. Add ¼ cup water into an Air Fryer safe dish. Put the apples in the dish.
3. Air fry for about 17 minutes at 340ºF (170ºC). Serve at room temperature. Enjoy!

Buttery Vanilla French Toast

Prep time: 10 minutes | Cook time: 7 minutes | Serves 3

2 tbsps. butter, melted
1 egg, whisked
3 slices bread
¼ cup coconut milk
1 tsp. vanilla paste
½ tsp. ground cinnamon
A pinch of grated nutmeg

1. Thoroughly combine the eggs, milk, butter, vanilla, cinnamon, and nutmeg in a mixing bowl.
2. Dip each piece of bread into the egg mixture, then put the bread slices in a lightly greased baking pan.
3. Air fry 4 minutes for 330ºF (165ºC). Turn them over and cook for 3 to 4 minutes more. Serve warm!

Vanilla Pumpkin Cake

Prep time: 5 minutes | Cook time: 13 minutes | Serves 2

2 eggs, beaten
⅓ cup pumpkin puree
½ cup peanut butter
1 tsp. vanilla extract
½ tsp. pumpkin pie spice
½ tsp. baking powder

1. Make the batter by mixing all the ingredients. Place the batter into a lightly oiled baking pan.
2. Put the pan in the air fryer basket.
3. Select the Desserts function, adjust time to 13 minutes, then press Start/Pause, until it is golden brown around the edges.
4. Enjoy!

Cinnamon Peaches

Prep time: 10 minutes | Cook time: 15 minutes | Serves 3

4 tbsps. coconut oil
3 peaches, halved
½ cup brown sugar
¼ cup water
1 tbsp. fresh lime juice
½ tsp. ground cinnamon
½ tsp. grated nutmeg

1. Toss the peaches with the rest of ingredients, except for water.
2. Add ¼ cup water into an Air Fryer safe dish. Put the peaches in the dish.
3. Select the Desserts function, adjust time to 15 minutes, then press Start/Pause. Serve warm!

German Giant Apple Pancake

Prep time: 10 minutes | Cook time: 13 minutes | Serves 3

1 tbsp. coconut oil, melted
1 small apple, peeled, cored, and sliced
1 egg, whisked
¼ cup full-fat coconut milk
¼ cup plain flour
½ tsp. vanilla paste
¼ tsp. baking powder
A pinch of granulated sugar
A pinch of kosher salt

1. Spray the apple slices with the melted coconut oil, then spread the apple slices in a baking pan.
2. Make the batter by mixing the remaining ingredients. Add the batter over the apples. Take the baking pan to the air fryer basket.
3. Select the Desserts function, adjust time to 13 minutes, then press Start/Pause, until it is golden brown around the edges.
4. Enjoy!

Chocolate Cupcakes

Prep time: 10 minutes | Cook time: 15 minutes | Serves 6

1 stick butter, at room temperature
2 eggs, beaten
¾ cup milk
¾ cup all-purpose flour
¾ cup granulated sugar
¼ cup unsweetened cocoa powder
1 tsp. baking powder
¼ tsp. ground cinnamon
A pinch of sea salt

1. Preheat your Air Fryer to 330ºF (165ºC).
2. In a bowl, mix all the ingredients. Scrape the batter into silicone baking molds, then put them in the air fryer basket.
3. Select the Desserts function, adjust time to 15 minutes, then press Start/Pause, until a tester comes out dry and clean.
4. Let the cupcakes cool before unmolding and serving. Bon appétit!

Brown Sugar Fried Plums

Prep time: 5 minutes | Cook time: 17 minutes | Serves 4

2 tbsps. coconut oil
1 pound (454 g) plums,
halved and pitted
4 tbsps. brown sugar

4 whole cloves
4 whole star anise
1 cinnamon stick

1. Toss the plums with the rest of ingredients.
2. Add ¼ cup water into an Air Fryer safe dish. Arrange the plums in the dish.
3. Air fry for 17 minutes at 340ºF (170ºC). Serve at room temperature. Enjoy!

Authentic Thai Goreng Pisang

Prep time: 10 minutes | Cook time: 13 minutes | Serves 2

2 tsps. coconut oil
2 eggs, whisked
2 bananas, peeled and
sliced
4 tbsps. rice flour

4 tbsps. all-purpose flour
4 tbsps. coconut flakes
¼ tsp. ground cinnamon
A pinch of sea salt
A pinch of grated nutmeg

1. Preheat your Air Fryer to 390ºF (200ºC).
2. Thoroughly combine the two flours, cinnamon, salt, nutmeg, and coconut flakes in a mixing dish.
3. Now, place the coconut oil and eggs. Roll each slice of banana over the egg and flour mixture.
4. Select the Desserts function, adjust time to 13 minutes, then press Start/Pause, turning them over halfway through the cooking time. Enjoy!

Classic Spanish Churros

Prep time: 10 minutes | Cook time: 10 minutes | Serves 4

1 large egg
¾ cup all-purpose flour
¾ cup water
4 tbsps. butter

1 tbsp. granulated sugar
½ tsp. vanilla extract
½ tsp. baking powder
½ tsp. sea salt

1. Thoroughly combine all the ingredients in a mixing bowl. Put the batter in a piping bag fitted with a large open star tip.
2. Pipe the churros into 6-inch long ropes and place them onto the greased Air Fryer pan.
3. Air fry for about 10 minutes at 360ºF (180ºC), gently flipping them halfway through the cooking time.
4. Repeat with the remaining batter and serve hot. Enjoy!

Homemade Banana Fritters

Prep time: 5 minutes | Cook time: 10 minutes | Serves 1

1 tbsp. coconut oil
1 banana, mashed
1 egg, beaten

1 tbsp. brown sugar
¼ tsp. ground cinnamon

1. Thoroughly combine all the ingredients in a mixing bowl.
2. Scoop the batter into a lightly greased Air Fryer pan.
3. Air fry for about 10 minutes at 360ºF (180ºC), gently flipping it halfway through the cooking time.
4. Enjoy!

Simple Colorful Fruit Skewers

Prep time: 10 minutes | Cook time: 10 minutes | Serves 4

2 tbsps. coconut oil,
melted
1 cup pineapple, cut into
1-inch chunks
1 cup melon, cut into
1-inch chunks

1 peach, cut into 1-inch
chunks
1 banana, cut into 1-inch
chunks
2 tbsps. honey

1. Toss your fruits with the honey and coconut oil.
2. Thread the fruits onto skewers and put them in the air fryer basket.
3. Then air fry for about 10 minutes at 400ºF (205ºC), turning them over halfway through the cooking time.
4. Enjoy!

Classic American-Style Crullers

Prep time: 10 minutes | Cook time: 20 minutes | Serves 4

3 eggs, beaten
¾ cup all-purpose flour
½ cup full-fat milk
¼ cup butter

¼ cup water
A pinch of grated nutmeg
¼ tsp. kosher salt

1. Thoroughly combine all the ingredients in a mixing bowl. Put the batter in a piping bag fitted with a large open star tip.
2. Pipe your crullers into circles and place them onto the greased Air Fryer pan.
3. Air fry for about 10 minutes at 360ºF (180ºC), gently flipping them halfway through the cooking time.
4. Repeat with the remaining batter and serve warm. Enjoy!

Indian Unnakai Malabar

Prep time: 5 minutes | Cook time: 13 minutes | Serves 1

1 tbsp. ghee
1 plantain, peeled
¼ cup coconut flakes

2 tbsps. brown sugar
¼ tsp. cardamom powder
¼ tsp. cinnamon powder

1. Start by preheating your Air Fryer to 390ºF (200ºC).
2. Toss the plantain with the rest of ingredients.
3. Air fry for about 13 minutes at 390ºF (200ºC), gently flipping it halfway through the cooking time.
4. Enjoy!

Pumpkin Cake with Honey

Prep time: 10 minutes | Cook time: 13 minutes | Serves 3

1 egg, beaten
¼ cup canned pumpkin
¼ cup milk
4 tbsps. all-purpose flour
4 tbsps. almond flour

4 tbsps. honey
1 tsp. baking powder
1 tsp. pumpkin pie spice blend
A pinch of Himalayan salt

1. Make the batter by mixing all the ingredients. Add the batter into a lightly oiled baking pan.
2. Put the pan in the air fryer basket.
3. Select the Desserts function, adjust time to 13 minutes, then press Start/Pause, until it is golden brown around the edges.
4. Enjoy!

Autumn Walnut Pumpkin Pie

Prep time: 10 minutes | Cook time: 35 minutes | Serves 4

12 ounces (340 g) refrigerated 2 pie crusts
½ cup pumpkin puree, canned
½ cup granulated sugar
1 ounce (28 g) walnuts,

coarsely chopped
1 tsp. fresh ginger, peeled and grated
1 tsp. pumpkin pie spice mix

1. Put the first pie crust in a lightly greased pie plate.
2. Make the filling by thoroughly combining the remaining ingredients in a mixing bowl. Scoop the filling into the prepared pie crust.
3. Unroll the second pie crust and put it on top of the filling.
4. Select the Desserts function, adjust time to 35 minutes, then press Start/Pause, until the top is golden brown. Enjoy!

Sweet Vanilla Pears in Red Wine

Prep time: 5 minutes | Cook time: 17 minutes | Serves 3

3 pears, peeled and cored
1 cup caster sugar
1 cup red wine

2 to 3 cloves
1 vanilla pod
1 cinnamon stick

1. Add the pears, cinnamon, vanilla, cloves, sugar and wine in an Air Fryer safe dish.
2. Air fry for about 17 minutes at 340ºF (170ºC).
3. Serve at room temperature. Enjoy!

Homemade Cinnamon Rolls

Prep time: 5 minutes | Cook time: 10 minutes | Serves 4

1 tbsp. coconut oil
9 ounces (255 g) refrigerated crescent rolls

4 tbsps. caster sugar
1 tsp. ground cinnamon

1. Separate the dough into rectangles. Mix the rest of ingredients until combined well.
2. Brush each rectangle with the cinnamon mixture, then roll them up firmly.
3. Put the rolls in the air fryer basket.
4. Select the Desserts function, adjust time to 5 minutes, then press Start/Pause, turn them over and cook for 5 minutes more.
5. Enjoy!

Chocolate Cupcakes with Raisin

Prep time: 15 minutes | Cook time: 15 minutes | Serves 4

4 tbsps. coconut oil
2 eggs, whisked
¾ cup brown sugar
¾ cup all-purpose flour
¾ cup yogurt
½ cup unsweetened cocoa powder

2 tbsps. raisins
¼ tsp. grated nutmeg
½ tsp. ground cinnamon
½ tsp. vanilla extract
½ tsp. baking powder
A pinch of kosher salt

1. Preheat your Air Fryer to 330ºF (165ºC).
2. In a bowl, mix all the ingredients. Scrape the batter into silicone baking molds, then put them in the air fryer basket.
3. Select the Desserts function, adjust time to 15 minutes, then press Start/Pause, until a tester comes out dry and clean.
4. Let the cupcakes cool before unmolding and serving. Bon appétit!

Buttery Pears Sticks

Prep time: 5 minutes | Cook time: 17 minutes | Serves 2

2 tbsps. butter
2 pears, peeled, cored, and cut into sticks
1 tsp. fresh ginger, grated

½ tsp. ground cinnamon
A pinch of grated nutmeg
A pinch of sea salt

1. Toss the pears with the rest of ingredients.
2. Add ¼ cup water into an Air Fryer safe dish. Put the pears in the dish.
3. Air fry for about 17 minutes at 340ºF (170ºC). Let cool before serving. Enjoy!

Banana Fritters

Prep time: 10 minutes | Cook time: 10 minutes | Serves 4

4 tbsps. butter
1 banana, mashed
¾ cup all-purpose flour
¾ cup water

1 tbsp. rum
1 tbsp. caster sugar
¼ tsp. grated nutmeg
¼ tsp. salt

1. Thoroughly combine all the ingredients in a mixing bowl.
2. Pour a spoonful of batter onto the greased Air Fryer pan. Air fry for about 10 minutes at 360ºF (180ºC), gently flipping them halfway through the cooking time.
3. Repeat with the remaining batter and serve hot. Enjoy!

Healthy Blueberry Fritters

Prep time: 10 minutes | Cook time: 10 minutes | Serves 4

2 tbsps. melted butter
1 egg
¾ cup all-purpose flour
½ cup coconut milk
2 ounces (57 g) fresh

blueberries
2 tbsps. coconut sugar
1 tsp. baking powder
A pinch of sea salt

1. Thoroughly combine all the ingredients in a mixing bowl.
2. Pour a spoonful of batter onto the greased Air Fryer pan. Air fry for about 10 minutes at 360ºF (180ºC), gently flipping them halfway through the cooking time.
3. Repeat with the remaining batter and serve hot. Enjoy!

Cinnamon Banana Slices

Prep time: 5 minutes | Cook time: 13 minutes | Serves 1

1 tbsp. coconut oil
1 banana, peeled and sliced

2 tbsps. granulated sugar
½ tsp. ground cinnamon
½ tsp. ground cloves

1. Start by preheating your Air Fryer to 390ºF (200ºC).
2. Toss banana slices with the rest of ingredients.
3. Air fry for about 13 minutes at 390ºF (200ºC), gently flipping them halfway through the cooking time.
4. Enjoy!

Simple Beignets

Prep time: 10 minutes | Cook time: 10 minutes | Serves 4

2 tbsps. coconut oil, melted
2 eggs, beaten
¾ cup all-purpose flour

¼ cup yogurt
¼ cup granulated sugar
1 tsp. baking powder
¼ tsp. kosher salt

1. Thoroughly combine all the ingredients in a mixing bowl.
2. Pour a spoonful of batter onto the greased Air Fryer pan. Select the Desserts function, adjust time to 10 minutes, then press Start/Pause, gently flipping them halfway through the cooking time.
3. Repeat with the remaining batter and serve hot. Enjoy!

Old-Fashioned Stuffed Apples with Pecans

Prep time: 10 minutes | Cook time: 17 minutes | Serves 2

2 tbsps. butter, at room temperature
2 medium apples
4 tbsps. pecans, chopped

4 tbsps. Sultanas
½ tsp. cinnamon
¼ tsp. grated nutmeg

1. Slice the apples in halves and scoop out some of the flesh.
2. Thoroughly combine the remaining ingredients in a mixing bowl. Stuff the apple halves and take them to the air fryer basket.
3. Add ¼ cup water into an Air Fryer safe dish. Put the apples in the dish.
4. Air fry for about 17 minutes at 340ºF (170ºC). Serve at room temperature. Enjoy!

Quick French Dessert

Prep time: 10 minutes | Cook time: 7 minutes | Serves 2

2 tbsps. coconut oil, melted
2 eggs
4 thick slices baguette

¼ cup milk
½ tsp. vanilla extract
¼ tsp. ground cinnamon
⅛ tsp. ground nutmeg

1. Thoroughly combine the eggs, coconut oil, milk, vanilla, cinnamon and nutmeg in a mixing bowl.
2. Dip each piece of bread into the egg mixture, then put the bread slices in a lightly greased baking pan.
3. Select the Desserts function, adjust time to 4 minutes, then press Start/Pause, turn them over and cook for 3 to 4 minutes more. Enjoy!

Honey Yogurt and Walnut Stuffed Pears

Prep time: 10 minutes | Cook time: 17 minutes | Serves 2

2 pears
2 ounces (57 g) Greek-style yogurt
2 tbsps. honey
2 tbsps. walnuts,

chopped
¼ tsp. ground cinnamon
¼ tsp. cloves
⅛ tsp. grated nutmeg

1. Slice the pears in half and scoop out some of the flesh.
2. Thoroughly combine the remaining ingredients in a mixing bowl. Stuff the pear halves and take them to the air fryer basket.
3. Add ¼ cup water into an Air Fryer safe dish. Put the pears in the dish.
4. Air fry for about 17 minutes at 340ºF (170ºC). Let the pears cool before serving. Bon appétit!

Cinnamon Cherry

Prep time: 5 minutes | Cook time: 20 minutes | Serves 4

1 tbsp. coconut oil
2 cups cherries, pitted
4 tbsps. brown sugar

¼ tsp. ground cinnamon
2 tbsps. bourbon

1. Toss the cherries with the rest of ingredients, then arrange cherries in a lightly greased baking dish.
2. Air fry for about 20 minutes at 370ºF (188ºC).
3. Let the cherries cool before serving. Bon appétit!

Favorite Chocolate Fudge Cake

Prep time: 10 minutes | Cook time: 20 minutes | Serves 5

nonstick cooking spray
3 eggs
1 cup turbinado sugar
½ cup butter, melted
½ cup all-purpose flour
5 ounces (142 g)

chocolate chips
¼ cup almond flour
1 tsp. vanilla extract
½ tsp. ground cinnamon
¼ tsp. ground cloves
¼ tsp. salt

1. Preheat your Air Fryer to 340ºF (170ºC). Now, lightly spray the sides and bottom of a baking pan with a nonstick cooking spray.
2. Beat the butter and sugar until fluffy in a mixing bowl. Next, gently fold in the eggs and beat again until combined well.
3. After that, place the remaining ingredients. Mix until everything is well combined.
4. Select the Desserts function, adjust time to 20 minutes, then press Start/Pause. Enjoy!

Appendix 1: Measurement Conversion Chart

Volume Equivalents (Dry)

US STANDARD	METRIC (APPROXIMATE)
1/8 teaspoon	0.5 mL
1/4 teaspoon	1 mL
1/2 teaspoon	2 mL
3/4 teaspoon	4 mL
1 teaspoon	5 mL
1 tablespoon	15 mL
1/4 cup	59 mL
1/2 cup	118 mL
3/4 cup	177 mL
1 cup	235 mL
2 cups	475 mL
3 cups	700 mL
4 cups	1 L

Temperatures Equivalents

FAHRENHEIT (F)	CELSIUS(C) (APPROXIMATE)
225 °F	107 °C
250 °F	120 °C
275 °F	135 °C
300 °F	150 °C
325 °F	160 °C
350 °F	180 °C
375 °F	190 °C
400 °F	205 °C
425 °F	220 °C
450 °F	235 °C
475 °F	245 °C
500 °F	260 °C

Volume Equivalents (Liquid)

US STANDARD	US STANDARD (OUNCES)	METRIC (APPROXIMATE)
2 tablespoons	1 fl.oz.	30 mL
1/4 cup	2 fl.oz.	60 mL
1/2 cup	4 fl.oz.	120 mL
1 cup	8 fl.oz.	240 mL
1 1/2 cup	12 fl.oz.	355 mL
2 cups or 1 pint	16 fl.oz.	475 mL
4 cups or 1 quart	32 fl.oz.	1 L
1 gallon	128 fl.oz.	4 L

Weight Equivalents

US STANDARD	METRIC (APPROXIMATE)
1 ounce	28 g
2 ounces	57 g
5 ounces	142 g
10 ounces	284 g
15 ounces	425 g
16 ounces (1 pound)	455 g
1.5 pounds	680 g
2 pounds	907 g

Appendix 2: Recipes Index

A

Alaskan Pink Salmon
Pink Salmon Patties   101

Almond
Coconut Almond Chocolate Cake   132

Apple
Apple and Walnut Muffins 15
Cinnamon Apples Stuffed with Granola   20
Cinnamon Apple Wedges   120
Lemony Apple Cake   133
Raisin Apple Turnovers   133
Lemony Apple Pie 134
Vanilla Apple Wedges   137
German Giant Apple Pancake   137
Old-Fashioned Stuffed Apples with Pecans   140

Artichoke
Easy Parmesan Coated Artichokes   37

Asparagus
Asparagus, Bell Pepper and Carrot Strata   11
Asparagus and Goat Cheese Frittata 21
Easy Asparagus with Tarragon   30

Avocado
Authentic Quesadillas   19
Crispy Avocado Fries   122

B

Baby Back Rib
Paprika Baby Back Ribs   75

Bacon
Crispy Bacon   15
Cheddar Muffins with Bacon   15
Quick Breakfast Bacon Sandwiches 22
Bacon Lettuce Salad with Croutons 65
Garlic Bacon Cheese Pizza 109
Chili BLT Sandwich   115

Banana
Fried PB&J with Banana   14
Healthy Banana Bread   108
Coconut Banana Chia Bread   110
Peanut Butter Banana Bread   113
Authentic Thai Goreng Pisang   138
Homemade Banana Fritters   138
Banana Fritters   140

Cinnamon Banana Slices   140

Beef
Ritzy Beef Steak with Mushroom Gravy   77
Cheesy Lasagna   78
Glazed Beef Cheese Cups 79
Cheddar Roasted Stuffed Bell Peppers   79
Light Herbed Beef Meatballs   79
Beef Taco Wraps 80
Beef and Bell Pepper Risotto   81
Thai Curry Lime Beef Meatballs   86
Tasty Beef Burgers   87
Simple Beef Sliders   87
Sicilian Beef and Tomato Stuffed Peppers   88
Spicy Beef Burgers   89
Cheesy Beef Sandwich   115

Beef Brisket
Classic Onion Beef Brisket 82
Authentic Mexican Carnitas   83
Ketchup Pulled Beef   85
Classic Corned Beef Brisket 86
Tasty Barbecue Beef Brisket   86
Garlic Pulled Beef 90

Beef Chuck
Old-Fashioned Shallot Meatloaf   83
Classic BBQ Cheeseburgers   85
Traditional Mexican-Style Meatloaf 87
Beef Patties with Mushroom   88
Garlicky Chuck Roast   88

Beef Chuck Eye
Chuck Eye Roast with Jalapeno Pepper   89

Beef Filet Mignon
French Filet Mignon   83
Mustard Filet Mignon   85
Herbed Filet Mignon   90

Beef Flank Steak
Beef Satay with Cilantro   77
Quick Paprika Flank Steak 86

Beef Flap Meat
Spicy Beef with Fajita Veggie   79

Beef Rump
Italian Rump Roast with Onion   85
Brandy Paprika Rump Roast   87

Beef Sausage
Beef Sausage and Bell Peppers   86

Beef Shoulder

Beef Shoulder and Onion   88

Beef Sirloin

Peruvian Stir-Fried Beef and Tomato with Fries   81
Spicy Chimichurri Beef Empanadas 107

Beef Steak

Sherry Beef Steak and Broccoli   81

Beef Tenderloin

Saucy Mongolian Beef   80
Chinese-Style Spiced Beef Tenderloin   90

Beef Top Sirloin

Sirloin Roast with Carrots and Herbs89

Bell Pepper

Bell Peppers Salad with Feta   27
Spicy Beef and Brown Rice Stuffed Bell Peppers   80

Bella Mushroom

Bella Mushrooms with Bacon   36

Blueberry

Blueberry Muffins   19
Simple Blueberry Muffins 20
Healthy Blueberry Fritters 140

Bottom Round Beef

Parsley Roast Beef   83

Bratwurst

Honey Bratwurst and Brussels Sprouts   74

Broccoli

Parmesan Broccoli Crust with Alfredo Sauce 34
Broccoli Salad with Bacon 35
Sesame Broccoli Florets   37
Cheesy Broccoli Cornbread114

Brussels Sprouts

Air-Fried Brussels Sprouts 35

Butternut Squash

Butternut Squash Frittata with Ricotta   13
Cinnamon Butternut Squash   25
Sweet Butternut Squash   39

Button Mushroom

Bread Crumbs Stuffed Button Mushrooms   128
Button Mushrooms   33

C

Calamari

Garlic Calamari with Sherry Wine   97
Mustard Coated Calamari 97
Parsley Calamari 98
Quick Fried Calamari Rings 98
Classic Mediterranean Calamari   98

Chili Calamari with Red Chili   100
Pepper-Brined Fried Calamari   119

Carrot

Carrot and Raisin Muffins with Brown Sugar 12
Sweet Glazed Carrot   33
Garlicky Baby Carrot with Sesame Seeds   34
Crispy Carrot Chips   122

Cauliflower

Mole-Braised Cauliflower with Sesame Seeds29
Simple Caesar Whole Cauliflower   29
Air-Fried Cauliflower with Tahini Sauce   30
Quick Lemony Cauliflower 37
Classic Gobi Manchurian   38

Center Cut Pork

Hot Center Cut Pork Roast 66

Center Cut Pork Chop

Chili Breaded Pork Chops 65
Worcestershire Center-Cut Pork Chops   73

Center Cut Rib Pork Chop

Pork Chops and Bell Peppers   72

Cherry

Cinnamon Cherry 141

Cherry Tomato

Maple Cheery Tomatoes with Thyme   36

Chicken

Spicy Barbecue Chicken Flatbreads 21
Spicy Chicken Chimichangas   41
Simple Chicken Hand Pies 42
Buffalo Egg Rolls with Blue Cheese Dip   45
Authentic Taquitos   47
BBQ Chicken Burgers   59
Chinese Chicken Patties   60
Buffalo Cheesy Meatballs   117

Chicken Breast

Fiesta Chicken Plate with Refried Beans   42
Chicken Cordon Bleu with Ham   43
General Tso's Chicken   44
Fried Chicken Breast with Buttermilk Waffles 45
Lemony Chicken Souvlaki   46
Butter Coated Chicken Breast   47
Chicken Breast with Dark Cherries   49
Airy Breaded Chicken   50
Marinara Chicken Breast Parmesan 52
Cheesy Chicken Breast   53
Chicken and Onion with Pineapple   55
Super Cheesy Chicken   56
Mozzarella Chicken Fritters with Garlic Dip   56
Chicken and Bell Peppers Fajita Roll-Ups   56
Greek Chicken Salad with Kalamata Olives   57
Garlic Breaded Chicken Breast   57

Spicy Chicken and Corn Stir-Fry   58
Spinach and Cheese Stuffed Chicken   58
Smoked Paprika Chicken Breasts   59
Mayo Chicken and Carrot Salad   59
Garlic Chicken Breasts   60
Chicken English Muffin Sandwiches 114

Chicken Drumstick

Buttermilk-Fried Chicken Drumsticks   41
Sweet Chicken Drumsticks 53
Five-Spice Chicken Drumsticks   60
Breaded Fried Chicken Drumsticks   61

Chicken Leg

Teriyaki Paprika Chicken Legs   58

Chicken Sausage

Chicken Sausage and Cream Cheese Biscuits 21

Chicken Tender

Garlic Chicken Tender   41
Breaded Chicken with Spaghetti and Marinara Sauce 42
Coconut Chicken Tender with Apricot-Ginger Sauce   43
Quick Marinaded Chicken Strips   48
Spicy Chicken Fries   55
Simple Mustard Chicken Tenders   58
Quick Panko-Crusted Chicken Chunks   61
Chicken Tender with Blue Cheese   127

Chicken Thigh

Golden Panko-Crusted Chicken Nuggets   43
Peanut Butter-BBQ Chicken   47
Simple Spicy Chicken Thighs   49
Chili Peanut Chicken   50
Buttermilk-Fried Chicken   50
Italian Lemony Chicken Thighs   54
Garlic Cream Chicken Thighs   54
Peruvian-Style Chicken with Herb-Mayonnaise   55
BBQ Chicken Thighs   59

Chicken Wing

Sweet Gochujang Chicken Wings   54
Quick Buffalo Chicken Wings   56
Garlic Honey Chicken Wings   60
Honey Glazed Chicken Wings   120
Sweet-Spicy Chicken Wings   125
Garlic Coated Chicken Wings   127
Asian-Style Chicken Wings 127

Chickpea

Simple Curried Chickpeas 124
Ranch Chickpeas 126

Chocolate

Chocolate Crescent Rolls with Almond   10
Spoon Chocolate Brownies 132

Chocolate Chip

Frosted Chocolate Cookie with Peanut Butter   133

Coconut Chia Chocolate Cake   135
Favorite Chocolate Fudge Cake   141

Cod

Breaded Cod Fish Fingers 102
Codfish Fillet Tacos with Avocado-Mayonnaise   102

Corn

Air-Fried Corn on the Cob 36
Fragrant Jerk Rubbed Corn on the Cob   36

Corn Kernel

Chile Cornbread with Cheddar   25
Cheesy Corn in a Cup   31

Cornish Hen

Simple Seasoned Cornish Hen   57
Honey Glazed Cornish Hens   57

Coulotte Roast

Parsley Coulotte Roast   87

Country-Style Rib

Country-Style Ribs with Red Wine   71
Country-Style Ribs with Sriracha   72

Cranberry

Cranberry Bran Muffins   12

D

Date

Fluffy Oat Bran Muffins   13

Dill Pickle

Cheesy Dill Pickles   121
Hot Fried Dill Pickles   125

Duck Breast

Hoisin Duck Breast   59

E

Eggplant

Stuffed Eggplant Shell with Spinach 35
Panko Breaded Eggplant Fries   124
Mozzarella Eggplant Chips 129

F

Fish

Fish Fillet with Crumb Coating   92

G

Grape Tomato

Cheesy Mushroom and Tomato Pita Pizza   115

Green Bean
Air-Fried Green Beans and Bacon   35
Spicy Green Beans   39

Green Pea
Green Peas with Lettuce   35

Green Tomato
Green Tomatoes with Sriracha Mayo   26

H

Halibut
Buttery Halibut Steaks   97
Garlic Halibut Burgers   103

Ham
Cheesy Egg English Muffins   9
Cheddar and Ham Muffins 18
Ham and Tomato Sandwiches   20
Picnic Ham with Tamari Sauce   66

Heirloom Carrot
Heirloom Carrots with Orange Zest 38

J

Jalapeño Pepper
Cheesy Bacon Wrapped Jalapeño Peppers   117

K

King Prawn
Mayonnaise King Prawn Salad   100

L

Lamb
Paprika Lamb, Green Olive and Cheese Pizza 112

Leek
Spicy Turkish Leek Fritters 30

Lobster Tail
Buttery Lobster Tail   104

London Broil
Parsley London Broil   86
Lemon Marinated London Broil   87

M

Mackerel

Lime Mackerel Fillets   96

Mahi-Mahi
Basil Mahi-Mahi Fillets   96

Meat
Red Rolls with Meat   10

Monkfish
Greek Monkfish Fillet Pita with Avocado   105
Italian Cheesy Monkfish Fingers   105

Mushroom
Bread Boat Eggs with Mushroom   8
Fluffy Cheddar Mushroom Loaf   37
Mushroom and Carrot with Grated Eggs   38

N

New York Strip Steak
Herbed New York Strip Steak   83

O

Okra
Breaded Okra   28
Spicy Indian Okra 34

Olive
Cheesy Olives and Roasted Red Pepper Bread   113
Greek Street Feta and Hummus Tacos   126

Onion
Onion Rings   33
Masala Onion Rings with Lemon-Mayo Dip   120

Orange Roughy Fillet
Garlic Orange Roughy Fillets   100

Oyster Mushroom
Smoked Mozzarella and Oyster Mushroom Pizza   113

P

Peach
Crispy Fried Peaches   124
Tasty Caramelized Peach Shortcakes 131
Cinnamon Peaches   137

Pear
Sweet Vanilla Pears in Red Wine   139
Buttery Pears Sticks   140
Honey Yogurt and Walnut Stuffed Pears   141

Pearl Onion
Pearl Onions with Rosemary   35

Pecan

Sweet Cinnamon-Glazed Butter-Pecan Roll   12

Pineapple
Simple Colorful Fruit Skewers   138

Pistachio
Bottom Rice with Pistachios   34

Plantain
Indian Unnakai Malabar   139

Plum
Brown Sugar Fried Plums   138

Plum Tomato
Quick Shakshuka with Tomato Sauce   14

Poblano Pepper
Chiles Rellenos with Tomato Sauce 31

Pollock
Chili Pollock   96

Pork
Spicy Vietnamese Pork Sausages   63
Sweet-Sour Pork Chunks   64
Caribbean-Style Pork Patties with Brioche Hamburger Buns   65
Pork Dinner Rolls 66
Dijon Pork Burgers   70

Pork Back Rib
Chinese Pork Back Ribs   70

Pork Belly
Herbed Pork Belly 71
Country-Style Pork Belly with Tomato Sauce 75

Pork Butt
Pork Butt with Fresh Rosemary   66
Mexican-Style Pork and Chile Tacos 67
BBQ Pork Butt   68
Cuban Cheesy Pork Sandwich   68
Herbed Pork Butt 71

Pork Center Cut
Pork Center Cut with Red Pepper   70

Pork Center Cut Rib
Hot Pork Rib Roast   68

Pork Chop
Coconut Pork Chops with Salad   67

Pork Cutlet
Thin Pork Cutlets with Aloha Salsa 63
Tasty Tortilla Chips Coated Pork Cutlets   73

Pork Loin
Garlic Rosemary Pork Loin Roast   68
Easy Beer Pork Loin   70
Pork Loin Fillets and Mushroom with Blue Cheese   73

Balsamic Pork Loin with Red Pepper 74

Pork Loin Chop
Lemony Breaded Schnitzel 63
Paprika Pork Loin Chops   72
Pepper Pork Loin Chops with Onions   73

Pork Loin Porterhouse
Chinese-Style Pork Loin Porterhouse   73

Pork Loin Rib
Pork Loin Ribs with Zucchini   72

Pork Sausage
Scotch Eggs with Sausage 14
Quiche Cups with Pork Sausage   17
Pork Sausage and Fennel   70
Smoked Pork Sausage with Onions Rings   75

Pork Shoulder
Vietnamese Pork Shoulder with Roasted Peanuts   64
Tasty Pork Bulgogi   65
Spicy Pork Gyros 67
Pulled Pork Sliders with Fish Sauce   72

Pork Shoulder Chop
Pork Shoulder Chops with Rosemary   73

Pork Sirloin Chop
Breaded Pork Sirloin Chops   68

Pork Sparerib
Sweet Pork Spareribs   68
Spareribs with Sriracha Sauce   71

Pork Tenderloin
Air-Fried Pork and Creamer Potatoes   64
Pork Tenderloin, Plum and Apricot Kebabs   64
Tasty Souvlaki   67
Honey-Lemon Pork Tenderloin   71
Mustard Breaded Pork Tenderloin   71
Cheesy Pork Taquitos   72
Pork, Eggplant and Bell Pepper Skewers   74
Pork Tenderloin with Apple   74
Sliced Pork Tenderloin and Mixed Greens Salad   74

Pork Top Loin
Paprika Pork Loin Roast   66
Pork Loin with Dijon Mustard   66

Potato
Spicy Hash Browns   17
Fried Potatoes with Onion and Bell Peppers 17
Cinnamon Sweet Potato Toast   22
Mashed Potato Tots with Bacon   25
Tart and Spicy Potatoes   26
Crispy Latkes with Sour Cream and Applesauce   26
Hasselback with Sour Cream and Pesto   27
Fingerling Potatoes with Parsley   30
Potato Wedges 33

Super Colorful Vegetable Rolls   36
Samosa Potato Pot Pie   110
Crispy Potato with Spicy Tomato Ketchup   119
Loaded Potato Skins with Bacon   122
Crispy Yellow Potato Chips 124
Potatoes Wedges 126
Crispy Potato Chips   128

Prawn

Exotic Hot Paprika Fried Prawns   97

R

Raisin

Fluffy Fruity Beignets   15
Chocolate Cupcakes with Raisin   139

Red Beet

Spicy Red Beets Chips   128

Red Potato

Fried Smashed Red Potatoes   28
Cheddar Red Potato Pot   31

Rib Pork Chop

Orange Glazed Pork Chops 67

Ribeye Steak

Quick Ribeye Steak   82
Garlic Ribeye Steak   82
Traditional Montreal Ribeye Steak   85
Ribeye Steak with Blue Cheese   90

S

Salami

Cheesy Salami and Kale Pizza   110

Salmon

Salmon and Pork Sausage Omelet   22
Honey Mustard Breaded Salmon Fillet   94
Herb Salmon Fillets   98
Old-Fashioned Fish and Olive Salad 103

Sausage

Coated Eggs with Sausage 19
Sweet Italian Sausage Sandwich   115
Sesame Seasoned Sausage Rolls   121

Sea Bass

Italian-Style Sea Bass with White Wine   103

Sea Scallop

Buttery Garlic Sea Scallops 96
Sea Scallops with Rosemary   100
Sea Scallop and Tomato Salad   100
Breaded Sea Scallops   101

Shallot

Fried Shallots   38

Shrimp

Coconut Shrimp and Tomato Po' Boys   92
Spicy Bang Bang Shrimp   93
Fried Shrimp with Peanut Mix   93
Authentic Cajun Fried Shrimp with Remoulade   93
Marinaded Shrimp and Grits   94
Lush Stuffed Tail-on Shrimp   94
Louisiana Shrimp Po Boy with Remoulade   95
Crispy Marinaded Shrimp 95
One-Pot Shrimp and Egg Fried Rice 95
Lemon Shrimp and Broccoli Floret   97
Pepper Air-Fried Shrimp   98
Buttermilk Coconut Shrimp   100
Jumbo Shrimp with Chives 101
Tandoori Shrimp with Cilantro   101
Panko Breaded Shrimp   102
Shrimp and Cucumber Salad Sandwich   105
Panko-Crusted Shrimp with Bang Bang Sauce 105
Shrimp Cucumber Pirogues   118

Sirloin Strip Steak

Beef, Mushroom and Broccoli   78

Sirloin Tip Steak

Beef, Orange and Pineapple Stir-Fry 78
Salsa Sirloin Tip Steak   80

Skirt Steak

Authentic Carne Asada   77
Garlic Skirt Steak 82
Skirt Steak Sliders with Mustard   83

Slab Baby Back Rib

Chinese Slab Baby Back Ribs   70

Spinach

Salmon and Spinach Frittata   19
Spinach and Turkey Bacon Rollups   22
Eggs Florentine with Spinach   23
Cheesy Spinach Dip with Bread Knots   117

Squid

Chili Squid with Capers   97
Easy Old Bay Calamari   104

Squid Tube

Mediterranean Cheesy Squid   96

St. Louis-Style Rib

Garlic St. Louis-Style Ribs   67

Strawberry

Strawberry Bread 112
Strawberry Scone Shortcake with Powdered Sugar   131
Honey Basil Strawberry Tart   135

String Bean

Crispy String Bean Fries   122

Swordfish

Lemon Cilantro Swordfish Steak   96
Swordfish Steaks with Red Wine   103

T

T-Bone Steak

T-Bone Steak and Tomato Salad   89

Tenderloin Steak

Tenderloin Steaks with Mushrooms 89

Tiger Prawn

Old Bay Tiger Prawns with Sherry Wine   104

Tilapia

Cheesy Tilapia Fish Fillets Burgers   98
Simple Tilapia Fillet and Chips   101
Herbed Tilapia Fillet Nuggets   102
Coated Tilapia Fillet   104

Tofu

Crispy Tofu with Tamari   9

Tomahawk Steak

Juicy Tomahawk Steaks with Bell Pepper   90

Tomatillo

Authentic Tomatillo Salsa Verde   127

Tomato

Cheesy Eggs with Bacon and Tomato Sauce   13
Healthy Crushed Tomato Pizza   112

Top Round Beef

Herbed Roast Beef   82
Parsley Top Round Roast   85

Top Sirloin Steak

Beef Steak Sliders with Horseradish Mayonnaise   118

Tuna

Cheesy English Muffin Tuna   102
Light Asian Tuna Steak   103
Tuna and Spinach Salad with a Twist 104

Turkey

Black Bean and Turkey Burgers with Cumin-Avocado Spread   44
Poblano Pepper with Turkey   48
Turkey and Zucchini Meatballs with Chili Sauce   52
Easy Turkey Burgers   58
Turkey, Pineapple and Bell Pepper Burger Sliders   126

Turkey Breast

Herbed Turkey Breast   46
Herbed Turkey Breast with Cherry Glaze   46
Simple Herbed Turkey Breasts   59

Turkey Sausage

Egg and Turkey Sausage Roll-Ups   10

Turkey Wing

Easy Turkey Wings   57

W

Walnut

Autumn Walnut Pumpkin Pie   139

White Fish

Pesto White Fish and Spinach Pie   92

Whole Chicken

Lime Curried Chicken with Coconut Rice   48
Chicken and Dill Pickle with Nashville Hot Sauce   49
Lemony Chicken with Sage 52
Paprika Fried Chicken   53

Y

Yellow Onion

Stuffed Onion with Garlic-Lemon Breadcrumb   121

Yellow Squash

Breaded Yellow Squash   28

Yuca Root

Yuca Roots Fries   27

Z

Zucchini

Blackened Zucchini with Kimchi Sauce   29
Parmesan Zucchini Gratin with Parsley   37
Zucchini Chocolate Bread   112
Parmesan Zucchini Fries   128

Made in United States
Orlando, FL
02 October 2023

37506174R00087